"Ortiz challenges cherished mythologies and traditions of American exceptionalism and innocence to re-envision a history in which working-class people organized themselves to fight oppression and racial capitalism. Instead of offering a history of white elites and manifest destiny, Ortiz seeks to construct a new 'origin narrative.' . . . A far more inclusive, alternative history—one developed from the bottom up—that does not worship the cult of Europe."

—W. GLASKER, *CHOICE*

"A welcome antidote to the poison of current reactionary attitudes toward people of color, their cultures, and place in the US . . . As Ortiz demonstrates, in their overlapping histories, black and brown people have always inspired each other in their parallel struggles toward emancipation."

—SARA MARTINEZ, *Booklist*

"Ortiz shows the history of the workers for what it really was: a fatal intertwining of slavery, racial capitalism, and imperialism. . . . A sleek, vital history that effectively shows how, 'from the outset, inequality was enforced with the whip, the gun, and the United States Constitution.'"

—*KIRKUS REVIEWS*, starred review

"*An African American and Latinx History* is a historical refutation of the imperialist and white supremacist myths most US residents accept as fact and history. . . . A work of liberation."

—RON JACOBS, *Counterpunch*

"A challenging and necessary approach to understanding our history. A must-read for those who want a deeper perspective than is offered in the traditional history textbook."

—*LIBRARY JOURNAL*

"Paul Ortiz delivers us the history of the United States from the viewpoint of black and brown people, from Crispus Attucks and José Maria Morelos to César Chávez and Martin Luther King Jr. The result is simultaneously invigorating, embarrassing, and essential to anyone interested in what the revolutionaries of years past can teach us about struggles for freedom, equality, and democracy today."

—WILLIAM P. JONES,
author of *The March on Washington: Jobs, Freedom, and the Forgotten History of Civil Rights*

"Paul Ortiz's new book is a crucial read for our current moment. Like Howard Zinn's *A People's History of the United States*, which popularized a radical new approach to history written from 'the bottom up,' Ortiz's multifaceted work brings together a little-known history of Black and Brown collaborative struggle against white supremacy and imperialism from the very origins of the American Revolution through the ascension of Donald Trump."

—DONNA MURCH,
author of *Living for the City*

"*An African American and Latinx History of the United States* is a gift. Paul Ortiz wields the engaging power of a social historian to bring vividly to life so many Black and Brown fighters for human rights in the Americas. Ambitious, original, and enlightening, Ortiz weaves together the seemingly separate strivings of Latinx and Black peoples into a beautiful tapestry of struggle."

—IBRAM X. KENDI,
National Book Award–winning
author of *Stamped from the Beginning:
The Definitive History of Racist Ideas in America*

"Paul Ortiz is a true people's historian, and his new book, *An African American and Latinx History of the United States*, is essential reading for our times. Ortiz, with graceful prose and a clear, compelling narrative, shows that what is exceptional about America is exactly what those who proclaim American exceptionalism the loudest want to bury: a history of struggle, international in its dimensions, inspiring in its audacity, of Black and Brown people fighting for the right to live with dignity."

—GREG GRANDIN,
author of *Empire of Necessity: Slavery,
Freedom, and Deception in the New World*

"Paul Ortiz has written an epic, panoramic account of class struggles in the Western Hemisphere. At center stage are the Black, Latinx, and Indigenous people who built the 'new world,' suffered, survived, and shattered human bondage, resisted imperialism, made revolutions, saved democracy, fought for power and social justice, and found a possible road to freedom—together."

—ROBIN D. G. KELLEY,
author of *Freedom Dreams: The Black Radical Imagination*

"A fierce and masterful work of historical scholarship. Extraordinary in its depth and breadth, this book transforms not only the history we think we know about Black and Latinx freedom struggles but also the very lens through which we understand them. *An African American and Latinx History of the United States* reveals shared revolutionary imaginations across the Americas linking Mexico and Haiti, Cuba and the US South, and exposes powerful visions of justice, peace, and the promise of abolition in the face of racial capitalism."

—GAYE THERESA JOHNSON,
author of *Spaces of Conflict, Sounds of Solidarity*

"An imaginatively conceived, carefully researched, beautifully written, and passionately argued book that places the emancipatory internationalism of Black and Latinx peoples at the center of the national past and present . . . Accessible, engaging, and enlightening."

—GEORGE LIPSITZ,
author of *The Possessive Investment in Whiteness*

"A groundbreaking book about African Americans and Latino/a Americans whose ancestors came from Africa, the Americas, and the Caribbean. Paul Ortiz highlights their respective roles in the shaping of the US working class from the days of the International Workers of the World in the 1800s to its rebirth in the present historic moment. He has captured the historic drama of their collective experience in their struggles for social justice, writing from the perspective of an activist scholar engaged in the current issues facing both peoples."

—CARLOS MUÑOZ JR.,
author of *Youth, Identity, Power: The Chicano Movement*

AN AFRICAN AMERICAN AND LATINX
HISTORY OF THE UNITED STATES

BOOKS IN THE REVISIONING AMERICAN HISTORY SERIES

A Queer History of the United States
by Michael Bronski

A Disability History of the United States
by Kim E. Nielsen

An Indigenous Peoples' History of the United States
by Roxanne Dunbar-Ortiz

AN
AFRICAN
AMERICAN
AND LATINX
HISTORY
OF THE UNITED STATES

PAUL ORTIZ

ReVisioning American History

BEACON PRESS BOSTON

BEACON PRESS
Boston, Massachusetts
www.beacon.org

Beacon Press books
are published under the auspices of
the Unitarian Universalist Association of Congregations.

21 20   8 7 6 (PBK)
21 20   8 7 (HC)

Beacon Press's ReVisioning American History series consists
of accessibly written books by notable scholars that reconstruct
and reinterpret US history from diverse perspectives.

This book is printed on acid-free paper that meets the uncoated paper
ANSI/NISO specifications for permanence as revised in 1992.

Text design and composition by
Wilsted & Taylor Publishing Services

LIBRARY OF CONGRESS CATALOGING-IN-PUBLICATION DATA

Names: Ortiz, Paul, author.
Title: An African American and Latinx history of the United States / Paul Ortiz.
Description: Boston : Beacon Press, [2018] | Series: ReVisioning American
history series | Includes bibliographical references and index.
Identifiers: LCCN 2017020565 (print) | LCCN 2017052998 (ebook)
ISBN 9780807013908 (e-book)
ISBN 9780807005934 (paperback)
ISBN 9780807013106 (hardcover)
Subjects: LCSH: Hispanic Americans—History. | African Americans—History. | United
States—Race relations. | United States—Ethnic relations. | Blacks—Caribbean Area—
Politics and government. | Anti-imperialist movements—United States. | Working
class—United States—History. | Internationalists—United States—History. | United
States—Relations—Latin America. | Latin America—Relations—United States.
Classification: LCC E184.S75 (ebook) | LCC E184.
S75 O79 2018 (print) | DDC 305.800973—dc23
LC record available at https://lccn.loc.gov/2017020565

For Sheila Payne:
compañera and sister in struggle

CONTENTS

AUTHOR'S NOTE

I was born in 1964 and it was in fourth grade that I remember the words being used against me for the first time. It was dinnertime at the kitchen table when my new, white, stepfather announced that if I wanted to continue eating meals with the family I would have to "stop eating like a spic, and stop drinking like a nigger." Until I learned proper table manners I was forbidden to eat with my mother and baby sister. My stepfather referred to incidents where I defied his authority as "Mexican standoffs" and he washed my mouth out with hot sauce as a lesson. He forced me to change my name from Paul Ortiz to Mick MacDonald, MacDonald being his surname. I was taught by the white adults around me that "the Blacks and Mexicans" (the two groups were constantly paired in derision in the discourse of the post–civil rights era) had contributed nothing to the United States. To "real Americans," we were all thieves. We stole good Americans' jobs, but at the same time we were terribly lazy. Somehow we had also stolen their country, even though we had no idea how any of this had happened.

There is a popular academic text on race and ethnicity titled *How the Irish Became White*, but much of my early childhood years could be called *How a Mexican American Boy Became Irish*. My mother's marriage to MacDonald ended in my mother's second divorce, and I spent my teenage life trying to reclaim my original name as well as my ability to speak in public—in those years I was struck with a severe speech impediment. Racism was a pervasive fact of life for my Chicano and Black peers in San Leandro, California, and Bremerton, Washington—the towns where I spent most of my youth. Racism robbed us of our childhoods, and it destroyed our families.

I wrote this book because as a scholar I want to ensure that no Latinx or Black children ever again have to be ashamed of who they are and of where they come from. Collectively speaking, African Americans and Latinx people have nothing to apologize for. Every democratic right we enjoy is an achievement that our ancestors fought, suffered, and died for. When I was growing up, their struggle was not part of the curriculum. We were not taught that Mexico abolished slavery long before the United States did. We did not learn that African Americans organized an international solidarity campaign to support the Cuban War of Liberation against Spain. No one seemed to know that Haiti was viewed by many of our ancestors as a beacon of liberty during the grimmest moments of our own independence wars against the Europeans. We were ignorant of the fact that every country in Latin America, the Caribbean, and Africa has a history of democratic struggle to be proud of. The descendants of these epic movements are today's reviled "freeloading" immigrants.

This book is rooted in nearly two decades of university teaching, years of labor and community organizing, and my experiences coming of age as a Chicano in the United States. At Duke University, I offered a seminar titled Black/Latino Histories, Cultures and Politics, as part of a one-year visiting assistant professorship after I finished my history doctorate there in 2000. I had already taught separate courses in African American and Latinx studies as a graduate student. However, Duke students involved in labor organizing, human rights, and health advocacy told me that what they desperately needed was a new kind of course that placed the histories of the Black and Latinx diasporas in dialog. Students were searching for a course of study that addressed the upsurge of immigration by people from Central America and Mexico to North Carolina. Lacking in critical discourse were insights into how these demographic shifts would impact the potential for social change in a state where African Americans had historically been oppressed. Even now, students in my African American and Latinx Histories research seminar at the University of Florida are asking questions about the history of the Americas that cannot be answered using historical frameworks that have been rendered obsolete by the forces of globalization.

I first learned the craft of social history as an organizer with the United Farm Workers of Washington State. In the midst of the eight-year boycott of Chateau St. Michelle Wines, where vineyard workers were struggling for union representation, I was frequently asked to give workshops about the history of the labor movement, the United Farm Workers, and earlier worker-consumer boycotts and strikes. This taught me the importance of historical research as a tool to pursue the truth on behalf of justice. People depended on me to "get the story right," to frankly discuss the flaws of the labor movement, and to present American history as a usable narrative, warts and all. This meant trying to explain why agricultural workers in the centuries between Christopher Columbus and Ronald Reagan were generally impoverished while their employers were fabulously rich. Answering this question informs the direction of this text.

My experiences as a paratrooper and radio operator in the United States Army in the early 1980s formed a crucial part of the intellectual trajectory that led me to write this book. Herman Melville famously said, "A whale ship was my Yale College and my Harvard." For me, service in the US Special Forces in Central America was an epiphany. In combat zones I learned that the edifying story I had learned about my nation as a guardian and promoter of democracy was false. It took me many more years to explain exactly what was wrong with that history, and how a new and more accurate story might be told.

AN AFRICAN AMERICAN AND LATINX
HISTORY OF THE UNITED STATES

"KILLED HELPING WORKERS TO ORGANIZE"

REENVISIONING AMERICAN HISTORY

This book draws from the voices and experiences of people from the African and Latinx Diasporas in the Americas to offer a new interpretation of United States history from the American Revolution to the present.

This is a story about how people across the hemisphere wove together antislavery, anticolonial, pro-freedom, and pro-working-class movements against tremendous obstacles. Historians have often used Alexis de Tocqueville's *Democracy in America* and other European texts to discuss the development of American institutions and culture. How does our interpretation of American history change when we take our cues more from organizers such as Cuba's José Martí, Jamaica-born Amy Jacques Garvey, and the abolitionist Reverend Henry Highland Garnet—as well as the movements that they were a part of?

In stark contrast to President Donald Trump's "America First" approach that involves building a wall between the United States and Mexico, Black and Latinx intellectuals and organizers have historically urged the United States to build bridges of solidarity with the nations of the Americas. "The people of Latin-America ethnologically are very little different from the Afro-American of this country," a columnist for the *Chicago Defender*, a Black newspaper, wrote in 1915. "They have Indian blood in their veins; so have we. They have African blood in their veins; so have we. They have European blood in their veins; so have we. It is only a difference in degree."[1] When the United States deployed occupying armies into the Caribbean and Central America, the *Chicago Defender* demanded an immediate withdrawal: "The United States cannot expect to succeed in establishing friendly relations or gain commercial growth and influence in Latin America until they have rightly and forever settled the race problem in this country, and further the Anglo-Saxon will continue to borrow trouble throughout the world just so long as they exploit their claim of superiority over other groups of dark-skinned people."[2]

In a time of endless war, with democracy in full retreat, I argue that we must chart pathways toward equality for all people by digging deep into the past and rediscovering the ideas of Emancipation Day lecturers, Mexicano newspaper editors, abolitionists, Latin American revolutionaries, and Black anti-imperialists who dreamed of democratic ways of living in the Americas. We have too often forgotten the connections that movement organizers built between people's movements for freedom in the United States, Central America, and the Caribbean. The recovery of these truths is more vital than ever as the United States erects barriers to divide humanity from itself in a fit of historical amnesia. In *Border Odyssey: Travels Along the U.S./Mexico Divide*, Charles D. Thompson Jr. reminds readers, "Stories are the opposite of walls; they demand release, retelling, showing, connecting, each image chipping away at boundaries."[3] *An African American and Latinx History of the United States* seeks to chip away at the barriers that have been placed in the way of understanding between people, between nations.

THE PROBLEM OF AMERICAN EXCEPTIONALISM

The abolitionist Frederick Douglass sought to reenvision American history as he took to a podium in Boston to explain the origin of the Civil War to an audience of Northerners in 1862. While his audience likely expected him to heap invective against the Confederacy, Douglass came to demand that Northerners take responsibility for their part in the making of the catastrophe. Douglass toiled to change his listeners' understanding of their history in order to make them realize the damage their politics had wrought. Above all, Douglass had to dismantle what Americans have always treasured most:

their innocence, and the sense that their history was so exceptional that they had managed to avoid the problems other nations faced. Douglass began by observing that the Civil War had been ushered in by decades of settler colonialism, corruption, and the promotion of slavery. In a rush to expand slavery's profits, the United States had transformed the Americas into a gigantic war zone:

> We have bought Florida, waged war with friendly Seminoles, purchased Louisiana, annexed Texas, fought Mexico, trampled on the right of petition, abridged the freedom of debate, paid ten million to Texas upon a fraudulent claim, mobbed the Abolitionists, repealed the Missouri Compromise, winked at the accursed slave trade, helped to extend slavery, given slaveholders a larger share of all the offices and honors than we claimed for ourselves, paid their postage, supported the Government, persecuted free negroes, refused to recognize Hayti and Liberia, stained our souls by repeated compromises, borne with Southern bluster, allowed our ships to be robbed of their hardy sailors, defeated a central road to the Pacific, and have descended to the meanness and degradation of negro dogs, and hunted down the panting slave escaping from his tyrant master—all to make the South love us; and yet how stands our relations?[4]

In one damning sentence, Douglass placed slavery and imperialism at the center of the nation's development. He sought to make his listeners recognize that the United States' egregious behavior vis-à-vis Latin America, the Caribbean, and Africa was decisive in the republic's precipitous collapse. Douglass believed that the United States needed to surrender the image of itself as an exceptional icon of liberty in order to deal with the self-inflicted problems that had driven the country into bloody civil war. He also reminded his Yankee audience that their pursuit of profits at the expense of human rights had had lasting consequences. The Black abolitionist insisted that his nation must abandon its claims to innocence. The problems that Douglass identified—the United States' propensity to wage self-destructive offensive wars on other nations, avarice, racism, and the suppression of dissent—continue to plague the nation into the twenty-first century. Little wonder that Douglass—the Lion of

Anacostia, referring to the area of Washington, DC, where Douglass resided—often faced physical violence in public from enraged spectators who took issue with his incisive attacks on the republic's most sacred myths.[5]

A century later, the editors of *El Malcriado*, the newspaper published by the Filipino and Chicana/o farmworker movement, otherwise known as the United Farm Worker Organizing Committee (UFWOC), interpreted the assassination of the Reverend Martin Luther King Jr. as shedding critical light on US history. The entire April 15, 1968, edition of *El Malcriado*—literally, "The Troublemaker"—was dedicated to the life of the fallen civil rights leader, who had been gunned down in Memphis earlier that month. The issue's cover featured a drawing of King leading a protest march with the Memphis sanitation workers' iconic "I Am a Man" picket sign in the background. The editors titled this special issue "Killed Helping Workers to Organize," and they printed telegrams of support and solidarity that had been exchanged by UFWOC cofounder César Chávez and King. In one article, "The Man They Killed," King was presented as a man who "fought against police brutality and the violence which grinds down the lives of our people and all the disinherited."[6]

El Malcriado reminded readers that King supported collective struggles against poverty through mass action and union organizing. The farmworkers' newspaper also emphasized how King linked domestic working-class struggles with international liberation:

> It was no accident that Martin Luther King placed himself in the center of the battle against the war in Vietnam. He saw the slaughter of Vietnamese farmworkers as an atrocious abuse of military power. He spoke out against the outrageous use of Black youth and all minority youth as cannon fodder in a war of *annihilation*. He chose to aim his movement at the war despite the advice of many that such a turn could destroy the movement for human rights.[7]

This was a twentieth-century version of Frederick Douglass's thesis that oppression and militarism destroyed the nation's ability to become truly democratic. Moreover, it was a primer on how poor people made history: *they organized themselves.* In contrast to the national origin story of heroic Founding Fathers who founded a nation where civil liberties were steadily expanding, *El Malcriado*'s theory of history took into account the exploitation of agricultural labor that stretched back to the slave labor camps of the early Americas. This bitter knowledge of the way that racial capitalism tyrannized farmworkers across centuries allowed *El Malcriado*'s editors to connect Black history to the struggles of farmworkers to create a new synthesis of US history. The UFWOC placed its faith in the power of poor people to join together and transform the society from the bottom up. This was the *union's* vision of historical progress: "We have a debt to Dr. King, a debt larger than to any living man. It can only be repaid by effectively organizing in the fields of our nation, so that farm workers can wrest their right to dignity and a decent life from the forces that have confined us so long."[8]

Here, we will retrace the odysseys of African American and Latinx thinkers as they theorized outside the nation's borders and beyond its mythologies of innocence and exceptionalism to challenge the crises facing them inside of the belly of the beast. *El Malcriado* did not believe that a return to the wisdom of the Founding Fathers or the principles of the US Constitution would solve their members' problems. The *Colored American*, one of the nation's first Black newspapers, had asserted quite frankly in 1840, "Now our Government is a government of slaveholders and has been so for more than forty years. Slavery has made war and peace for us, embargo and non-intercourse; it has set up and pulled down protective and banking systems."[9] Francisco P. Ramírez, the abolitionist founder of *El Clamor Público*, a Los Angeles–based Spanish-language newspaper, wrote in 1855, "The United States' conception of freedom is truly curious. This much lauded freedom is imaginary. . . . To buy a man for money, to hang or burn him alive arbitrarily, is another great liberty which any individual has here, according to his likes. This happens in the United States, where slavery is tolerated, where the most vile despotism reigns unchecked—in the middle of a nation that they call the 'Model Republic.'"[10]

Generations of Black and Latinx writers argued that the ability of oppressed people throughout the world to exercise genuine self-determination would strengthen liberty in the United States.

This idea of *emancipatory internationalism* was born of centuries of struggle against slavery, colonialism, and oppression in the Americas. When Martin Luther King connected the lives of Vietnamese villagers with the prospects of Black youths in South Central Los Angeles he was drawing on an extraordinary fountain of experiential wisdom. In her foreword to *Where Do We Go from Here: Chaos or Community?*, Coretta Scott King noted that her husband "spoke out sharply for all the poor in all their hues, for he knew if color made them different, misery and oppression made them the same."[11] In the midst of Reconstruction, the *Christian Recorder*, the national organ of the African Methodist Episcopal Church, exulted in the rising of Cuban people against the Spanish empire. The *Christian Recorder*'s editors believed that a Cuban victory would enhance freedom's march everywhere: "The Cuban Revolutionists still hold out against all the force the Spaniards are able to bring against them. A number of battles have been fought, in all which the Cubans show bravery worthy of the cause in which they fight. . . . Spain may as well keep her legions at home. They can never crush out the spirit of liberty in the Queen of the Antilles."[12]

Herein lies a new way to understand American history. The radical ideas of Frederick Douglass, the *Christian Recorder*, and the editors of *El Malcriado* were generated in social movements where people came together to learn how to overturn slavery and other forms of domination. Placing these struggles at the heart of the historical narrative allows us to reenvision a vibrant past that shines a path for every individual who yearns for a more democratic future.

CONFRONTING AMERICAN EXCEPTIONALISM

Students of color and working-class students in general lament their people's absence and inferior placement in this nation's historical record as reflected in history and other textbooks. The majority of students whom I have taught do not believe that their textbooks present a realistic story of how we reached this point in our history nor how we might use the past to address historically rooted problems. High school students often find history "boring," elitist, and worse.

One of my former students at the University of California, Santa Cruz, explained: "As a student of African heritage growing up in Santa Cruz, a predominantly Caucasian town, the role my ancestors played in the development of the country was never revealed. Slavery was always downplayed in favor of glorifying Abraham Lincoln and the Emancipation Proclamation. How was I to regard my heritage with confidence while the environment I was raised in depicted Africans as nothing but slaves saved by a white man? Believe me, no teacher ever let me forget that."[13]

All of this leads me to maintain that we need to create what Elizabeth "Betita" Martínez, a Chicana scholar and former Student Nonviolent Coordinating Committee organizer, calls a "new origin narrative" of American history.[14] Many of the events chronicled in the following chapters either occurred outside the boundaries of the United States or happened in such a manner as to make the idea of borders and boundaries seem absurd. Creating a new origin narrative of our history means following the African American writer Carl Hansberry as he traveled to Mexico in 1945 to report on a conference that proposed to end racism and militarism in the Americas. It means keying on individuals such as Geoconda Arguello Kline, who left Nicaragua in 1983 and helped to organize a labor union in Nevada composed of individuals from eighty-four nations. In his essay "A Chicano in Philadelphia," Danny Romero writes, "If there had never been a George Washington or Thomas Jefferson, I would still have been born in 'El Norte.' If there had never been a Woodrow Wilson, a Nixon, or Reagan, I still would have been born in (El Pueblo de Nuestra Señora Reina de) Los Angeles. My history stems from south to north, not east to west."[15] Today, the descendants of former slaves and the descendants of people in Latin America and the Caribbean are heirs to oft-forgotten lineages of democratic struggle that provide vital reminders of how linked our histories are in the Americas.

Those interested in the origins of democratic traditions in this country must look to Latin America, the Caribbean, and Africa as often as they look to Europe. In eras when fascism, eugenics, and apartheid dominated the nations of Europe and the Global North, it was often ideas from the Global South (referring here mainly to the nations of Latin America, the Caribbean, and Africa)—as well as the immigrants who brought those ideas to the United States—that rejuvenated US political culture.[16] The historian Greg Grandin has observed that "Latin America is famous for revolutionaries, but Latin America practically invented social democracy. The world's first fully realized social democratic constitution was [framed in] Mexico. The right to organize, the right to education, the right to health care: those rights disseminated throughout Latin America, and then they found their way into the UN Declaration of Human Rights. Latin America invented what we think of as modern social democracy, and it never gets credit for it."[17]

Readers will quickly see the debt I owe to Chicana/o and Black studies scholars who have taught us how to make critical knowledge accessible to the broadest possible audiences. This book draws on classic texts in the field of ethnic studies to emphasize themes including democratic striving, coalition building, and the dream of the self-emancipation of the working classes of all nations and peoples.[18]

Drawing deeply on scholarship in labor studies, this book reenvisions American history as working-class history. Standard approaches to the nation's story stressed a tale of steady progress toward the creation of a middle-class republic, but this progressive narrative does not square with the facts. Dr. Martin Luther King Jr. observed of most white people in the nation: "They believe that American society is essentially hospitable to fair play and to steady growth toward a middle-class Utopia embodying racial harmony. But unfortunately, this is a fantasy of self-deception and comfortable vanity. Overwhelmingly America is still struggling with irresolution and contradictions."[19] The United States has persisted in creating economic, legal, and political barriers to full citizenship for much of the nation's workforce.

Whether one studies the fate of African American workers at the nation's inception or the experiences of twelve million "undocumented" immigrant workers today, disenfranchisement has been a traumatic factor of life for millions of working-class people.[20] The imperial thrust of US military and trade policies—often pursued in tandem—has resulted in what journalist Juan González calls a "Harvest of Empire."[21] I witnessed this traumatic process firsthand as a Special Forces soldier in the 1980s carrying out foreign policies that forced numerous residents in Central America to leave their homelands for *El Norte*.[22] Pulitzer Prize–winning writer Junot Díaz, whose family originally hailed from the Dominican Republic, writes, "I'm here because the United States invaded my country in 1965, an illegal invasion, completely trumped-up excuse to invade the Dominican Republic and crush our democratic hopes. We've lived the consequences of that illegal invasion politically, economically, and in the bodies of the people who were wounded, in the bodies of the people who were killed. We've been living it for over 40 years."[23]

EXPLANATION OF TERMS USED IN THIS BOOK

Broad terms such as "Black" and "Brown" are necessary to describe groups of people who have struggled to survive in a society determined to keep them at the bottom rungs of the social order—but they are also problematic. In the 1960s, many young Mexican Americans or Spanish-speaking Americans began using terms like "*Chicano y Chicana*" to describe themselves. These had once been terms of derision, but a newly politicized generation of youths transformed "Chicano" into a term of pride. I began to describe myself as a Chicano when I became an organizer with the United Farm Workers of Washington State in the late 1980s. Elder activists in the United Farm Workers also taught me the term "La Raza" ("our people"), which acknowledged our Indigenous roots and five centuries of struggle against European imperialism. I learned later that the farmworker movement had long served as an incubator of political identity for people of Mexican descent. Likewise, the markers of self-identity used by residents of Puerto Rico, Cuba, and the Dominican Republic changed—sometimes dramatically—over time.[24] The Spanish language is a gendered language, and I have adopted the newer term "Latinx" to reflect my students' search for "a gender-inclusive way of referring to people of Latin American descent residing in the United States."[25]

In the early twentieth century, African Americans commonly referred to themselves and their loved ones as "Negroes" or "colored" people. During insurgent freedom movements in the 1960s, however, the terms "Black," "Afro-American," and "African American" were put forth by activists and writers. Because this is a historical study, I will generally use terms of identification invoked and preferred by individuals given their specific historical context and circumstances.

Black and Brown histories have always overlapped. The anthropologist Martha Menchaca notes that Mexican Americans have African, Indigenous, and European roots that go back centuries.[26] Literary scholar Marta E. Sánchez stresses that intercultural connections between Puerto Rican, African American, and Chicano cultures have been a pervasive aspect of life in the Western Hemisphere.[27] Millions of people in the Americas identify with multiple ancestries, including Afro-Latinx, Indo-African, *moreno*, mestizo, biracial, and multiracial, among many other conceptions of identity.[28] Today, many Latin American countries are acknowledging the cultural and civilizational debts they owe to African civilizations. Mexico has declared Africa to be Nuestra Tercera Raíz (Our Third Root) of the nation, and increasing numbers of Mexicans are identifying as Afro-Mexicans.[29]

CONNECTING THE STRANDS OF HISTORY

In the course of my research, I have learned that it is impossible to understand United States history as a singular entity. To comprehend where we are and how we got here, we must go outside the confines of the nation-state for answers. This book connects the stories of freedom fighters in the Mexican War of Independence to Africans and Indigenous people who challenged slavery in Spanish Florida, as well as Harlemites who railed against the US military occupation of Nicaragua in the 1920s. This movement-centered approach to history raises up the voices of the people who built democracy across borders and helps us overcome the paralyzing nationalistic myths that have divided people in this hemisphere for too long. There are many in the United States today who believe that there is only one way to be an "American," but history teaches us that this is not true. To quote Aimé Césaire, "There is room for all at the Rendezvous of Victory."

Connecting Black and Latinx historical experiences draws on Kimberlé Crenshaw's idea of "intersectionality," as well as the timeless idea that forms of oppression—as well as methods of resistance to that oppression—are linked.[30] This does not mean, however, that one can erase the distinctive experiences that mark centuries of exploitation in the Americas. Manuel Pastor and Angela Glover Blackwell urge us to avoid the trap of historical amnesia:

> In a time of increasing diversity, it might be tempting to look beyond the black-white framework that structures race relations and social and economic opportunity. To the contrary, as other racial minorities grow, it becomes increasingly important to address the fundamental question of fairness for African Americans, which affects the fortunes of the other groups. The black-white economic and social divide created by slavery and cemented through years of servitude and subjugation has endured and helped shape America.[31]

Shortly after *El Malcriado* published its tribute to Martin Luther King Jr.'s life, it announced that a series of educational workshops in Spanish would be held for the children of striking grape workers in Delano, California. Students would study Mexican folklore and art, and that they would be taught lessons about the lives of Emiliano Zapata, Pancho Villa, Malcolm X, Martin Luther King, "and the leaders of the farm workers' Cause."[32] It was a course of study emphasizing revolutionary struggle as well as pride in the cultures and survival of African Americans and Chicanos. It is just the kind of new origin narrative that *An African American and Latinx History of the United States* seeks to promote as a way to reenvision American history more accurately and more democratically.

CHAPTER 1

THE HAITIAN REVOLUTION AND
THE BIRTH OF EMANCIPATORY
INTERNATIONALISM, 1770s TO 1820s

The foremost issue facing the Americas in the Age of Revolution— roughly from the 1770s to the 1840s—was the future of slavery in a hemisphere bristling with anticolonial insurgencies. In 1780, Peru's José Gabriel Condorcanqui Noguera, claiming the mantle of the last King of the Incan Empire, rechristened himself Tupac Amaru II, and with his African-descent wife, Micaela Bastidas, launched a rebellion against Spanish rule. Tupac Amaru II recruited a massive army that included Indigenous Peruvians, mestizos, *libertos*, and slaves, in an effort to end European rule forever.[1] In this same period, a cohort of propertied elites in Great Britain's thirteen North American colonies organized a revolution to safeguard slavery, property, and political power.[2] Thomas Jefferson and his peers sought to preserve as much as they looked to overthrow. The Founding Fathers looked primarily to Europe for inspiration.[3] They drew on the ideas of the political theorist John Locke and other Enlightenment philosophers to construct rationales for racial slavery, the expropriation of Native lands, and control of the continent's unruly masses, disdainfully referred to by elites as "the people out of doors."[4]

The wealth built up by enslaved African labor gave English colonists the resources they needed to challenge British rule and to subsequently contest European powers for domination in the Western Hemisphere.[5] The slave plantation was the engine of early economic growth in the Americas, and the force behind the rise of global markets in tobacco, sugar, molasses, dyestuffs, cotton, and other commodities.[6] The pages of the Charleston-based *South Carolina Gazette* in the 1770s reveal an interior world of racial capitalism and the degradation of labor: "Anyone person who wants to hire a negro with a good breast of milk, and without a child—Enquire of the printer," reads a typical item.[7] Another advertisement noted that three "negroes" would be sold along with brandy, porter, and empty bottles.[8]

The *South Carolina Gazette* was typical of commercial newspapers that promoted the breeding, trading, recapture, and punishments of African Americans in order to sustain merchant profits.[9] Paradoxically, slave owners who placed advertisements in the *Gazette* to locate their runaway slaves revealed that the individuals they had reduced to private property were intelligent human beings. Refuting their captors' efforts to rob them of their humanity, enslaved Africans constantly struggled to keep families intact and escaped when possible in kin groups in efforts to reunite with family members sold away or left behind in the wake of sales. One advertisement concerning a fugitive from racial capitalism on the eve of the Revolution noted, "He speaks very good English and is very artful."[10] The cash rewards for turning in fugitives as well as the expectation that white people would offer the authorities information on runaways is a reminder that the minority of slave-holding colonists depended on the vigilance of the majority who did not own slaves to police the system.[11]

In their fight for freedom, African American communities rejected European theories of domination as surely as their revolutionary counterparts in Peru. Black writers looked to revolts in the Global South for inspiration because *these* revolutions challenged slavery, the caste oppression of Indigenous people, and the rule of the few over the many. This global vision of human rights was the core element of emancipatory internationalism, and it became a foundation of what Black scholar Cedric Robinson has called "the Black radical tradition," a set of ideas and practices rooted in grassroots insurgencies that challenged slavery and racial capitalism at its inception.[12] Robinson argued that "Black Radicalism critically emerges from African culture, languages, and beliefs, and enslavement. What emerged from that conjunction were powerful impulses to escape enslavement."[13] In the Age of Revolution, Black organizers and writers studied and celebrated Latin American and Caribbean revolutionaries such as Toussaint L'Ouverture, Simón Bolívar, and Vicente Guerrero for profoundly enlarging the meaning of freedom in the Americas. The strength of emancipatory internationalism was its rootedness in popular movements, its accessible language of justice, and its resiliency through generations of Black thought and action.[14]

A REVOLUTION OF GUILTY MASTERS

Given the role that plantation owners and merchant capitalists played in the American Revolution, it is not surprising that a war of independence became a war to preserve slavery.[15] The colonial upper class looked with trepidation at signs from Great Britain that foretold the demise of chattel bondage. Foremost among these was the English Court's *Somerset v. Stewart* case, decided in 1772. The decision resulted in the freeing of James Somerset, an enslaved African who had been brought by his master to England a few years earlier. The judge in the case found that slavery was not supported in the Common Law. Despite the debate in England about the ultimate meaning of *Somerset* in England, the decision was interpreted by many white leaders in the Thirteen Colonies as foretelling the doom of slavery in the British Empire.[16]

Threats of insurgencies from slaves and poor colonists also convinced these leaders that a break with Great Britain was necessary. As tensions escalated between colonists and Parliament, a South Carolina planter, William Drayton, accused the Royal Navy of offering sanctuary to runaway slaves.[17] The *South Carolina Gazette* published an ominous "Letter from London" in the winter of 1775 that accused the Crown of arming "[Negroes], the Roman Catholics, the Indians and Canadians" to put down the brewing colonial rebellion.[18] That spring, "a group of slaves, scenting freedom in the air," approached Lord Dunmore, the royal governor of Virginia, "and volunteered their services" against their increasingly restless masters.[19] Sensing that he was on precarious ground, the nervous governor initially turned the dissident slaves away. By the fall, however, Dunmore reversed course. In November, he issued a proclamation freeing slaves who promised to bear arms against the embryonic anticolonial revolt. Dunmore sealed the Patriots' decision to escalate the revolt to a full-blown war of independence. Indeed, the third draft of Thomas Jefferson's Declaration of Independence listed as primary grievances against King George III "prompting our negroes to rise in arms among us" and, in the next sentence, "endeavoring to bring on the inhabitants of our frontiers the merciless Indian savages, whose known rule of warfare is an undistinguished destruction of all ages, sexes, & conditions of existence."[20]

In 1775, the revolutionary pamphleteer Thomas Paine published *African Slavery in America*, which indicted slavery at all levels:

> So monstrous is the making and keeping them slaves at all, abstracted from the barbarous usage they suffer, and the many evils attending the practice; as selling husbands away from wives, children from parents, and from each other, in violation of sacred and natural ties; and opening the way for adulteries, incest, and many shocking consequences, for all of which the guilty Masters must answer to the final Judge.[21]

Paine wanted the rebellious colonists to look at themselves in the mirror: "With what consistency, or decency they complain so loudly of attempts to enslave them, while they hold so many hundreds of thousands in slavery; and annually enslave many thousands more, without any pretence of authority, or claim upon them."[22] Paine's pleas for moral consistency fell upon deaf ears and hearts hardened with the lucre of chattel bondage.[23] The English essayist Samuel Johnson wryly observed the ironies of a revolution led by guilty masters: "We are told, that the subjection of Americans may tend to the diminution of our own liberties; an event, which none but very perspicacious politicians are able to foresee. If slavery be thus fatally contagious, how is it that we hear the loudest yelps for liberty among the drivers of negroes?"[24]

LIBERTY FURTHER EXTENDED

African Americans fought with every weapon at their disposal to change the course of the American Revolution away from slavery and toward freedom for all. In the fall of 1776, Lemuel Haynes, a Revolutionary War soldier in Massachusetts, took up his pen to grapple with Thomas Jefferson's Declaration of Independence. Two years earlier, Haynes had enlisted in the Patriot cause. In April of the previous year, he and his fellow Granville, Massachusetts, militia members rushed to defend Lexington from British troops. The young Minuteman later served with Ethan Allen's Green Mountain Boys at the Battle of Ticonderoga.[25]

Private Lemuel Haynes was a free Black man and a soldier who believed that the American Revolution should be a war against slavery. He was born in 1753, the progeny of a Black father and white mother "of respectable ancestry" in Connecticut who publicly renounced him. Thus orphaned, Haynes was apprenticed to and raised by an intensely religious family in Granville. He became an ardent foe of slavery and titled his rebuttal to Jefferson's document "Liberty Further Extended: Or Free thoughts on the illegality of Slave-keeping; Wherein those arguments that Are used in its vindication Are plainly confuted. Together with a humble Address to such as are Concerned in the Practice."[26]

Haynes opened his challenge to the Continental Congress by quoting the highlight of the Declaration of Independence, its opening sentence: "We hold these truths to be self-evident, that all men are created Equal, that they are Endowed By their Creator with Certain unalienable rights, that among these are Life, Liberty and the pursuit of happiness." Haynes admonished his independence-minded comrades that they should be engaged in a war against oppression: "To affirm that an Englishman has a right to his Liberty," Haynes stated, "is a truth which has Been so clearly Evinced, Especially of Late, that to spend time in illustrating this, would be But Superfluous tautology." Building on this point, Haynes insisted that the goals of the revolution should not be constrained by race:

> But I query whether Liberty is so contracted a principle as
> to be confined to any nation under Heaven; nay, I think

> it not hyperbolical to affirm, that Even an African, has
> Equally as good a right to his Liberty in common with
> Englishmen. . . . And the main proposition, which I intend
> for some Brief illustration is this, Namely, That an *African*,
> or in other terms, *that a Negro may Justly Challenge, and
> has an undeniable right to his Liberty: Consequently, the
> practice of Slave-keeping, which so much abounds in this
> Land is illicit* [emphasis in original].[27]

The twenty-three-year-old citizen-soldier sought to imbue the Revolution with a vision much broader than that of Jefferson's and his proslavery countrymen.

Lemuel Haynes was one of many thousands of Black freedom fighters who have been forgotten in the story of the American Revolution. The Afro–Puerto Rican scholar Arturo Alfonso Schomburg dedicated his career to documenting Black sacrifices in the development of the United States. In "The Formation of the American Republic," Schomburg wrote: "The books on the history of the United States chronicle the events preceding the Revolution with fidelity and Patriotic fervor. A Negro reading those books finds them lacking the substance of recording the active part the African has played in the drama that brought to life the American nation."[28] Several years before Haynes picked up a rifle to defend an embattled country in the making, a whaler of African and Native American descent, Crispus Attucks, went to his death battling British Redcoats in the Boston Massacre. Speaking of this rebellious sailor, John Hancock of Boston, a lawyer and a Patriot, declared: "Who taught the British soldier that he might be defeated? Who dared look into his eyes? I place, therefore, this Crispus Attucks in the foremost rank of the men that dared."[29] A brigade of soldiers of African descent from Haiti served alongside the Continental Army at Savannah and other battles.[30] By the end of the war, historian Benjamin Quarles estimated that at least five thousand African American men served in the Patriot armies.[31]

African Americans delivered numerous petitions to Colonial legislatures in the years leading up to 1776 in which they argued that emancipation should be a central goal in the clash with the British Empire. These entreaties reveal the philosophical positions on democracy that Black communities had forged during the Colonial era.[32] African American petitioners noted that white Patriots invoked terms such as "liberty" and "slavery" to describe their conflict with England without satisfactorily explaining either concept. These petitions borrowed from but ultimately transcended white Revolutionary rhetoric. African American Framers demonstrated that they had an expansive vision of liberty that did not brook compromise with chattel bondage. Black Bostonians employed a keen sense of irony in their appeal to the Boston Patriots in 1773:

> The efforts made by the legislative of this province [Massachusetts] in their last sessions to free themselves from slavery, gave us, who are in that deplorable fate, a high degree of satisfaction. We expect great things from men who have made a noble stand against the designs of their fellow men to enslave them.
>
> We cannot but wish and hope Sir, that you will have the same grand object, we mean civil and religious liberty, in view in your next session. The divine spirit of Freedom seems to fire every human breast on this continent, except as are bribed to assist in executing the execrable plan [slavery].[33]

By 1776, nearly five hundred thousand African Americans, more than 90 percent of them enslaved, lived in British North America.[34] By the end of the Revolutionary War, nearly a hundred thousand slaves had braved great risks by escaping from their masters and seeking sanctuary with the British or Native Americans.[35] The historian Sylvia Frey notes, "Severe punishment, and often death, was a virtual certainty for an unsuccessful escape."[36] Benjamin Quarles aptly characterized African American insurgencies in the Age of Revolution: "The Negro's role in the Revolution can best be understood by realizing that his major loyalty was not to a place nor to a people but to a principle. Insofar as he had freedom of choice, he was likely to join the side that made him the quickest and best offer in terms of those 'unalienable rights' of which Mr. Jefferson had spoken."[37]

THE DUEL FOR LABOR CONTROL

The repressive contours of the new republic were visible in the efforts made by Alexander Hamilton and Thomas Jefferson to recapture former slaves who had escaped with Britain's Royal Navy at the end of the war. Hamilton moved, in a session of Congress, to protest "the British seizure of Negroes belonging to citizens of the United States," and Jefferson pressed the matter in a letter to George Hammond, the British envoy charged with establishing diplomatic relations between Great Britain and the United States after the war.[38] Secretary of State Jefferson was outraged at General Guy Carleton for overseeing the evacuation of North Americans, including former slaves. He argued that this was a violation of the Treaty of Paris, which prohibited "carrying away any Negroes or other property of the American inhabitants."[39] Jefferson belittled the general's argument that he was compelled by moral reasons to carry out the rescue of enslaved people, and he railed at the great indignities and financial inconveniences suffered by the Virginia gentry at the loss of their property.[40] Little wonder that Hammond observed of the former Patriot leaders, "I have reason to think most of them are Tories at heart."[41]

The Patriot ruling class designed the US Constitution to protect chattel bondage. As Staughton Lynd notes, the Constitution

> gave the South disproportionate strength in the House of Representatives by adding three-fifths of the slaves to the number of white persons in apportioning Congressmen to the several states; by Article I, Section 8, which gave Congress the power to suppress insurrections; by Article I, Section 9, which postponed prohibition of the slave trade until twenty years after the Constitution's adoption; by Article IV, Section 2, which provided for the return of Fugitive slaves.[42]

The Electoral College was a check on the rights of ordinary people to directly elect the president, as well as a guarantee that Presidents George Washington, Thomas Jefferson, James Madison, and James Monroe would protect their fellow Virginia plantation owners' interests for the first decades of the nation's history.[43]

Shortly after ratification of the Constitution, in 1789, Congress passed the Naturalization Act of 1790, which restricted the naturalization process toward citizenship in the United States to "any alien, being a free white person."[44] The Constitution and the Naturalization Act marginalized people of color for generations to come. The racialization and denial of citizenship to entire classes of workers became the blunt instrument that employers used to keep wages low in numerous occupations identified with undesirable African American and, later, immigrant labor.[45] The Naturalization Act worked to exclude nonwhite people from the benefits of citizenship even and entrenched racism as the philosophy of westward expansion. Thomas Law, "Washington's First Rich Man," explained to James Madison that racialized naturalization was a necessary weapon of settler colonialism: "I conceive that Virginia should particularly adopt every method to introduce more whites & if possible to diminish the blacks. . . . If emigrants were fixed to the Westward would they not combat against Indians & Negroes?"[46]

THE MAKING OF EMANCIPATORY INTERNATIONALISM

As the embers of the Revolutionary age died out, African Americans sought to rekindle the visions of liberation that had animated them in earlier decades. The historian Julius Scott notes that the next great sparks of liberty in the Americas came from the Caribbean. In 1791, enslaved people of Saint-Domingue, a fabulously profitable sugar colony of France on the island of Hispaniola, carried out an extraordinary insurrection. The uprising was inspired in part by the French Revolution. Some of its leaders had served with the Chasseurs-Volontaires de Couleur de Saint-Domingue in support of the American Revolution years earlier. History's only successful slave revolution was led by Toussaint L'Ouverture, a former house servant. The slaves defeated each of the European armies sent to crush their rebellion. Winning their independence in 1804, the revolutionaries christened their new nation Haiti in honor of the original Indigenous inhabitants' name for the island, Ayiti—much to the horror of US and European slave owners.[47] As African Americans quickly understood, and as historians have reconfirmed, the Haitian Revolution was a major impetus for the abolition of slavery and independence in the Americas.[48]

African Americans throughout the United States commemorated the Haitian Revolution in many ways. Black newspapers featured stories on the drama, and parents taught their children about the valiant Toussaint L'Ouverture, as well as his generals Dessalines and Christophe. Black communities named streets and neighborhoods after revolutionary Haitian heroes. Students at the Institute for Colored Youth in Philadelphia were required to learn and to recite Jean-Jacques Dessalines's "1804 Independence Address to the Haytians."[49]

African American slaves in Virginia and North Carolina organized revolts between 1800 and 1801 that drew on the Haitian and French Revolutions for inspiration. However, unlike their counterparts in Haiti, who enjoyed a decisive numerical majority vis-à-vis their white antagonists, enslaved Africans in the United States were a minority population in most parts of the country. Slave conspirators in Virginia acted in the expectation that poor white artisans would join them in rising against the upper classes. After all, didn't slaves and working class whites share the same common oppressor? It was not to be. The plots were discovered and mass executions followed. In the words of the rebel slaves, condemned to die at the gallows, one grasps the grimmest ironies of American history. "I have nothing more to offer than what General Washington would have had to offer," said one of the doomed revolutionaries. "I have adventured my life in endeavoring to obtain the liberty of my countrymen, and am a willing sacrifice in their cause."[50]

African Americans signaled their rejection of the new slave republic's ideology of white supremacy and Black racial inferiority through words and deeds. A former Haitian slave, Charles Deslondes, led the January 1811 German Coast Uprising in southern Louisiana. The slave rebels planned to seize New Orleans and declare it a free city.[51] After armed clashes north of the city, the rebellion was crushed and the participants were executed en masse. A few years later, Denmark Vesey, a free Black man, helped to organize an insurrectionary plot in Charleston, South Carolina. The revolt was planned for July 14, 1822, Bastille Day. The liberated slaves planned to escape to Haiti after the uprising. City officials caught wind of the plan ahead of time, and executed Vesey as well as many alleged co-conspirators who had been members of the African Methodist Episcopal church in Charleston, which Vesey had helped to found.[52]

Four years later, in 1826, a group of enslaved African Americans on a slave-trading vessel fresh out of the port of Baltimore bound for Georgia rose up and seized control of the slave ship *Decatur.* After throwing the captain and first mate overboard, the insurrectionists ordered the surviving crew members to steer a course for Haiti and liberty. Unfortunately, the ship was soon boarded by the crew of a Yankee whaling vessel. The mutineers were seized and brought to New York. Although most of the slave rebels managed to escape soon after landfall, William Bowser, one of the leaders of the revolt, was sentenced to death.[53]

In 1825, free African Americans in Baltimore gathered to celebrate the twenty-first anniversary of Haitian independence. Honoring the Haitian Revolution in Baltimore was especially meaningful in light of the grueling conditions that African Americans faced in Maryland. Maryland was a slave state that bordered nonslave states of the North, and Baltimore was a large slave entrepôt. Slave traders thrived in the region. They brokered the sale of thousands of slaves from Virginia and Maryland to toil on the plantations and slave labor camps of the booming South of the Mississippi River Valley. Black families were routinely broken apart by sales.[54] A Baltimore-based reporter noted in 1845:

> Dealing in slaves has become a large business—establishments are made in several places in Maryland and Virginia, at which they are sold like cattle. These places of deposit are strongly built, and well supplied with thumb-screws and gags, and ornamented with cowskins and other whips, *often-times bloody!* From these prisons they are driven in droves to the Southern market, and the cruelties and atrocities practiced upon them between Baltimore, Washington, and New Orleans, are scarcely excelled by the agonies of the middle passage.[55]

A spectator of a slave auction in Baltimore wrote, "I saw a mother whose very frame was convulsed with anguish for her first born, a girl of 18, who had been sold to this dealer and was among the number then shipped. I saw a young man who kept pace with the carriages, that he might catch one more glimpse of a dear friend, before she was torn forever from his sight. As she saw him, she burst into a flood of tears, sorrowing most of all that they should see each other's faces no more."[56] Frederick Douglass recalled of his youth in Baltimore, "In the deep still darkness of midnight, I have been often aroused by the dead heavy footsteps, and the piteous cries of the chained gangs that passed our door. The anguish of my boyish heart was intense."[57]

The historians Ned and Constance Sublette have argued, "No less than any other form of capitalism, slavery was premised on continual expansion."[58] Baltimore's proximity to Northern cities that were heavily invested in slavery's infrastructure of credit, insurance, shipbuilding, and land speculation in the South made the Maryland port a key junction point for providing slave labor and commodities to New Orleans and other Southern ports.[59] Approximately one million enslaved workers were shipped from cities such as Baltimore, Charleston, South Carolina, and Washington, DC, to the burgeoning plantations of the Deep South, which supplied the majority of the world's cotton to Great Britain, France, and other rapidly industrializing nations.[60] According to one historian, "In 1830, the aggregate value of United States slaves was about $577 million. The economic power value in 2014 dollars would be $9.84 trillion (56 percent of 2014 GDP)."[61]

Another observer wrote in anguish in 1828,

> When I reflect that such shocking and flagitious spectacles, as chains, handcuffs, soul drivers, and human victims, can be exhibited on the Christian Sabbath in the city of Baltimore, and with that impunity, nay, under the immediate inspection of professors of religion, many of whom contribute to the perpetuation of this hellish traffic, in their exercise of the elective franchise—when I reflect that the ministers of the gospel, for the most part, are as silent on this subject as the dead, I tell you, the blood runs cold in my veins, "I" indeed "tremble for my country."[62]

Slavery inflicted a state of terror in Black communities. Deceitful traders kidnapped free Blacks, often young children, in cities like

Philadelphia and transported them to Baltimore for sale. The *Pennsylvania Freeman* noted, "There is [*sic*] about 25 or more young men, or rowdies I ought to say, who make a practice of enticing away from Philadelphia poor neglected colored children, and bring them to this market [Baltimore]; and, from outward appearances here, they take into Slavery more every year than all the Anti-Slavery Societies take from it."[63] William Watkins, a Baltimore resident who was a prominent educator, leader of the free Black community, and the adoptive parent of a young girl, Frances Ellen Watkins, lamented, "When our children are out of our sight, we feel a painful anxiety for their safety, which none experience but those who are similarly circumstanced."[64] The *National Era* observed: "The laws of Maryland were framed with a special eye to the oppressor's interests, rather than to those of the oppressed—to protect the strong rather than the weak!"[65]

African Americans in Maryland struggled to keep their families intact. Nine-year-old Henry Highland Garnet's parents decided to flee Maryland to avoid being sold separately. After following the Underground Railroad to New York, young Henry served as a cabin boy on voyages to Cuba, where he witnessed firsthand the horrors of Spanish slavery.[66] Charity Still escaped with her four children in an effort to be reunited with her husband in New Jersey, only to be recaptured and returned to her master on Maryland's Eastern Shore. Shortly thereafter, Still escaped once again but had to leave two of her children behind in slavery, one of whom was later beaten to death.[67] Henry Stewart, who escaped slavery from Maryland in 1855, vividly recalled the time when his master had negotiated the sale of a young boy on his plantation to a Georgia slave trader. When the boy's mother discovered this, she barricaded the young child in her house and yelled at the dumbfounded slave monger, "You are after my son; but the first man that comes into my house, I will split his head open."[68] In 1849, Harriet Tubman escaped from Eliza Ann Brodess's Eastern Shore estate to freedom in Philadelphia. Barely a year later, Tubman made her way back to Maryland. The woman who became known as both "Moses" and "General Tubman" began liberating first her family members and later other enslaved people as she ingeniously helped to build up the foundation of the Underground Railroad in Baltimore.[69]

These self-emancipated abolitionists undermined slavery from within.[70] "Runaway slave" notices published in Southern newspapers bear witness to the struggle to keep kin and community together. The following notice was printed in the Baltimore newspaper the *Sun* in September 1842:

> 200 DOLLARS REWARD—Ranaway from the subscribers, living 4 1/2 miles from Baltimore, on the Frederick Turnpike, on Saturday night, Sept 3d, 1842, TEN NEGROES, answering to the following descriptions: REISIN, a very dark Negro Man, aged about 36 years, 5 feet 6 or 7 inches high; EVELINA, his wife, a bright mulatto, aged about 35 years, who also took with her son DANIEL, a bright mulatto, aged nine years; FLAVELLA, a dark mulatto, aged about 34 years; LUCY, a bright mulatto, aged about 18 years; GREEN, a bright mulatto, aged about 13 years; JOHN, a dark mulatto, aged about 10 years; with 1 Negro Boy 5 years, and 2 female children, one an infant.
>
> It is supposed that JOHN SMITH, (husband of Flavella), has absconded with them—he is a negro about 35 or 36 years of age, 6 feet 1 or 2 inches in height, lisps slightly when speaking.[71]

Free black people in Baltimore and Maryland endured the same punishing social conditions facing their counterparts throughout the South. They were accused of insolence, rampant criminality, and collusion with the Underground Railroad. Slaveholders pushed for the passage of laws to force free Blacks to move out of the region.[72] The Baltimore-based *Niles Weekly Register* magazine commented, "There is no State in this Union, in which the ingredients for civil strife, of the most fearful character, are so largely congregated as in the State of Maryland."[73] William Watkins remarked,

> We live among a professedly Christian people, whose comfort, prosperity and happiness, have been greatly promoted by our peaceable demeanor, our docility and industry; and yet, such is the inveterately bitter prejudice entertained against us—such the jealous suspicion with which we are

viewed—such the consequently illiberal, the unjust, the cruel policy exercised in relation to us, that we can scarcely feel, at any time, secure, either in our persons or property.[74]

State governments and private citizens used every weapon at their disposal to beat back Black resistance.[75] When a group of escaped slaves was spotted outside Rockville, Maryland, the town's white male populace mobilized and carried out an assault designed to strike fear into any would-be runaways. An account of the confrontation appeared in the *National Anti-Slavery Standard*: "I learn from a gentleman who was present at the arrest of the gang of runaway negroes, near Rockville, Maryland, that they were treated in the most brutal manner by their captors. When surrounded by the Rockville volunteers, they were commanded to surrender, and because one out of the forty showed a determination to resist a whole volley of balls from rifles and pistols was poured indiscriminately among them."[76] The proslavery correspondent who told this story reported that the white attackers "regretted that they 'could not make the damn niggers resist so that they might have the pleasure of shooting them all down.'" Whites who did not own slaves routinely served in slave patrols or sometimes in vigilante groups to lay claim to a tenuous white citizenship earned by the protection of private property—wealthier people's property.[77]

Even Blacks who had managed to purchase their freedom knew that the limited liberties they enjoyed could be taken from them in an instant. Free African Americans in Baltimore opened their newspapers one day in the summer of 1827 to read the following warning:

MAYOR'S OFFICE
—NOTICE TO PERSONS OF COLOUR.—
The city Watchmen are authorised and directed to arrest and convert to the Watch Houses of their districts, all persons of colour found in any of the streets, lanes, alleys, or any open grounds in their respective Wards, at or after the hour of 11 o'clock, P.M. unless such person shall have a written permit, from his or her master or mistress.[78]

Like their counterparts in other major cities, the free Black community in Baltimore built strong cultures of resistance by organizing churches, schools, and fraternal organizations for mutual aid and survival.[79] These institutions would serve African Americans well for the struggles to come. Generations later, the *Christian Recorder* asked: "Look back at 1816. What do we see? [Richard] Allen, Coker, and the little band of noble heroes in Baltimore and Philadelphia."[80] The Reverend Daniel Coker preached freedom from the pulpit of Baltimore's African Methodist Episcopal Church in the 1810s, and the Black community's persistence served as an inspiration for generations of abolitionists, including Benjamin Lundy, William Watkins, Frederick Douglass, William Lloyd Garrison, and many others. William Watkins was a graduate of Rev. Coker's Bethel Charity School and went on to found Watkins' Academy for Negro Youth in the 1820s.

Even as merchants promoted the city as a haven for profits in slavery, in the early 1800s, African Americans and their allies transformed Baltimore into a center of anti-slavery resistance.[81] Well into the twenty-first century, archeologists continued to discover hidden tunnels, camouflaged cisterns, and secret compartments in church basements that harbored fugitive slaves. Baltimore's white elite despaired of the ever-expanding Underground Railroad in Maryland and beyond.[82] Writing as "A Colored Baltimorean," William Watkins penned a series of commentaries beginning in the 1820s for *Freedom's Journal*, one of the first Black newspapers in the country, in which he predicted doom for the nation that perpetuated human servitude: "Slavery has destroyed kingdoms and empires, and what may we not expect will happen to those religious communities in which this crying evil is tolerated? The least evils that we can expect are disaffection and division."[83]

African Americans in Baltimore who gathered in August 1825 to commemorate Haitian independence and the first successful slave revolution in history knew firsthand what tyranny was; they lived every day with the fear of physical violence, economic insecurity, and re-enslavement. They looked to Haiti as a beacon of liberty unlike anything that existed in the United States. Local people had direct contact with Haitians whose masters had brought them to Baltimore decades earlier to flee the results of the revolution, and they were quite aware of the negative narrative that their white counterparts attempted to spin about the country of Haiti.[84] Haiti was viewed by the ruling classes of the United States, France, and Great Britain as a threat to slavery, colonialism, and white rule, a veritable "contagion of liberty." Thomas Jefferson had plotted against the Black revolutionaries and had urged Napoleon Bonaparte to re-enslave the upstart Haitians.[85] Event organizers in Baltimore designed their Haitian tribute to provide the kind of democratic education to each other and to their youth that could not be attained from their own nation's educational institutions.

They raised their glasses to "Washington, Toussaint, and Bolivar—Unequalled in fame—the friends of mankind—the glorious advocates of Liberty."[86] With this gesture, African Americans connected the fate of their own freedom with the emancipation of people in Latin America and the Caribbean. The toast reflected a distinct understanding of the connections between movements for freedom throughout the Americas. Simón Bolívar (1783–1830), the former slave owner in the land that was to become the Venezuelan republic, was an admired figure in African American communities because of his Decrees of 1816, which freed enslaved people willing to fight on behalf of the Third Republic of Venezuela. These declarations followed Bolívar's meeting with the Haitian president Alexandre Pétion, who pledged military and financial support to El Liberator contingent on his ending slavery. In gratitude, Bolívar proclaimed, "Should I not let it be known to later generations that Alexandre Pétion is the true liberator of my Country?"[87]

The port of Baltimore was situated at the nexus of Africa, Europe, the Caribbean, and Latin America. While slave traders and merchants attempted to turn the Eastern Seaboard into a springboard for a continental slave empire, African American freedom fighters sought to destabilize that empire from within. If cities such as Baltimore were conduits for slavery and racial capitalism, African Americans were determined to transform their neighborhoods into communities of struggle. The people of this booming port city were at the epicenter of the greatest questions bedeviling the young republic. Baltimore's Black churches, neighborhoods, hidden cellars, and shipyards nurtured freedom fighters who carried the African American freedom struggle out of embattled Baltimore and into the broader world. Charity Still, Harriet Tubman, William Watkins, Frederick Douglass, and so many others left Baltimore to become prophets of justice. Their children and their pupils carried on the struggle into the era of the Civil War. Frances Ellen Watkins, whose career as an abolitionist, Underground Railroad conductor, writer, and cofounder of the National Association of Colored Women spanned seven decades, spoke for Black Baltimoreans when, years after departing from the tormented city, she wrote the poem "Bury Me in a Free Land":

> *Make me a grave where'er you will,*
> *In a lowly plain, or a lofty hill;*
> *Make it among earth's humblest graves,*
> *But not in a land where men are slaves.*
>
> *I could not rest if I heard the tread*
> *Of coffee gang to the shambles led,*
> *And the mother's shriek of wild despair*
> *Rise like a curse on the trembling air.*
>
> *If I saw young girls from their mother's arms*
> *Bartered and sold for their youthful charms,*
> *My eye would flash with a mournful flame,*
> *My death-paled cheek grow red with shame.*
>
> *I ask no monument, proud and high.*
> *To arrest the gaze of passers by;*
> *All that my yearning spirit craves.*
> *Is bury me not in a land of slaves.*[88]

In 1827, *Freedom's Journal* joined Black Baltimoreans in promoting emancipatory internationalism by linking together the fate of African Americans with their embattled brothers and sisters in Latin America, stating:

> The truth is, the new Republics of North and South America have set us an example on the subject of slavery, which we should do well to imitate, under such modifications as our peculiar circumstances render necessary. If we remember right, the last slave in Colombia is to be emancipated within the present year. Peru has essentially lightened the

burden which for centuries had oppressed the poor Indians, and Mexico evinced by her decision in enforcing the
law on behalf of enslaved Africans, that she is determined
not to be behind her sister Republics in this cause of justice,
humanity and religion.[89]

African Americans paid tribute to slave rebellions, wars of independence, and revolutions against caste oppression that were firing
the Western Hemisphere's nights with the glow of freedom. The
steady drumbeat of anticolonial insurgencies filled African Americans with hope. Though the *Freedom's Journal*'s analysis of the outcome of the Latin American independence wars exaggerated their
immediacy—the final abolition of slavery in Colombia would not
occur until 1851—the newspaper's main argument was that one had
to study events in Mexico and Latin America if one hoped to gain
a greater understanding about the processes of emancipation and
democracy.

Meanwhile, the progress of antislavery insurgencies in Haiti,
Mexico, and Latin America filled US political leaders with dread.
Something would have to be done to limit the spread of liberty to
those whom it was not intended to grace. John Adams created a rigid
framework for US American exceptionalism by arguing that the
Black people of the Western Hemisphere did not have the capacity
for self-rule. In 1815, the former president of the United States asked,
"When the National Convention in France voted all the Negroes in
St. Domingo, Martinique, Guardaloupe [*sic*] St. Lucie [*sic*] & free at
a breath did the poor Democracy among the Negroes gain any thing
by the Change?" Contrasting the Haitian and American Revolutions, Adams depicted the Haitian masses as ignorant: "Did they not
immediately fall into the Power of Aristocrats of their own Colour?
Are they more free, from Toussaint to Petion & Christophe? Do
they live better? Bananas and Water, they Still enjoy, and a whole
Regiment would follow a Leader, who should hold a Salt fish to their
Noses."[90] John Adams associated democracy with whiteness and
tyranny with blackness.

African Americans, by contrast, lifted up the Haitian Revolution
as a great moment in world history to learn from. In 1827, in *Freedom's Journal*, it was stated, "There are very few events on record

which have produced more extraordinary men than the revolution in St. Domingo. The negro character at that eventful period, burst upon us in all the splendor of native and original greatness; and the subsequent transactions in that Island have presented the most incontestable truths that the negro is not, in general, wanting in the higher qualifications of the mind."[91] Decades later, the Baltimore *Afro-American* paid tribute to General Máximo Gómez, a leader of the Cuban insurrection against Spanish colonialism, by observing, "The brave and courageous words of Gomez bring before us the noble figure of Toussaint L'Ouverture."[92] Black writers urged their audiences to understand that the liberty had reached its summit not in the United States but in Haiti.[93]

Frederick Douglass spoke about the Haitian Revolution at the World's Columbian Exposition in Chicago in 1893. Douglass presented Haiti as the original beacon of liberty in the Americas. His audience responded affirmatively:

> Speaking for the Negro, I can say, we owe much to Walker for his appeal; to John Brown [applause] for the blow struck at Harper's Ferry, to Lundy and Garrison for their advocacy [applause], We owe much especially to Thomas Clarkson [applause], to William Wilberforce, to Thomas Fowell Buxton, and to the anti-slavery societies at home and abroad; but we owe incomparably more to Haiti than to them all. [Prolonged applause.] I regard her as the original pioneer emancipator of the nineteenth century. [Applause.][94]

Douglass's homage to Haiti reaffirmed what too many would forget in subsequent generations: the Haitian Revolution was the inspiration for the pursuit of liberty in the Americas.

In the nineteenth century, slavery was understood to be the cornerstone of American exceptionalism. The proslavery *New York Daily News* mocked slavery's detractors as not understanding the foundations of American business prosperity: "If slavery was so great a sin, how comes it that through its agency this country attained the greatest amount of prosperity in the shortest space of time any nation ever attained?"[95] The pursuit of profit at the expense of Black lives was the central theme in early US history. As C. L. R. James, an Afro-Trinidadian historian, observed, "Negro slavery seemed the very basis of American capitalism."[96] The single-minded pursuit of wealth and power launched by the Patriot leaders and their descendants engulfed the continent in a series of violent conflicts culminating in the bloodiest civil war in human history.[97]

In the wake of the Haitian Revolution, African Americans envisioned a new kind of freedom that transcended national borders. They urged the opening of a global liberation front. Emancipatory internationalism gained momentum as the abolition of slavery spread throughout the world, and as Black organizers strengthened ties with activists outside of the United States. William Whipper, a key Black abolitionist, credited the activity of the oppressed in their own behalf—not the enlightenment of the British—with abolition in the Caribbean:

> How was the emancipation of the slave, and the enfranchisement of the free colored people effected there? We unhesitatingly affirm, that it was chiefly through the influence of colored men—the oppressed; by that restless discontentment that changed deeply injured slaves into insurgent runaways, by that manly bearing and living purpose, with which the free people of color contended for their rights, and which, especially in Jamaica, led the noble [Edward] Jordan and his compeers to some of the most daring and heroic acts in the annals of the race; which confer honor upon the people who seconded him, and which ultimately will give him an emblazoned immortality.[98]

For African Americans and their abolitionist allies, the anti-slavery movement did not begin or end in the United States; it was conceived of most broadly as an anti-imperial cause. The *National Anti-Slavery Standard* opined, "Slavery kills; it commits adultery; it steals; it bears false witness; it covets Texas, Mexico, and Indian Territory, all that is its neighbors, and says aloud—perish all the commandments."[99] As the battle against slavery caught fire across the Americas, the people of Mexico prepared to strike a blow against the Spanish Empire, while their counterparts in the United States fine-tuned the praxis of resistance.

CHAPTER 2

THE MEXICAN WAR OF INDEPENDENCE AND US HISTORY

ANTI-IMPERIALISM AS A WAY OF LIFE, 1820s TO 1850s

In the summer of 1815, José María Morelos, leader of the Mexican War of Independence, wrote to President James Madison requesting the support of the United States in his people's struggle against Spanish colonialism. A former *arriero* (mule driver) and Roman Catholic priest turned revolutionary general, Morelos, a man of African, Indigenous, and European descent, had presented "Los Sentimientos de la Nación" at the historic National Constituent Congress in Chilpancingo in southern Mexico. The "Feelings of the Nation" called for the abolition of slavery and for an end to the de jure caste oppression of Indigenous people as well as independence from Spain.[1] "Los Sentimientos" banned torture, forbade military invasions of other nations, promised the "education of the poor," and was the banner that the barefoot armies of African, Indigenous, and mestizo guerrilla fighters carried in their war of liberation.[2]

The axioms presented in "Los Sentimientos" were a rejection of three centuries of European colonialism. Just a few years earlier the German explorer and scientist Alexander von Humboldt had described the racial caste system of New Spain that Morelos and his soldiers were now risking their lives to overthrow: "In a country governed by whites, the families reputed to have the least mixture of Negro or mulatto blood are also naturally the most honored. In Spain it is almost a title of nobility to descend neither from Jews nor Moors. In America the greater or less degree of whiteness of skin decides the rank which man occupies in society. A white who rides barefooted on horseback thinks he belongs to the nobility of the country."[3] As a priest, Morelos had engaged in an act of resistance during the 1804 *padron* (census) by refusing to categorize people by race.[4]

Morelos, Miguel Hidalgo, Vicente Guerrero, and their comrades recruited fighters to the Mexican War of Independence by invoking the ideals of "civil rights and racial equality."[5] The war began on September 16, 1810, and "the first addition which he [Morelos] received to this force, on arriving on the coast, was a numerous band of slaves from Petatlán, and other towns, eager to purchase their liberty on the field of battle: arms were, however, so scarce, that twenty muskets, which were discovered in Petatlán, were considered as a most invaluable acquisition."[6] This insurgency was condemned by royalist leaders in New Spain as "an uprising against the rich people."[7] While some elite leaders—like their counterparts in the United States—schemed to maintain their suzerainty over the rest of the society in the transition to independence, "the peasants and workers who formed the bulk of the insurgent ranks had very different goals, such as access to land and improved working conditions."[8] The royalist general Félix María Calleja wrote to King Ferdinand that Morelos's soldiers wished for "the Independence of the country, and the proscription of all the Europeans, whom they detest."[9] Morelos seized every opportunity to publicly denounce slavery as well as caste repression against Indigenous people; his troops revered him for his moral and physical courage. Morelos's education to the priesthood gave him educational advantages his soldiers could only dream of; according to one chronicler in the *Negro Digest*, however, "He had not forgotten the 20-odd years spent as an unlettered mule driver. . . . He never became so well educated that the poor and uneducated peasants could not understand him and he them."[10] Awed at his adversary's ingenuity and the morale of José Morelos's fatally outgunned troops at the Siege of Cuautla in 1812, General Calleja called Morelos "a second Mahomet."[11]

José María Morelos attempted to gain President James Madison's support for the cause of Mexican independence against the Spanish Empire. But how could this priest turned battle-hardened general fighting to abolish caste oppression connect with Madison, a political philosopher who refused to end slavery in his own new nation? Morelos opened his communication with Madison by reminding

Madison of America's own independence struggle by foregrounding the evils of European colonialism, writing:

> Dear Sir: The Mexican people, tired of suffering under the enormous weight of the Spanish domination, and forever losing their hope of being happy under the government of their conquerors, broke the dikes of moderation, and braving difficulties and dangers that seemed insurmountable for those of an enslaved colony, raised the cry of liberty and courageously undertook the work of their regeneration.[12]

José Morelos urged President Madison to see that the Mexican people were following in the footsteps of the Thirteen Colonies in their desperate battle for freedom:

> I could not forsake the obvious Justice of our cause, nor abandon the righteousness and purity of our intentions aimed exclusively for the good of humanity: we trust in the spirit and enthusiasm of our patriots who are determined to die first rather than return to the offensive yoke of slavery; and finally we trusted in the powerful support of the United States, who has guided us wisely with example. . . . We have sustained for five years our fight, practically convincing ourselves that there is no power capable of subduing a people determined to save themselves from the horrors of tyranny.

Morelos offered a vision of emancipatory internationalism to James Madison and asked the American statesman to imagine the combined power they could wield against all foreign enemies: "The sincerity and philanthropic spirit that characterize both Nations: the ease and speed that they can mutually communicate their assistance to each other: the beautiful bond that will result between the two peoples, the one privileged by fertility and productions so rich and varied from its soil, and the other distinguished by its industry, by its culture, and by its genius." This potential alliance between "the North Americas and Mexicana," in the words of Morelos, would make the two peoples "invincible to the aggressions of greed, ambition, and tyranny."[13] José María Morelos's efforts to recruit

Madison to support the Mexican War of Independence represented a moment of unparalleled opportunity for the United States to place itself on the side of liberty for all—not just in its rhetoric, but in its actions.

"SOUTH AMERICAN LIBERTY"

If Mexico's looming abolition of slavery disturbed US leaders, rebellions of African Americans and Native Americans in Spanish Florida terrified them. Secretary of State John Quincy Adams gave the pretext for launching the First Seminole War (1816–19) by claiming that during the War of 1812, British commanders in Florida "in their invitations and promises to the slaves to run away from their masters and join them, did not confine themselves to the slaves of the United States. They received with as hearty a welcome, and employed with equal readiness, the fugitives from their masters in Florida as those from Georgia."[14] John Quincy Adams frequently clashed with General Andrew Jackson in the political conflicts of the early republic; however, Adams agreed with the general on the need to secure the nation's southern borders against the threat of slave revolt.[15]

Adams denigrated the insurgencies in Latin America in letters to his family as well as in his diplomatic correspondence with Spain. These missives illuminate the attitude of Secretary Adams on race, democracy, and citizenship. Adams contrasted the American Revolution, which he characterized as a "war of freemen," with the Latin American wars of independence:

> The struggle in South-America, is savage and ferocious almost beyond example. It is not the tug of war between Greek and Greek, but the tyger-conflict between Spaniard and Spaniard—The Cause has never been the same in any two of the revolting Colonies—Independence has not even been the pretext during great part of the time—Sometimes they have fought for Ferdinand; sometimes for the Cortes— Sometimes for Congresses and Constitutions, and sometimes for particular leaders, like Morales [sic] Hidalgo,

Artigas, or Bolivar—The resemblance between this Revolution and ours is barely superficial. In all their leading
characters the two Events, present a contrast, instead of a
parallel—Ours was a War of freemen, for political Independence—This is a War of Slaves against their masters—
It has all the horrors and all the atrocities of a servile War.[16]

Adams revealingly compared the Latin American wars of independence with the Servile Wars, slave revolts in the late Roman
Republic, which according to the historian Plutarch contributed to
its fall.[17] The future president of the United States told his father,
John Adams, that while some Americans sympathized with the wars
of independence in South America, the Latin American insurgents
"by their internal elements of the exterminating war between black
and white, present to us the prospect of very troublesome and dangerous associates, and still more fearful allies. Such are the ingredients of the caldron, *which will soon be at boiling heat* [italics in
original]."[18]

For John Quincy Adams, General Andrew Jackson served as the
perfect weapon to keep the caldron from boiling over. As secretary
of state, Adams made expansion of the nation's borders one of his
foremost goals. Adams defended Jackson's controversial conduct in
the First Seminole War, including his summary execution of two
British subjects because, as Adams told George William Erving, the
US minister to Spain, they had "invited by public proclamations,
all the runaway negroes, all the savage Indians, all the pirates and
all the traitors to their country, whom they knew or imagined to
exist within reach of their summons, to join their standard, and
wage an exterminating war against the portion of the United States
immediately bordering upon this neutral and thus violated territory of Spain."[19] Adams instructed Erving to explain to the Spanish government that Jackson's destruction of the Negro Fort on the
Apalachicola River was necessary because the redoubt had become
a "receptacle for fugitive slaves and malefactors, to the great annoy-
ance of the United States and of Spanish Florida."[20]

While negotiating the treaty that allowed the United States to
acquire Florida (Florida became a state in 1845), Secretary Adams
used the language of empire in explaining his country's military

conduct to Spain.[21] Adams claimed that the African American and
Native American men, women, and children who peopled the Negro
Fort were engaged in a "savage, servile, exterminating war against
the United States."[22] Leaders of the early American republic were
concerned with the destabilizing effect of African and Indigenous
resistance on slavery's southeastern frontier; the US "international"
border was at Georgia's southern border. Adams railed at what he
called the Negro Fort's "fugitive slaves and Indian outlaws; these
perfidies and treacheries of villains incapable of keeping their faith
even to each other; all in the name of South American liberty, of the
rights of runaway negroes, and the wrongs of savage murderers all
combined and projected to plunder Spain of her province, and to
spread massacre and devastation along the borders of the United
States." Adams lectured Erving that although outsiders may have
judged Jackson's prosecution of the war in Florida to be extreme,
"The justification of these principles is found in their salutary effi-
cacy for terror and for example. It is thus only that the barbarities of
the Indians can be successfully encountered."[23]

John Quincy Adams's rationale for waging war to protect the
United States from the dangers of "South American liberty" reveals
much about race and the political ideology of the United States.
Adams's denigration of the Mexican War of Independence demonstrates that a central motivation for US imperial expansion into the
West—the concept of manifest destiny—was that it would preempt
the threat of revolt in the United States and keep the institution of
slavery intact.[24] At the same time, Adams disparaged Mexicans as
inferior—he could not accept that they were capable of waging a genuine war of independence. His point of view would have shocked José
María Morelos and those who fought for liberation from European
colonialism *and* an end to slavery—all without plotting to annihilate
their former masters. Adams racialized people in Mexico and Latin
America in ways that would haunt their descendants in the United
States well into the twenty-first century. José Morelos's vision of a
"beautiful bond" between Mexico and the United States was doomed
by the imperatives of racial capitalism. When the most powerful leaders in the early republic era looked to what we now call the Global
South, they saw disorder; they could not accept that the region's people were the equals of the heirs of the American Revolution. What

scholars call the "racialization" of Mexican Americans in the nine-teenth century was rooted in the imperatives of imperial slavery.[25]

Shortly after negotiating the Adams-Onis Treaty in 1819, which allowed the United States to acquire Florida, Adams helped to frame the Monroe Doctrine. The goal was to aid US investors in the island's sugar plantations by keeping the British Royal Navy from interfer-ing with slavery in Cuba.[26] While armies of liberation were disman-tling slavery all throughout Latin America, the Monroe Doctrine gave the slave trade a new lease on life in Cuba. Once again, Adams invoked the specter of race to argue that Cubans were incapable of fighting a genuine war of independence.[27] Adams warned that there was much to fear from Cuban independence, especially the possibil-ity that a slave rebellion in Cuba could potentially destabilize slavery in the United States. Race and trade trumped all other consider-ations in Secretary Adams's diplomatic mind.[28] In a rush to expand the frontiers of slavery and racial capitalism, James Madison, John Adams, and John Quincy Adams foreclosed the possibility of coop-eration with the independence movements in Latin America and the Caribbean.

EMANCIPATORY INTERNATIONALISM VS.
THE BLOODY BANNER OF SLAVERY

Mexicans, African Americans, and their abolitionist allies con-ceived of a hemispheric liberation movement that would not be tied to nationality nor constrained by borders. They also knew that slav-ery's relentless cycle of growth would destroy democracy. If "addi-tional territory had been denied to the slavery of the old slave States," noted the abolitionist paper *National Era*, "it would have been at least in process of abolition. But it was allowed to propagate itself, and, in so doing, it gathered new life. Not only were the new States, formed out of the territory originally possessed by the Union, given up to its ravages, but Florida, and the immense territory of Louisi-ana, were opened to it."[29] *National Era* grieved, "Why deceive our-selves? The establishment of slavery in California, in New Mexico, or a part of it, and throughout Texas, will invest the slave-holding class with a power, from which there can be no escape."[30]

African Americans linked Black struggles with anticolonial movements in the Caribbean and South America.[31] *Freedom's Journal* argued that the liberation armies of Latin America were multiracial: "What is the complexion of the common soldiery of these states? Has not the independence of their country from the vassalage and bondage of Old Spain, been accomplished by troops composed of negroes, mulattoes and indians?"[32] Celebrating emancipation in the British West Indies, Frederick Douglass presented the brief for emancipatory internationalism: "Neither geographical boundaries, nor national restrictions, ought, or shall prevent me from rejoicing over the triumphs of freedom, no matter where or by whom achieved."[33] Douglass challenged the notion that it was possible to confine the idea of freedom within the boundaries of one nation: "On this question, we are strangers to nationality. Our platform is as broad as humanity. We repudiate, with unutterable loathing and disgust, that narrow spirit which would confine our duties to one quarter of the globe, to the exclusion of another."[34]

Internationalist visions of emancipation thrived in the early antebellum era. The abolition of slavery in Mexico, timed to coincide with the anniversary of Mexican independence in 1829, was a shattering blow against the United States. The antislavery spirit stoked by José Morelos, Vicente Guerrero, and the Mexican War of Independence persisted, and made Mexico a sanctuary for African Americans fleeing from the burgeoning slave labor camps of the Southwest. Sensing the possibility of finding freedom in Mexico, enslaved African Americans as far away as Florida escaped to the Republic of Mexico. This newest trunk line of the Underground Railroad was so successful that it provoked congressional action even before Mexico's formal abolition of slavery. In 1826, Congressman William Brent of Louisiana spearheaded a successful resolution before the House of Representatives demanding

> that the President of the United States be requested to inform this House whether any measures have been taken to obtain the runaway negro slaves from Louisiana and elsewhere, which have taken *refuge* in the territories of that Government [of Mexico]; and also whether any measures

have been taken with the Government of Mexico to enable citizens of the United States to recover debts from those who have fled from the United States to the territories of Mexico.[35]

The United States attempted to negotiate a treaty with Mexico for the "surrender of such fugitive slaves as might seek refuge on the soil of that Republic. But the treaty was rejected by the Mexican Congress, which denounced slavery as a 'palpable violation of the first principles of a free republic.'"[36]

Even as Mexico was shutting down slavery, the United States was expanding it. The *National Anti-Slavery Standard* described how imperial slavery worked during the Mississippi land boom of the 1830s. As cotton prices rose, "Immediately a clamor was raised in Georgia and Mississippi for the Indian lands. Georgia has a surplus slave population, which she must send out of the State, or find employment for by opening new lands." As long as Native Americans lived in their ancestral homelands, however, white settler-colonists could not make money. "To this end, as well as to reap the benefit of the high price of cotton, [Georgia] must oust the Cherokees. Mississippi, influenced more especially by the cotton fever, and a desire to increase the population of the state by the emigration of planters and others [from the East], must oust the Choctaws." Slavery's advocates also pointed to alliances between Indigenous people and slaves as another reason for pursuing the path of genocidal removal. The historian William Loren Katz argues that "I believe that one of the reasons the Native American nations were moved out in the removal that began in the 1830s . . . is because these nations had become a harbor—a safe haven—for slaves that were escaping."[37]

The *National Anti-Slavery Standard* noted that Yankee entrepreneurs promoted the expansion of slavery in the Mississippi Valley:

Northern merchants and capitalists, some in person, and some by their agents, rushed to the spot. Some Bostonians went, authorized to buy up lands, on northern paper, to be sure, to the extent of half a million of dollars. . . . That was the beginning of the land speculation mania. It went from Mississippi to other states. . . . But the new lands were valueless, and could yield no fortunes, unless they were cultivated. The cultivators were not there. They must be had.[38]

This was where slave traders in the Upper South entered the scene: "So, in came the cultivators, in the shape of 90,000 slaves, valued at $90,000,000[,] imported in the space of three years or so, from Virginia, Maryland, Kentucky, and other slave-breeding states."

Slavery's financiers built the economy by convincing the nation to wage war and to clear out new areas for exploitation.[39] The *Sacramento Daily Union* explained how racial capitalism worked: "The slave owner being a capitalist, must also have the best land, or the labor of his slave cannot be made as profitable as to loan out the $1,200 paid for him."[40] "What does the past teach?" asked another abolitionist newspaper, and answered the question:

That slavery lives by expansion. Slave labor cannot, on the whole, be profitably used in manufactures, commerce, or farming. In the growth of sugar, cotton, tobacco—that is, in planting—it may be turned to pecuniary account; but planting is an exhausting process, and, to be conducted with permanent advantage to the planter, requires constant accessions of territory. Deny it these, and see the results. The soil is impoverished; the free population of moderate means is forced out of the State.[41]

"The native inhabitants of Mexico, are, almost to a man, opposed to slavery," wrote the abolitionist editor Benjamin Lundy shortly after Mexican emancipation. "The system has been *totally* abolished in every section of the Republic, except in Texas."[42] In 1832, an ex-slave named Richard Moran praised Mexico as offering an "asylum" from slavery and told William Lloyd Garrison, "That republic, we know, is as extensive as our own, and although at a greater distance than Canada, yet it is near enough. I have long wondered why it is that my colored brethren do not turn their attention to that republic. There is no distinction of color in politics or law. It seems to me that the Province of Texas, in that republic, must attract the attention of my colored brethren in these States." This former slave informed Garrison, "Nothing keeps me from that country [Mexico] but a total loss of health for many years, and consequently abject poverty. I have seen persons who have travelled pretty extensively in it, and from their report it is certainly a desirable part of the world to live in."[43]

These visions of freedom in the Southwest received a tremendous boon with emancipation in the British West Indies in 1833. Drawing strength from British abolition, antislavery partisans built a new line of the Underground Railroad to the Bahamas.[44] Freedom fighters struck with force all across the empire's expanding borders. An alliance of formerly enslaved African Americans and Indigenous people in Florida kept the United States pinned down in the Second Seminole War (1835–42), which has been compared by some historians to the American War in Vietnam.[45] "The Seminole made a desperate stand for his Florida home," one historian wrote in the nineteenth century. "He was exacting from the whites a terrible price for the acres they coveted. And even more desperately than the Indian, fought the negro fugitive. Defeat for him was not the loss of land, but of liberty; to yield meant not exile, but bondage.[46] General Thomas Jessup, commander of the US military forces, wrote, "This . . . is a negro, not an Indian war," and echoed Andrew Jackson's assessment decades earlier that if the army was unable to put down the resistance, then slavery in the Deep South was imperiled. At the outset of the Second Seminole War, nearly one thousand enslaved African Americans rose in a concerted effort to join Seminole allies in fighting the United States.[47]

The epic battle for freedom being waged in the borderlands drew John Quincy Adams, now a US congressman representing Massachusetts, into the fight. Adams rose in the House of Representatives in 1836 to give one of the landmark speeches in the history of that body.[48] The erstwhile supporter of the slave republic delivered an hours-long stinging repudiation of the coming war with Mexico as well as a brief against the aggression of Anglo settler colonists against Mexicans, Seminoles, and African Americans. The former president of the United States spoke without notes and ignored his colleagues' jeers and angry cries to sit down and to be quiet. Congressman Adams quickly established the issue at the heart of the conflict stoked by US imperialism: "Do not you, an Anglo-Saxon, slave-holding exterminator of Indians, from the bottom of your soul, hate the Mexican-Spaniard-Indian, emancipator of slaves, and abolisher of slavery? And do you think that your hatred is not with equal cordiality returned?"[49]

Barely two decades earlier, Secretary Adams had been a servant of empire, and he had belittled Mexicans for striking against their colonial masters. Now, Adams, called the "madman of Massachusetts" by his enemies, declared that he had joined the resistance.[50] Adams paid tribute to the resolute antislavery feeling among the Mexican people, and he beseeched his fellow citizens to consider the moral bankruptcy and depravity of their motives in attacking Mexico: "And again, I ask, what will be your *cause* in such a war? Aggression, conquest, and the re-establishment of slavery where it has been abolished. In that war, Sir, the banners of *freedom* will be the banners of Mexico; and your banners, I blush to speak the word, will be the banners of *slavery*."[51] Adams warned, "Your Seminole war is already spreading to the Creeks, and in their march of desolation, they sweep along with them your negro slaves, and put arms in their hands, to make common cause with them against you; and how far will it spread?" Adams urged his countrymen to retreat from their disastrous path. "Go to the city of Mexico—ask any of your fellow-citizens who have been there for the last three or four years whether they scarcely dare show their faces, as Anglo-Americans in the streets? Be assured, Sir, that however heartily you detest the Mexican, his bosom burns with an equally deep-seated detestation of you."[52] The widely translated Manifesto of the Mexican Congress, published in July 1836 in response to the uprising of proslavery Anglo settlers in the Texas Revolution, confirmed John Quincy Adams's thesis that Mexicans understood exactly why their neighbors to the north coveted their lands.[53]

An essayist writing in *Frederick Douglass' Paper*, an abolitionist journal, observed, "We began by robbing the Indians, then the Texans, then the Californians, N. Mexicans, and Utahs, and then we provoked the thunders that now roll over the relics of Mexico, and send their echo from Darien to Magellan." The exasperated essayist noted, "One more Presidential term, with a Scots or Pierce at the helm, in pursuit of these platforms and this policy, and . . .

there will not be a spot visible where the black and bloody banner of slavery and the fugitive slave law does not wave."[54] The abolitionist press referred to the Seminole Wars as "bloodhound wars" for the vicious attack dogs used by Anglo soldiers to hunt Native Americans. The *Colored American* wrote: "The conduct of General Jessup in decoying the Indians within his power by means of 'the flag of truce,' and then sending them to a dungeon is in the highest degree abominable."[55]

African Americans kept Mexico at the forefront of their hopes for future liberation.[56] The *Colored American* was outraged when, during the so-called Pastry War of 1838–39, the United States assisted France in the blockade and invasion of Veracruz. The newspaper criticized King Louis-Philippe's aggression and urged the Mexican people to resist the latest European invaders:

> The present position of Mexico is one of intense interest to the lover of liberty. All the dissension so industriously created and fomented in her by foreign emissaries, are [*sic*] giving way to a spirit of union in the defense of Mexican rights against French aggression. The sentiment 'you are a Mexican' is the call which unites the most opposite parties in that republic, to oppose the unprovoked and gratuitous attacks of the bullying Louis Philippe.[57]

At the National Negro Convention, held in Buffalo in 1843, the Reverend Henry Highland Garnet came forward with an audacious plan to stoke the flames of anti-imperial rebellion. The twenty-seven-year-old minister had already lived an eventful life. His family had barely escaped being recaptured in New York and returned to their owner when he was fourteen. His biographer noted, "Such onslaughts on colored families were not infrequent at the time: no colored man's home was secure against them."[58] In 1835, young Garnet attended Noyes Academy in New Hampshire, an integrated institution of higher learning founded by abolitionists. When the enterprising student discovered that area whites were gathering to destroy the school, Henry "spent most of the day in casting bullets in anticipation of the attack, and when the whites finally came he replied to their fire with a double-barreled shot-gun, blazing from his window, and soon drove the cowards away." Garnet's covering fire forced the whites to retreat and allowed his fellow students to escape. However, the mob later returned and destroyed the school.[59]

Before his audience in Buffalo, Garnet adamantly stated: "If you would be free in this generation, here is your only hope. However much you and all of us may desire it, there is not much hope of redemption without the shedding of blood. If you must bleed, let it all come at once—rather die freemen, than live to be slaves." The young man moved the delegates to tears with his relentless eloquence; however, many of those present—including Frederick Douglass—believed his "Call to Rebellion" proposal of a mass slave uprising would alienate supporters of the abolitionist cause and lead to immense bloodshed. Garnet, however, argued that there was no escaping the fact that the United States had an imperial plan to spread slavery everywhere it went: "The Pharaohs are on both sides of the blood red waters!" Garnet exclaimed. "You cannot move en masse, to the dominions of the British Queen—nor can you pass through Florida and overrun Texas, and at last find peace in Mexico. The propagators of American slavery are spending their blood and treasure, that they may plant the black flag in the heart of Mexico and riot in the halls of the Montezumas."[60]

Frederick Douglass spoke in Belfast, Ireland, in 1845 on the causes of US aggression against Mexico. Along with Morelos, Guerrero, and his countrywoman Harriet Tubman, Douglass arrived at the understanding that the enslaved themselves would have to deliver the decisive blows against slavery. Douglass was one of the greatest proponents of emancipatory internationalism. Now, for his Irish audience, the Lion of Anacostia proceeded to tear down decades of lies and distortions in the telling of American history. He began by paying homage to the Mexican War of Independence, discussing the 1845 US annexation of Texas and revealing how the government of Mexico had tried to compromise with Anglo-American settlers in Texas in order to institute a gradual emancipation. Douglass's Irish audience punctuated his lecture with great applause: "We do not hear of much confusion in Texas, until 1828 or 1829, when Mexico after having erected herself into a separate government and declared herself free, with a consistency which puts to the blush the boasted 'land of freedom,' proclaimed the deliverance of every captive on her soil."[61]

Back on American soil, Douglass connected the US invasion of Mexico with the oppression of labor, the extension of slavery, and the evils of militarism:

> You know as well as I do, that Faneuil Hall has resounded with echoing applause of a denunciation of the Mexican war, as a murderous war—as a war against the free states—as a war against freedom, against the Negro, and against the interests of workingmen of this country—and as a means of extending that great evil and damning curse, negro slavery. Why may not the oppressed say, when an oppressor is dead, either by disease or by the hand of the foeman on the battlefield, that there is one the less of his oppressors left on earth? For my part, I would not care if, to-morrow, I should hear of the death of every man who engaged in that bloody war in Mexico, and that every man had met the fate he went there to perpetrate upon unoffending Mexicans.[62]

When the US invasion of Mexico commenced in 1846, Black newspapers and abolitionist journals printed devastating critiques of President James Polk and the war; they denounced the idea that the assault on Mexico was about anything other than preserving and extending slavery. Martin Delany, speaking to members of the Sixth Congregational Church in Cincinnati, excoriated the United States for imperialism and "affirmed that the war was instigated for the acquisition of slave territory, at the behest of Southern slaveholders."[63]

In a letter published in the *National Anti-Slavery Standard*, Douglass wrote,

> The real character of our Government is being exposed. . . . The present administration is justly regarded as a combination of land-pirates and free-booters. Our gallant army in Mexico is looked upon as a band of legalized murderers

and plunderers. Our psalm-singing, praying, pro-slavery priesthood are stamped with hypocrisy; and all their pretensions to a love for God, while they hate and neglect their fellow-man, is branded as impudent blasphemy.[64]

Frederick Douglass' Paper reprinted a petition that the American Anti-Slavery Society had submitted to Congress demanding that the United States compensate Mexico for what was essentially an illegal war:

> Believing that the existing war between this country and Mexico originated in a desire to extend the area of Slavery, and that it is still prosecuted with the same object: We, the undersigned, inhabitants of ———— county and State of ————, respectfully request your honorable body to take immediate Measures to recall our armies from Mexican Territory, and to make full Reparations to Mexico for the wrongs we have done her.[65]

The triumph of US arms did not break the antislavery spirit of the majority of the Mexican people. The American diplomat Nicholas Trist discovered that "the Mexicans not only understood the project of forcing slavery into the territory sought to be acquired from them, but viewed it with an abhorrence which strangely contrasts with the pro-slavery proclivity of [the United States]."[66] Later, during the American Civil War, a reporter for *Californio*, Ramón Hill, affirmed that a Southern victory would mean the reestablishment of slavery in Mexico: "If a monarchy is established in the United States, Mexico will be contaminated with the cursed plague of slavery; and this would be the ultimate misfortune that the nation could suffer, for death is a thousand times preferable to regressing to the point of tolerating slavery."[67]

Resistance fighters continued battling slavery in every corner of the empire. Enslaved African Americans escaped into Mexico individually as well as in groups: "The People of Texas bordering on the Mexican provinces have also been bitterly complaining of the escape of their slaves across the Rio Grande, and the impossibility of recapturing them, threatening to redress themselves by force."[68] A correspondent from Mexico reported to the *National Anti-Slavery Standard*, in a story headlined "A New Plot of the Slave-Drivers," that slave drivers were "trying to acquire Mexican territory, to own slaves there, but to also keep those regions from being available to fugitive slaves to hide."[69] Harold Preece wrote, "In 1856—almost on the eve of the Civil War—a Mexican farmhand, remembered only as Frank, was flogged and burned with rebellious Negroes at Columbus, Texas, for organizing the slave in a movement aimed at overthrowing the white planters and confiscation of the estates originally stolen from Mexicans. After the lynchings, the planters held a meeting and ordered the Sheriff to run all Mexicans out of the county lest they continue to stir up the Negroes."[70]

In 1852, B. F. Remington, a Black abolitionist, wrote that the United States aimed to shut down the Underground Railroad and bring an end to antislavery sanctuaries in Canada and Mexico.[71] At the same time, groups of American citizens known as "filibusters"—irregular military adventurers—began launching invasions of countries throughout Latin America, seeking to reimpose slavery or take over existing plantation societies such as that in Cuba. "General" William Walker, a US filibuster who briefly seized control of Nicaragua, wrote: "The introduction of negro-slavery into Nicaragua would furnish a supply of constant and reliable labor requisite for the cultivation of tropical products."[72] The proslavery *Richmond Enquirer* urged that the federal government annex Cuba to stave off the possibility of the British intervening militarily to end slavery in Cuba:

> Our views of the policy of this measure as, of every other, is determined by the paramount and controlling consideration of Southern interests. It is because we regard the acquisition of Cuba as essential to the stability of the system of slavery, and to the just ascendency of the South. . . . We must re-enforce the powers of slavery as an element of political control, and this can only be done by the annexation of Cuba. In no other direction is there a chance for the aggrandizement of slavery.[73]

African Americans and abolitionist newspapers believed that the filibusters received unofficial backing from the highest circles of government in Washington, DC.[74] Regarding the Cuban filibuster movement, *Frederick Douglass' Paper* commented, "Our voracious eagle is whetting his talons for the capture of Cuba. This beautiful Island has long been a coveted treasure, and, at last, has so excited our national cupidity that we are no longer able to restrain it. The value of the prize, and the probability of success in securing it, alike conspire to sharpen our over keen and almost insatiable appetite for that which can only be attained by plunder." Basing its analysis on the outcome of the US invasion of Mexico, *Frederick Douglass' Paper* believed that "all difficulties will be encountered, all dangers braved, and though it may cost millions of treasure and rivers of blood, Cuba will be conquered and severed from the Spanish crown, and sooner or later annexed to the United States."[75]

Mexican writers in newly conquered California shared this contempt for imperial slavery as well as for the US filibusters. Antonio Mancillas, writing in *La Voz de Méjico*, wrote, "Each acre of territory that the South gained, made the price of slaves rise in the market; and consequently this [phenomenon] was duplicated with the acquisition of Texas. From this arose that insatiable desire of the Southern filibusters to take over Cuba and Nicaragua."[76] Francisco P. Ramírez's *El Clamor Público* fiercely criticized the US filibusters and their quest to reestablish slavery in Latin America.

Abolitionists kept close tabs on US misadventures in the United States' backyard and elsewhere. Martin Delany, a Black abolitionist, prepared a special international report for a meeting of antislavery activists in Pittsburgh in 1855. Delany rejoiced in the failure of US forces to annex either the Sandwich Islands or Haiti, citing as the reason that "the Haytien people are too intelligent and too conversant with the outlandish prejudices of the Americans, for a moment to entertain any such proposition." Delany likewise detailed the failure of US efforts to seize Cuba, and predicted that the Nicaraguan people were now on their guard against further US incursions on their soil, stating, "We trust this may be so, since the sole object of the Americans in desiring a foot hold in foreign territories, is the servitude and enslavement of the African and colored races."[77]

African Americans engaged in the resistance to empire understood that their uncompensated labor power was the fundamental force building the nation. "We were stolen from our mother country, and brought here," Bishop Richard Allen cried out. "We have tilled the ground and made fortunes for thousands, and still they are not weary of our services."[78] Slave testimonies reveal that Black workers carefully gauged their market value. In 1855, N. A. Matheas, a fugitive slave, was interviewed shortly before he fled America to find freedom in Canada. Matheas "estimated his value in Virginia at $900."[79] Frederick Douglass introduced himself as a "thief and a robber" for "stealing" his own body to freedom and away from his erstwhile owner. The ex-slave Richard Moran spoke for many when he recounted the ways that slave labor had enriched the United States:

> We have felled almost all the forest that is felled in the south, and a deal elsewhere. We have cultivated, and do cultivate the fields of the south, and much elsewhere. The annual millions of exports from the south, and part of the west, in cotton, rice, hemp and tobacco, are, I might say, exclusively the labor of our hands. Is it unreasonable, after all this accumulation of wealth in the hands of the whites, that here we should be men—be respected? My heart sickens when I reflect, that thousands of men calling themselves philanthropists, republicans, nay more, Christians, can entertain the feelings and views they do towards the colored man.[80]

"It is idle to talk of preventing the extension or circumscribing the limits of slavery," Dr. J. McCune Smith told his Philadelphia audience at the Colored National Convention in 1856. "There is no foot of American Territory over which slavery is not already triumphant, and will continue triumphant, so long as there remains any foot of American Territory on which it is admitted that man can hold property in man."[81] This was a clear rejection of the idea that the United States was uniquely democratic and served as an exemplar to other nations. Smith asserted that it would take external pressure to stop the United States:

> In spite of the resistance of public sentiment, from the Seminole robbery and massacre, the conquest and purchase of

Texas, the Mexican robbery, to the Compromise and the Fugitive Slave Law, those parties have dragged the country down, until the opposing force in the parties is all spent, and nothing but an external resistance can now prevent them from descending still to the lowest depths of dishonor, injustice and oppression.[82]

REENVISIONING AMERICAN HISTORY

Black thinkers attempted to link the Mexican War of Independence, the antislavery movement in the United States, and the ongoing efforts to end racial and caste oppression in the Americas. José María Morelos and Frederick Douglass were born in two very different times and places, but their separate struggles were truly united in purpose. The efforts of Black communities to pay homage to Morelos, Guerrero, Toussaint L'Ouverture, and other freedom fighters suggests a political culture where the pursuit of liberty outranks nationalism or commercial imperialism. Emancipatory internationalism weathered the onslaught of American nativism and the anti-immigrant "Know-Nothing Party" in the 1850s; it reemerged in the midst of the Civil War, when African Americans continued to think expansively about the relationship between citizenship and liberation.[83]

African Americans, Native Americans, Mexicans, and other groups waged intense battles against slavery in the first half of the nineteenth century. The determination to fight the slave republic and create a culture of anti-imperialism is a singular achievement and requires a reenvisioning of US history. African Americans repeatedly pointed out that slavery and imperialism were fatally intertwined and encoded in the nation's institutions from the very beginning, with grave consequences for all of the citizens of the Americas. Inundated with propaganda about the superiority of Anglo-Saxon institutions, freedom fighters against slavery looked to Haiti, Mexico, and other nations in the Global South for political wisdom on how to grapple with racial capitalism.[84]

Unfortunately, too many Americans have forgotten Mexico's rich history of social democracy, and how African Americans, Latinx people, Native Americans, and citizens of the Americas have made the practice of anti-imperialism central to their way of life. Mexican immigrants brought traditions of mutual aid, solidarity, and democracy with them to the United States. These values have too often been squandered by their adoptive country. Instead, these immigrants have been asked to assimilate to a nation that was ignorant of the role they had played in eradicating slavery and in waging a heroic war of independence against the Spanish Empire.

Of course, not all Americans were ignorant of this history. Speaking with gratitude toward a nation where former slaves were welcomed, the Reverend Henry Highland Garnet, one of the foremost abolitionists in American history, described Mexicans as "liberty-loving brethren" and "ultra-abolitionists."[85] Garnet's understanding of the role that Mexican and Latin American abolitionists played in the struggle against slavery fired his own international solidarity work, which lasted for the rest of his life.

Manifest destiny was, among other things, a preemptive strike to ensure that the freedom movements rising in Mexico, Florida, the Caribbean, and elsewhere did not spread to the United States. The Cuban revolutionary José Martí noted that US imperialism was rooted in the nation's "tradition of continental dominion perpetuated in the Republic."[86] Generations later, Jack O'Dell, a radical scholar, connected the histories of slavery, the US war on Native Americans, and its invasion of Mexico: "This was the main path by which the American power structure ascended to the position of a world power, by the turn of the 20th century."[87] More recently, William Appleman Williams reaffirmed that "Empire as a way of life," has been a central theme of US history.[88] It is equally true, however, that African Americans, Latinx people, Native Americans, and people of the Global South practiced anti-imperialism as *their* way of life.

CHAPTER 3

"TO BREAK THE FETTERS OF
SLAVES ALL OVER THE WORLD"

THE INTERNATIONALIZATION OF THE CIVIL WAR,
1850s TO 1865

Every major political gain that African Americans and Latinx people have made has been countered by waves of violence and statutory countermeasures designed to abrogate their human rights and claims to citizenship.[1] To officially end the Mexican War, on February 2, 1848, the United States and Mexico negotiated the Treaty of Guadalupe Hidalgo. This accord was designed to confer citizenship rights on Mexicanos in the territories that the United States had seized from Mexico in the wake of the war.[2] In response to the possibility of Latinx people becoming citizens, however, states passed measures to ensure that most Mexican Americans and their descendants remained permanent outsiders. White vigilantes engaged in armed assaults on Mexican American communities, lynched Mexican Americans, and stole land from rightful owners. While Mexicans were driven off of farms and gold mining claims, African Americans were banned from entire regions.[3] The territorial governor of New Mexico advocated the proscription of African Americans, claiming, "Free negroes are regarded as nuisances in every State and Territory in the Union; and where they are tolerated, society is most degraded. . . . The disgusting degradation to which society is subjected by their presence, is obvious to all, and demands a prohibitory act of the severest character."[4]

The West was now, in Alexander Saxton's terminology, a white republic whose fields were patrolled by settler colonialists, as John Steinbeck illustrated in *Grapes of Wrath*:

Once California belonged to Mexico and its land to Mexicans; and a horde of tattered feverish Americans poured in. And such was their hunger for land that they took the land—stole Sutter's land, Guerrero's land, took the grants and broke them up and growled and quarreled over them, those frantic hungry men; and they guarded with guns the land they had stolen. They put up houses and barns, they turned the earth and planted crops. And these things were possession, and possession was ownership.[5]

African Americans in the North were besieged by segregation laws, re-enslavers, and anti-Black race riots.[6] Dr. John S. Rock, a Black abolitionist, elicited bitter laughter from his audience when, in 1862, he reminded them,

In Philadelphia, where there is a larger free colored population than is to be found in any other city in the free States, and where we are denied every social privilege, and are not even permitted to send our children to the schools that we are taxed to support, or to ride in the city horse cars, yet even there we pay taxes enough to support our own poor, and have a balance of a few thousand in our own favor, which goes to support those "poor whites" who "can't take care of themselves."[7]

Dr. Rock described slavery as a business that enforced a false unity between whites of different classes:

The educated and wealthy class despise the negro, because they have robbed him of his hard earnings, or, at least, have got rich off the fruits of his labor; and they believe if he gets his freedom, their fountain will be dried up, and they will be obliged to seek business in a new channel. Their "occupation will be gone." The lowest class hates him because he is poor, as they are, and is a competitor with them for the same labor. The poor ignorant white man, who does not understand that the interest of the laboring masses is mutual, argues in this wise: "Here is so much labor to be performed,—that darkey does it. If he was gone, I should have his place."

During the antebellum period, Francisco P. Ramírez mobilized his Los Angeles–based Spanish-language newspaper, *El Clamor Público*, to challenge the march of slavery and white supremacy across the continent. "But here in this fabulous country," Ramírez argued in 1855, "he who robs and assassinates the most is he who enjoys freedom. Certain people have no kind of freedom—this freedom, we say, is that which the courts deny to all individuals of color."[8] The young editor wielded *El Clamor* as an educational tool to counter the views of the majority of white Angelenos who were ardently proslavery. Ramírez attacked the Supreme Court's *Dred Scott* decision in 1857, in which it was ruled that African Americans had no rights that white people were bound to respect; echoing abolitionist movement warnings, Ramírez predicted that slavery would tear the United States apart.[9] He "angered whites, many of whom were Southern sympathizers, with his attacks on slavery and calls for racial equality for Mexicans, blacks, Chinese and Indians."[10] *El Clamor Público* posited that slavery was the linchpin of the apocalyptic violence sweeping the continent. As a result of *El Clamor Público*'s agitating, the *San Francisco Herald* labeled *El Clamor Público* as one of the state's "Free Nigger organs," one that endangered white rule.[11]

Anglo theft of Mexican and Indian lands was the order of the day. The Treaty of Guadalupe Hidalgo was supposed to protect the status of the approximately 115,000 former Mexicans who lived within the newly conquered territories of the West.[12] Instead, existing anti-Indian and anti-Black laws were amplified to undermine the human rights of Mexicans who could not prove that they were definitively white. The California Gold Rush and Anglo hunger for land combined to create what the anthropologist Martha Menchaca calls "the racialization of the Mexican population," as state authorities created laws that defined Mexicans overall as an inferior people with minimal claims on citizenship and land tenure.[13] There were certainly exceptions to this rule. Some wealthy Mexicanos and Tejanos, Mexicans who lived in newly conquered Texas, managed to hold on to Spanish and Mexican land grants through the late nineteenth century.[14] However, the overall trend of land loss in the West was so devastating that the popular image of the typical Mexican American in mid-twentieth-century America was that of a landless laborer.[15] Anglo racism against Mexicans, Chinese, Indians, and free Blacks was interconnected, and numerous state laws were passed to deny each group basic rights such as due process, public assembly, and voting rights as well as equal access to property ownership and employment.[16]

The Anglo-Saxon "march of civilization" in the West was accomplished through a mix of legal and extralegal measures. In 1850, the State of California used a "foreign miner's tax" to drive Chinese and Mexican miners out of precious-metals mining. A few years later, Francisco P. Ramírez connected the California legislature's anti-Mexican Vagrancy Law, widely known as the "Greaser Act," with anti-Black racism and manifest destiny.[17] One historian has written, "The antivagrancy law provided one more justification for expropriating lands belonging to Mexicans in northern California."[18] Though California was admitted to the United States as a "free state" in 1850, slavery was tacitly tolerated throughout the state, and California passed a fugitive slave law in 1852.[19] Whites impatient with the pace of legal disenfranchisement launched assaults against Mexicans and Indians. In California, hundreds were lynched in the decades after California statehood, while in Texas, Afro-Mestizo landowners were driven off of their lands by white usurpers.[20] In the late nineteenth century, from Southern California to Seattle, Washington, vigilantes and law enforcement launched nearly three hundred pogroms, or organized massacres, against Chinese workers.[21] California state policy toward Native Americans was indentured servitude, slave labor, and extermination.[22]

The rise of agriculture in the West was premised on the creation of an impoverished working class unable to defend itself in the courts, in politics, or in the fields.[23] In an overview of two centuries of agricultural history, Ernesto Galarza argued that twentieth-century farmworkers were disenfranchised politically and economically because their ancestors did not own land. Galarza argued, "The black slave, the sharecropper, the hired hand, the migratory harvester, the wetback, the bracero, and all the intermediate types of land workers in America never had any institutional connections with the government because they had never possessed land."[24] In his study of Chicanos in Santa Barbara, California, the historian Albert Camarillo writes, "The incorporation of Mexican workers into the capitalist labor market locked them into the status of a predominantly unskilled/semiskilled working class at the bottom of the occupational structure."[25] Oliver Cromwell Cox, a Trinidadian American sociologist, posited that the dynamics of racial inequality were to be found in capitalism's "need for slaves, or peons, or unorganized common laborers—a need for 'cheap, docile labor.'" Furthermore, "The fact of crucial significance is that the racial exploitation is merely one aspect of the problem of the proletarianization of labor, regardless of the color of the laborers. Hence, racial antagonism is essentially a political-class conflict. The capitalist exploiter, being opportunistic and practical, will utilize any convenience to keep his labor and other resources freely exploitable. He will devise and employ race prejudice when that becomes convenient."[26] Not hatred but racial capitalism drove this system of exploitation. Indeed, employers not infrequently waxed elegiac about how much they loved "their workers"—so long as they did not complain or go out on strike.

States mercilessly attacked the rights and economic well-being of free Blacks in the North and in the South. Several states and territories, including Illinois, Indiana, and Oregon, passed "exclusion laws" and other anti-immigrant measures prohibiting Black settlement in their jurisdictions.[27] Rooted in the racial logic of the 1791 Naturalization Act, such laws made whiteness a valuable birthright.[28] Oregon was organized as a white homeland. In 1844, the Provisional Government of Oregon banned slavery and ordered all free blacks age eighteen or older to leave the territory. To enforce Black expulsion, provisional authorities established the "Lash Law," whereby recalcitrant Black Oregonians received twenty to thirty-nine lashings every six months "until he or she shall quit the territory." This punishment was soon replaced by a more profitable penalty: forced labor.[29]

When Oregon gained statehood, in 1859, its bill of rights contained a Negro Exclusion Law, which remained on the state's law books until 1926. During the Oregon Constitutional Convention that preceded statehood, the number of votes against admitting African Americans to the state exceeded even the number of votes against slavery.[30] Three years after statehood, Oregon passed a "race tax" that required African Americans, Hawaiians, Chinese, and "Mulattos" (individuals of mixed race) to pay an annual five-dollar penalty for residing in the state.[31] In 1868, the state legislature abrogated the Fourteenth Amendment to the Constitution just in case African Americans had not received the message that they were persona non grata in the Pacific Northwest.[32]

Learned Americans crafted theories of racial hierarchy that were used to promote white supremacy. Dr. Samuel George Morton, known by the *New York Tribune* as the most noted "scientific man in America," published his popular book, *Crania Americana*, in 1839. Ranking human groups by their skull size, Morton argued that Native Americans were inferior because "they are crafty, sensual, ungrateful, obstinate and unfeeling, and much of their affection for their children may be traced to purely selfish motives."[33] Morton collected hundreds of human skulls and measured them for the stated purpose of judging the intelligence of each racial group he named. Remarkably, the skulls perfectly affirmed America's racial order: the white "Teutonic Family" skulls enjoyed the largest cranial capacity, while African Americans and what Morton called the "Toltecan Family" (including Mexicans) ranked near the very bottom. Scientific racism became a well-funded tendency in educated circles, one that endures to this day.[34]

The duel between enslaved workers and their masters for control of workers' labor was the most important political issue of the antebellum period. This battle for Black labor power determined land values in vast areas of the republic, set profit margins for entire industries, generated new political parties, and drove constitutional debates in the Congress. Slavery exhausted land and bodies at a frightening rate; hence, for survival, it depended on policies of territorial expansion that were justified in terms of imperial manifest destiny. The slave republic mobilized the resources of the nation to maintain chattel bondage by offensive wars, the numerous fugitive slave acts (both state and federal), the suppression of slave revolts, and other expenditures of money and blood.

The investments that were required to sustain and to expand

slavery defy imagination. In 1848, the *North Star*, which became *Frederick Douglass' Paper* a few years later, set the amount from the nation's coffers used to expand slavery at approximately $227.25 million.[35] The *Sacramento Daily Union* contended that the figure was no less than $100 million by the eve of the Civil War. This included the costs of annexing Texas, invading Mexico, waging war on Indian nations, purchasing millions of acres from Spain and France, and securing slavery's borders. In addition, "from the date of the Constitution until the treaty with Mexico was signed, every foot of territory acquired by purchase and negotiation was, when so acquired, occupied by slaveholders."[36]

The *Daily Union* described the foundation of the nation's economy in one concise sentence: "In political economy a negro is considered as property—capital invested. He is as much a machine as the spinning jenny, and the profits of his labor are considered as the interest paid to the owner upon the money invested."[37] The weaponized labor relations that underwrote this system would color race and class relations in the United States for centuries to come.[38]

Antislavery's partisans rejected the inhuman calculus of racial capitalism, and they tirelessly built new way stations of the Underground Railroad, eventually connecting Montreal, Pittsburgh, El Paso, Tampa, Mexico City, Haiti, and the Bahamas in a grand trunk line of liberation. In the early 1850s, the Mexican government welcomed Black Seminoles, veterans of the Seminole Wars, as border guards to defend Mexico from Texas Rangers, slave catchers, and outlaws.[39] In turn, these veterans began helping scores of slaves find freedom in Mexico in what whites, infuriated by these actions, called "The Mexican Border Troubles."[40]

Genevieve Payne Benson, a descendent of Black Seminoles who evacuated from Florida at the end of the Second Seminole War, recounted how generations of her family found freedom in Mexico. In the 1850s, Benson's grandfather, Isaac Garden, dug his way out of a Texas prison along with two of his brothers and received sanctuary in Mexico with the help of sympathetic Tejanos.[41] Zaragosa Vargas notes that Tejanos "rescued runaway slaves, hid them, fed them, and at great risk guided them to safe passage across the Rio Grande at Laredo and Eagle Pass. When the Texas Rangers captured Tejano abolitionists, they immediately executed them."[42]

Slave catchers and law enforcement officials faced increasingly determined slaves, free Black communities, and vigilance committees determined to resist recapture—by force of arms if necessary. On November 5, 1850, near Quincy, Illinois, "about fifty negroes, of all ages and sexes, with teams, stampeded from the Missouri side of the river. . . . The slaves were overhauled on Saturday morning, and after a desperate resistance and the loss of their leader, they were captured." The following year, a fugitive slave was apprehended in Syracuse, New York, "but he was rescued by a mob from the officers who had charge of him, and the result was that he escaped to parts unknown."[43] In 1857, the efforts of United States marshals to recapture a single fugitive slave from Kentucky led to a series of shootouts and an incident called "the Civil War in Ohio."[44] Anthony Burns, a man owned by Charles F. Suttle of Alexandria, Virginia, was seized by US marshals in Boston. While Wendell Phillips, Theodore Parker, and other abolitionists were making indignant speeches about the incident at Faneuil Hall, it was suddenly "announced that there was a mob of negroes in Court Square, attacking the Court House where the prisoner was confined." US troops were called out to disperse a reported gathering of over 1,000 people who attempted to free Burns. Church bells in Manchester "and many of the interior towns" tolled in mourning after a final rescue effort failed. Shortly afterward, images of the officials responsible for re-enslaving Burns were wrapped on the flagstaff in Boston Common with the following messages: "I: Marshal FREEMAN. Chief of the Boston Ruffians, Slaveholders and Bloodhounds. II. BENJAMIN F. HALLETT. U.S. District Attorney and Attorney General to the Prince of Darkness. Commissioner LORING, The Ten Dollars Jeffries of 1854."[45]

The resistance of African Americans, Tejanos, and white abolitionists was decisive in the advent of the Civil War. C. L. R. James wrote, "The agitation of the abolitionists, the sensational escapes by the Underground Railway, the ferment among the Negroes, all helped to focus public attention on slavery. But long before the Civil War the great issues were becoming clear."[46] Antislavery insurgencies gravely threatened racial capitalism and forced the hand of Southern politicians. Southern elites viewed the preservation of slavery and the enforcement of the Fugitive Slave Act to be nonnegotiable. The leading white women of Broward's Neck, Florida, informed the *Jacksonville Standard* shortly after the election of 1858, "In our humble opinion the single issue is now presented to the Southern people, will they submit to all the degradation threatened by the North toward our slave property and be made to what England has made white people experience in the West India Islands—the negroes afforded a place on the same footing with their former owners, to be made legislators, to sit as Judges." In the spring of 1860, Democrats in Jacksonville stated that regardless of who was nominated to run for president, "The amplest protection and security to slave property in the territories owned by the General Government" and "the surrender [of] fugitive slaves when legally demanded" were vital to Florida's interests. If these terms were not met, they asserted, "then we are of the opinion that the rights of the citizens of Florida are no longer safe in the Union, and we think that she should raise the banner of secession and invite her Southern sisters to join her."[47] The following year, John C. McGehee, the president of the Florida Secession Convention, gave the most concise reason why the majority of his colleagues supported secession: "At the South, and with our People of course, slavery is the element of all value, and a destruction of that destroys all that is property."[48]

The United States drove itself to civil war because the society valued profits over Black humanity, as the following story illustrates. When plantation owners vacationed in the North, they often brought their slave servants with them, and many Northern communities became dependent on Southern tourist dollars. The town of Manchester, New York, near Niagara Falls, was a popular destination. Allegedly, local African Americans approached one Southern tourist's female servant in the first week of July 1847 to help her escape. Local whites mobilized in opposition. They beat the African Americans who were involved in the rescue effort, and it was reported that members of law enforcement led the attack. One correspondent noted, "The mobocrats however were not satisfied with beating the men, who for the sake of the liberty of a woman would run the risk of injuring the business of the village. They gathered together again in the evening, and tore down the grocery shop of J.M. Anderson, destroyed his goods, and broke up his furniture."[49] The correspondent who wrote about the riot emphasized the pecuniary impetus behind the mob's actions: "The people of that neighborhood, it seems, take a peculiar interest in the support of the system of Slavery, flattering themselves, of course, that it is a patriotic love of the Union, and of justice, but like all the patriotism that goes by the name now-a-days, it is easily resolved into a base love of dollars and cents."

The *Christian Recorder* explained the coming of the Civil War as a culmination of decisions made by the nation's leaders at the founding of the nation:

> The slave power has always ruled the continent. It ruled the colonies, it ruled the British cabinets as long as we were colonies; it was no small element in causing the revolution, as Jefferson said in his declaration. . . . The Constitution recognized it. Washington signed a fugitive slave bill, and Jefferson annexed Louisiana in its interest. It caused the war of 1812, the war with Mexico, and the present war. It is met to-day on its own merits. Our statesmen do not yet avow it, but they feel it. We may have to fight for political existence, for personal liberty even.[50]

"UNTIL FREEDOM IS PROCLAIMED THROUGHOUT THE WORLD"

Because their resistance to slavery had occurred on an international stage, many African Americans viewed the Civil War through a global lens. Black Southerners' and Northerners' "self-activity"— self-determined activism in their own behalf—in waging a war for liberty radically enlarged the meaning of the war. Ideas of emancipation without borders were grounded in everyday flesh-and-blood struggles. The truth of this was personified in the Civil War odyssey of Garland H. White. White was a slave of Senator Robert Toombs of Georgia. In explaining the reason for his state's secession from the Union, Toombs, a future Confederate general, vowed: "We want no negro equality, no negro citizenship; we want no negro race to degrade our own; and as one man [we] would meet you upon the border with the sword in one hand and the torch in the other."[51]

White escaped from Toombs in 1860 and reached Canada. A few years later the former slave returned to the United States and recruited African Americans to the Union Army.[52] "It is no longer a question of doubt as to what the American people think of us," White, now chaplain of his regiment, wrote from Corpus Christi, Texas, in 1864. "From Fortress Monroe to the Rio Grande, colored pickets can be seen watching the approach of every ship, and the nation intends to use us in restoring peace, order and national tranquility. The very position we occupy to-day in the army of our country has a voice much louder than the organs of a thousand demoralized cities."[53] This man, a slave only five years earlier, now dreamed of an international liberation struggle. Reflecting on his regiment's triumphant march into Richmond, the capital of the Confederacy, in the spring of 1865, Chaplain White stated, "I was with them, and am still with them, and am willing to stay with them until freedom is proclaimed throughout the world. Yes, we will follow this race of men in search of Liberty through the whole Island of Cuba."[54]

The French invasion of Mexico in 1861 raised alarm bells in African American and Mexican American communities across the continent. An emperor, Maximilian I of Mexico, had been imposed on Mexico by France. The popular assumption in the abolitionist press was that Maximilian's ultimate goal was to reestablish slavery in Mexico, as well as to negotiate an alliance with the Confederate States of America.[55] The Black press echoed the tenor of the *Hartford Daily Courant*'s headline "Brilliant Achievements of the Mexicans" in resisting the French invasion.[56] At times, coverage of the French invasion preempted reporting on American Civil War battles. The *Christian Recorder* published "A letter from Vera Cruz," which reported "that the Mexicans, after holding out so long, and fighting with desperate bravery, are now taking the offensive. . . . Twice the French were driven from the city. The Mexicans have fought admirably, and the French are depressed by their defeat."[57]

The *Christian Recorder* exulted in the gallant Mexican defense at Puebla between 1862 and 1863 and marveled at the besieged garrison's ability to hold out against French artillery. "It is reported that the French army has been again repulsed and driven back from before Puebla with great loss," the *Recorder* reported on January 31, 1863. "General Berthier's van-guard, 4000 strong, was completely surprised by 800 Mexican cavalry, and about 2000 of the French were killed and wounded. Several French officers were taken by the lasso and dragged off. The prospects of the French look exceedingly bad."[58] Even after Puebla—after most of the country had fallen to the French onslaught—the *Christian Recorder* quoted sources that claimed, "Over seventy guerilla bands, of about two hundred men each, harass the roads leading to [Mexico City]. The renegade Mexicans are rapidly deserting the French."[59] The popular holiday Cinco de Mayo, initiated by Mexican American Union Army veterans in the Southwest to commemorate the Mexican victory over the European invaders, joined together themes of Mexican independence, resistance to imperialism, and slavery abolition. It would become a major commemoration in American culture more than a century later.

David E. Hayes-Bautista writes, "Slavery, many Latinos understood, was the major issue of the Civil War." Francisco P. Ramírez used the pages of *El Nuevo Mundo* in California to denounce the Confederacy's support of the French invasion of Mexico:

> It is not strange that the rebels of the South in the United States should be in favor of the establishment of Maximilian's imperial power in Mexico; for men fanatically attached to the slavery system—who have rebelled against the most liberal republican government in the world and started the current war . . . are capable of anything. . . . Napoleon III, Maximilian, and Jefferson Davis maintain relations of the closest friendship. They support one another, for all of them have an interest in dominating the people, though it be over the bodies of the dead and through rivers of blood.[60]

As Emperor Maximilian's invading army cut a destructive path through Mexico, the Reverend Henry McNeal Turner urged the United States to raise an army to drive the European monarch back across the Atlantic Ocean. "I believe this government can drown Jeff Davis and his hosts in the Red Sea, and send three hundred thousand men to Mexico to welcome Maximilian to his imperial throne, with as much canister and grape as would blow him into another region."[61] Turner's invasion plan was never enacted, but small numbers of African American soldiers, including the future historian George Washington Williams, crossed the border to join republican forces in the struggle against the European emperor.[62]

The *New Orleans Tribune*, a Black newspaper, coupled the fate of people in the United States with that of the citizenry of Mexico in its moment of crisis: "For us, men of African Descent, we cannot forget that this undertaking was coupled with the attempt to perpetuate slavery and the Black Code in the United States. We cannot forget that the prospect was to re-establish servitude in Mexico."[63] A few months after the end of the Civil War, the *South Carolina Leader*, a Black newspaper based in Charleston, waxed enthusiastic about the prospects of abolition in Cuba but warned about the threat of slavery reemerging in Mexico under Emperor Maximilian's rule. What happened in Cuba and Mexico mattered greatly to Black South Carolinians as they mapped out their own strategies for freedom.[64]

Black military service changed the very meaning of the war. Northern leaders marveled at the élan of Black troops and the willingness of African American civilians to risk their lives for the Union in a variety of capacities, from fighting on land and sea to providing the United States' most dependable wartime military intelligence network in the South.[65] Secretary of State William Seward observed, "Everywhere the American General receives his most useful and reliable information from the Negro who hails his coming as the harbinger of Freedom."[66] After the Army of the Potomac seized the high ground at Gettysburg thanks to the intelligence of a Black spy, General Robert E. Lee lamented, "The chief source of information to the enemy is through our Negroes."[67]

Black men in the ranks drew from their experiences to frame the broader significance of the war. Private William B. Johnson of the Third United States Colored Infantry was one such soldier. As he wrote toward the end of the war, "One particular and interesting feature in Lake City [Florida], is a pond about a mile from town, where the rebels drove the Blacks into, in the summer of '64, to keep our scouts from bringing them into our lines. Many lost their lives in this way; but thank God they had their time, and now comes ours." Johnson believed that the Civil War must have a redemptive meaning: "By good behavior, we will show them that we are men, and able to fill any position in life that we may be placed in. There is only one thing I want, that is my vote; let us see what time will do."[68]

Junius Browne, a Northern war correspondent who escaped from a Confederate prison camp, recognized Black civilians for saving his life and the lives of Union soldiers. African Americans had created a new branch of the Underground Railroad which aided US prisoners of war: "God bless the negroes! say I with earnest lips. During our entire captivity and after our escape, they were ever our firm, brave unflinching friends. We never made an appeal to them that they did not answer. They never hesitated to do us a service at the risk even of life; under the most trying circumstances revealed a devotion and a spirit of self-sacrifice that were heroic."[69]

Harriet Tubman, whom John Brown had called General Tubman, performed all of these duties and more. Harriet Tubman helped lead troops into battle in a series of daring raids in the Sea Islands region of South Carolina, where US forces destroyed plantations, liberated slaves, and recruited the former "contrabands" (slaves) into the Union Army.[70] Toward the end of the war Tubman traveled to Camp William Penn in Pennsylvania to talk with the soldiers there about her exploits. One observer noted,

> During her lecture, which she gave in her own language, she elicited considerable applause from the soldiers of the 24th regiment, U.S.C.T., now at the camp. She gave a thrilling account of her trials in the South, during the past three years, among the contrabands and colored soldiers, and how she had administered to thousands of them, and cared for their numerous necessities.[71]

Tubman's effectiveness as a recruiter was rooted in her ability to create a discourse of the dispossessed. She drew slaves away from the plantations by proclaiming, "Uncle Sam is rich enough to give you all a farm," affirming her people's belief that their labor had built the nation.[72]

Senator John Sherman of Ohio depicted the impact of Black troops and civilians—men and women—in battle and behind the lines to achieve victory for the United States: "These slaves have won their freedom by their devotion to our cause. They have from the beginning been true friends. They have borne our flag in battle.

They have carried our arms. They have been slaughtered for our cause. They have aided our sick and wounded. They have fed our soldiers when in prison, and have guided their escape. They have performed the humble offices of the camp and the hospital."[73] Senator Sherman wanted it clearly understood that Black war service was saving the Union: "They have never fought against us. They have relied upon our promise, and have performed their part. Without them, and without their presence as a weakness to the enemy, we might not have succeeded." Sherman argued that Negro manhood suffrage was a minimal precondition for the Reconstruction of the South: "If we put negro regiments there and give them the bayonets, why can't we give votes? They have joined in putting down the Rebellion; and now to place them at the mercy of those they have helped us to subdue—to deny them all political rights—to give them freedom but leave them entirely subject to laws framed by Rebel masters—is an act of injustice against which humanity revolts."[74]

The political significance of Black military service became clearer with each passing day. Abraham Lincoln was deeply moved—and transformed—by the sacrifice of African American men on the field of battle. He told John T. Mills, a Delaware judge, "There have been men base enough to propose to me to return to slavery the Black warriors of Port Hudson and Olustee, and thus win the respect of the masters they fought." Lincoln flatly refused. "Should I do so, I should deserve to be damned in time and eternity. Come what will, I will keep my faith with friend and foe. My enemies pretend I am now carrying on this war for the sole purpose of abolition. So long as I am President, it shall be carried on for the sole purpose of restoring the Union."[75] President Lincoln wanted Mills and his readers to understand that the hope of a Union victory in the Civil War was now inextricably bound up with Black emancipation and freedom. Facing the prospects of losing the presidency in the 1864 election, he told Frederick Douglass that he wanted him to organize a slave revolt in the South, what one historian calls his "John Brown plan."[76] It was now the only way Lincoln could see of saving the United States in its moment of deepest crisis.

W. E. B. Du Bois interpreted the mass exodus of slaves from Southern plantations as the first national general strike in US history and emphasized that "without the blacks the war would not have been won."[77] Du Bois asserted, "This was not merely the desire to stop work. It was a strike on a wide basis against the conditions of work. It was a general strike that involved directly in the end perhaps a half million people."[78] C. L. R. James fleshed out the political significance of the slaves' general strike: "What I want to emphasize is that it was not only that the blacks brought their forces into the Northern army and gave labour. It was that the policies that they followed instinctively were the policies ultimately that Abraham Lincoln and his cabinet had to use in order to win the war."[79]

This rising of the workers was a hundredfold more important than enlightened statecraft; it was the motive force compelling Emancipation and the remarkable period of Reconstruction that followed after the end of the Civil War. At no time in American history has the working class occupied such a position of awesome power. In a speech given toward the end of 1863, Frederick Douglass made it clear that Lincoln's leadership would not win the war: "We are not to be saved by the captain this time, but by the crew. We are not to be saved by Abraham Lincoln, but by the power behind the throne, greater than the throne itself."[80] Without the uprising of the plantation workers, the nation would have been permanently broken in two: they were not merely heroes—they were the saviors of the republic.[81]

The movement of ordinary African Americans doing extraordinary things fired the nation's imagination. One writer juxtaposed the bravery of Black troops on battlefields like Fort Pillow with their precursors in Latin America:

> In the United States, *Nat Turner* . . . Port Hudson, Fort Wagner, Fort Pillow, etc., in Spanish America, against the Spanish hordes during the War of Independence; in Cuba Aponte, Placido, the greatest Cuban poet; F. Vargas Captain of the Cuban Colored Militia . . . and hundreds coldly murdered by Gen. O'Donnell—some of them on the scaffold, and the great majority under the terrible lash; and above all, the numberless victims slain in Hayti by the French soldiery; that most noble specimen of the human race, Toussaint L'Ouverture, murdered by the first Napoleon in the dark dungeon of Fort Joux![82]

In invoking the name Plácido—nom de plume of Gabriel de la Concepción Valdés, an Afro-Cuban poet executed by the Spanish for his role in the so-called Ladder Conspiracy—the writer was drawing connections between the massacre of Black Union soldiers at Fort Pillow, Tennessee, and the Spanish suppression of Cuban antislavery insurgents in 1844.[83] This act of historical imagination linked the progress of democracy not to events in Europe but to those taking place in Latin America and the Caribbean.

In a speech given to an African American audience in Boston in the final weeks of the war, Wendell Phillips pointed to the global implications of Black self-activity: "In the hands of the four millions of blacks in the Republic was the fate of the black race all over the world. With the ballot the colored men could ensure not only their own redemption but also that of their race from Cuba to Ethiopia. From this rebellion the black men would clutch the power to break the fetters of slaves all over the world." The atmosphere that evening was electric: "Repeated bursts of enthusiastic applause testified the admiration of the audience during Mr. Phillips's brilliant oration." Like Harriet Tubman in South Carolina's Sea Islands, Wendell Phillips spoke the language of his hopeful listeners; the great abolitionist had captured the zeitgeist of emancipatory internationalism. At the dawning of Emancipation, the Day of Jubilee, African Americans were ready to raise the bar of emancipation higher than ever.[84]

CHAPTER 4

GLOBAL VISIONS OF RECONSTRUCTION
THE CUBAN SOLIDARITY MOVEMENT,
1860s TO 1890s

African Americans decided that emancipation in one country was not enough. How they came to this belief is instructive for students of democracy. The creative energy unleashed by the African American general strike against slavery transformed the idea of emancipatory internationalism into a powerful social movement. Experience was a great teacher. The way in which Black workers had earned their citizenship was crucial because it now informed their understandings of how politics worked. African Americans had gained their individual rights working together in a great cause for liberation. Black soldiers had withstood the enemy's onslaughts on the battlefield as disciplined members of regiments, battalions, and rifle squads. Black laborers had downed their tools, quitting Southern plantations first in small groups and then in vast numbers, thus denying the Confederacy the means to provision its armies. African American men and women labored together to dig fortifications, to build roads, and to feed and care for wounded prisoners and escaped Union soldiers.

In religious gatherings, mass assemblies, and state legislatures, African Americans insisted that their newly won citizenship rights could form the basis of a global fight against tyranny. From the beginning, Black churches were critical sites of these discussions. Church meetings—whether held publicly in buildings or outdoors, or held in secret—were events where African Americans had taught each other mutuality, striving, and love for their fellow human beings, values that were always under siege in the nightmarish world of slavery.[1] Carrying forward the African ethics of their forebears, slaves revolutionized the slave master's religion into a belief system that served, in Howard Thurman's words, "the poor, the disinherited, the dispossessed."[2] Drawing on the wellsprings of these traditions, the Reverend W. B. Derrick asked if his country was willing to lend a hand to the struggling people of Cuba:

> Can it be possible that the offensive, aye, miserable carcass of slavery still lurks around the threshold of our Republic? And treading upon the necks of over a half million blacks. At our very threshold, is Cuba, only a few hours' sail from us; and the unwholesome stench can be inhaled. . . . At our own door the cry is heard, "Come and help us." Where are the four millions of our people lately emerged from the house of bondage? Can we remain still? Are we going to act as the brothers did to Joseph? Can we not hear the cry coming up from the slaves of those Islands?[3]

Radical abolitionists believed that the defeat of the Confederacy did not mean the end of slavery in the United States or abroad.[4] When William Lloyd Garrison proposed to close down the American Anti-Slavery Society, the *Christian Recorder* dissented: "Although we love Mr. Garrison as much as ever, and feel that he will work as faithfully in our cause as ever, we by no means endorse his opinion that the Anti-Slavery Society should be disbanded. The Anti-Slavery Society should keep in existence as long as slaves breathe the air anywhere in the world."[5] The *Christian Recorder* associated triumphalism in the United States with the betrayal of oppressed people in Latin America: "Disband the Anti-Slavery Society when Cuba, with over half a million of slaves lies at our gates! Disband the Anti-Slavery Society when Maximilian's government may be permanent, and be made slaveholding. . . . It may be said 'These are out of the United States.' But these men—slaves, are our brothers." Frederick Douglass amplified this theme in a speech to the American Anti-Slavery Society in 1869. Douglass argued that slavery was not yet defeated in the United States and that "we are here to-night in the interest of the negro, but we are here also in the interest of patriotism, in the interest of liberty in America, liberty in Cuba, liberty the world over."[6]

African Americans viewed abolition in the United States as a springboard to challenge subjugation everywhere. The Reverend J. B. Sanderson used his 1868 Emancipation Day speech in San Francisco to link the campaign for Black equality to Italian independence, the end of serfdom in Russia, and the liberation of Ireland. Sanderson exulted that "Cuba, the 'Gem of the Antilles,' has taken the initiatory steps towards the entire emancipation of her five hundred thousand slaves. The Emperor of Brazil has begun the good work of gradually converting four millions of bondmen into loyal, grateful subjects and citizens."[7] The *Christian Recorder* wrote, "Steadily is the area of human liberty being enlarged. A few years ago, it was Russia that threw off the manacles of her twenty million white serfs; then, by means of the fiery ordeal of war, America struck the manacles from nearly five million black ones. And now Spain is gradually moving in the same direction."[8]

African American communities placed global emancipation in concert with their celebrations of the ratification of the Fifteenth Amendment to the US Constitution. Aaron L. Jackson, the keynote speaker at a ratification celebration in Sacramento, California, swept up his listeners in the history they had all had a hand in making: "I feel to-day, that it has come full and complete, to gladden the hearts of millions of my oppressed people. Then roll on, thou great power of deliverance, guided by the hand of deity, regardless of all obstacles that the puny hand of man can erect to stay thy onward progress!" Jackson believed that the work of emancipation was incomplete: "Stop not within the confines of America, but leap across the briny deep, and encircle the bleeding isle of Cuba, thence to the Brazils, where thousands of human beings are yet groaning under the cruel yoke of slavery!"[9]

While expressing gratitude for the rights they had earned, African Americans also demanded that their government support human rights abroad. Participants at the 1870 Fifteenth Amendment ratification celebration in Virginia City, Nevada, drew up a list of resolutions that included the following statement: "RESOLVED: That our thanks are due to the Congress of the United States of America for the wise enactment, and maintaining of laws which makes all men free and equal; and that this Government, at no distant day, will extend its might and protecting arm of mercy to the struggling patriots of Cuba."[10]

African Americans were creating an idea of citizenship that linked national civil rights and international human rights, deeming one insufficient without the other. These Fifteenth Amendment commemorations open a window into a new theory and practice of American freedom. Black speakers and their audiences articulated the idea that their individual rights were intimately connected with the rights of oppressed people in Latin America, the Caribbean, and other parts of the world. This was an ideology based on the harsh experience of seeing slavery and racial capitalism extinguishing liberty everywhere it went. African Americans understood that the United States had torn itself apart due to its allegiance to a theory of profit-based individualism shrouded in slavery. The nation must never again define freedom in such a way as to place property rights above human rights. Furthermore, Americans could not preserve their liberty at home while crushing it abroad as slavery's imperial advocates had demanded.

Because of the connections between Black abolitionists and Cuban revolutionary emigrés in the United States, African Americans placed Cuba at the center of their concerns. Port cities such as Baltimore continued serving as strategic nodes of communication for receiving and spreading word about the progress of the antislavery and independence movements in Cuba. New Orleans, San Francisco, and New York were also places where African Americans could receive news directly from seafaring crews about goings-on in Cuba.

THE MAKING OF THE CUBAN SOLIDARITY MOVEMENT

As the Civil War was ending, the New Orleans *Black Republican* insisted that the period which came to be known as "Reconstruction" must be global in scope. The paper insisted, "We have great work to accomplish before we can rest satisfied. There are thousands of our brethren now upon the Island of Cuba, wearing the yoke of bondage, and they too must be free."[11] The Cuban War of Liberation, also known as the Ten Years' War, fought between 1868 and 1878, inspired African Americans and infused Black Reconstruction with special meaning. The desperate struggle of Cuban patriots against the Spanish reminded African Americans of their own harrowing journey to freedom. Numerous US cities passed resolutions in support of Cuba Libre, and newspapers published accounts of atrocities inflicted by the Spanish on the inhabitants of the island. However, it would fall to Black organizers and institutions to build a nationwide Cuban solidarity movement based on the principles of emancipatory internationalism.[12] Efforts to build a coordinated campaign in support of the Cuban struggle quickened in the wake of the election of Ulysses S. Grant, because Grant had publicly denounced Spanish conduct in the Ten Years' War.[13]

The centerpiece of the campaign was the national petition drive, which was facilitated by the Cuban Anti-Slavery Committee. Organizers circulated petitions in support of Cuban independence at religious gatherings, Emancipation commemorations, and Fifteenth Amendment ceremonies, among other settings. The goal was to obtain as many signatures as possible and hand-deliver the signed petitions to Congress and President Grant. The national petition operation kept organizers, churches, fraternal societies, labor organizations, and other supportive groups in contact with each other while creating measurable benchmarks of success. This newest antislavery crusade also mobilized Black voting power to convince legislatures in key Southern states, such as South Carolina, Louisiana, and Florida, to pass strongly worded resolutions in support of Cuban liberation that would then be sent to the White House.

A Black assemblyman and Union Army veteran, Robert Elliot, introduced resolutions in support of Cuban independence before the South Carolina House of Representatives in 1869. Elliot's resolutions reveal the early goals of the Cuban solidarity movement, including resolutions to recognize the "independence of the Republic of Cuba" and a promise to support military action against the Spanish:

> *Resolved* by the Senate and House of Representatives of the State of South Carolina, now met and sitting in General Assembly, that it would be eminently right and proper [for]

the Government of the United States to recognize the independence of the Republic of Cuba, without further delay;
and we hereby appeal to our Government to accord such
recognition at the earliest possible day.[14]

On its way to the US Congress, the South Carolina resolution joined
a similar one that had been submitted by an African American
assembly in New York.[15]

As the Cuban solidarity movement took shape, resolution
demands changed over time. Proposals for US military intervention
for Cuba Libre were scaled back in favor of the granting of belligerency status and the recognition of Cuban independence—which
would make the insurgent forces eligible to receive arms and support from the outside world. Working with members of the Cuban
Junta in New York, which helped coordinate international support
for the insurgents, Black petitioners emphasized the ability of the
resistance forces to defeat the Spanish, if only they received material
support from the outside world.[16] African Americans did not trust
the United States to embark on a military operation without impos-
ing its imperial will on Cuba.

Frederick Douglass, Governor P.B.S. Pinchback, William Wells
Brown, George L. Ruffin, and other luminaries spoke at the Colored
National Convention held in New Orleans in 1872.[17] "The wildest
applause greeted Mr. Ruffin's proposition to make a move on Cuba
for the abolition of the horrible slavery that prevails there. He said
that if the Fenians could cross the Atlantic to fight for the freedom
of their countrymen, the colored men can cross the narrow strip of
water that separates Florida from Cuba."[18] An African American
correspondent in Salt Lake City, Utah, admonished the readers of
the *Elevator* on the Fourth of July weekend,

> While we are rejoicing over our national anniversary,
> let us not forget the patriotic sons of Cuba in the struggles
> for their national existence, from the misruling of the gov-
> ernment of Spain; whose troops, brute-like and fiendish in
> disguise, have perpetuated acts of brutalities and cruelties
> on the Cuban patriots; not for the first time have they dis-
> graced her banner and civilization.[19]

At the height of Reconstruction, the Reverend Henry Highland Garnet delivered the keynote address at the founding convention of the Cuban Anti-Slavery Committee held at Cooper Union in New York City, the epicenter of the national Cuban solidarity movement, in December 1872. African Americans, Cuban émigrés, reporters, and curious onlookers bristled with excitement as they filled the Great Hall to overflowing. Black leaders in New York could remain in close contact with members of the Cuban "Junta," Cuban exiles in the United States who published educational materials on the anticolonial struggle in Cuba from their New York office.[20] During the Civil War, whites had rioted and killed scores of African Americans in protest of the institution of the military draft in the city. Garnet had recruited Black Union soldiers during the war and had narrowly escaped with his life.[21] He spoke with an authority based on decades of sacrifice, and his audience revered him. The Spanish government sent special emissaries to disrupt the meeting, but Garnet smiled over the crowd as the Spanish king's special agents were shouted down by enthusiastic participants.[22]

The Cuban patriot José Martí said of Garnet, "His eyes evinced honesty, his lips truth, his whole person respect. He rendered it and inspired it."[23] Garnet began his speech by assuring New Yorkers that the work of the antislavery movement was far from completed. He warmly welcomed the freedom fighters from Cuba, saying, "I see before me tonight many native Cubans, who, driven by the fierce fires of Spanish oppression, have sought and found shelter in our free land." There was a sense of urgency in the air, and nearly every sentence that Garnet uttered was punctuated by tremendous applause. "Permit me to assure you, my exiled friends," Garnet continued, "that I know that I am justified in saying to you that this meeting, and millions of American citizens, bid you God speed in your noble cause."[24]

Garnet drew on his observations of slavery in Cuba when he had sailed to the island years earlier as a young cabin boy. Quoting the great Cuban poet Gabriel de la Concepción Valdés (Plácido), Garnet combined experience and analysis to argue that liberation was attainable in Cuba:

> I have seen slave ships enter the port of Havana, and
> cargoes of miserable men and women, some dying and

some of them dead, dragged and hurried from the decks of slavers and thrown upon the shores. ([from the audience] *"Shame!"*) You cannot forget, Cubans, the immortal mulatto poet of your country, the brave and heroic Plácido (*"Bravo!" and continued cheers*). . . . When he was led forth to death he cried:

> *"O, Liberty! I hear thy voice calling me*
> *Deep in the frozen regions of the North, afar,*
> *With voice like God's and vision like a star."*[25]

Garnet used every rhetorical tool at his disposal to weld together his multiracial, multilingual, and multinational audience into supporters of one common cause. The meeting ended with the creation of a national coordinating committee. As cheers pulsed through the Cooper Union's Great Hall, the meeting's organizers circulated the national petition calling on the federal government "to accord to the Cuban Patriots that favorable recognition that four years' gallant struggle for freedom justly entitles them to."[26] The headquarters of the Cuban Anti-Slavery Committee were established at 62 Bowery. Organizers immediately set about planning an educational campaign to support the petition drive, and the assembled pledged to spread the campaign throughout the country. Mass meetings were immediately called in Boston, Philadelphia, Baltimore, San Francisco, Washington, DC, and other cities.

Ultimately, Garnet planned to present the petitions to President Grant for immediate action in the cause of Cuban liberty. "The colored citizens of New York are doing a good thing in protesting against the conduct of Spain to Cuba," the *Christian Recorder* wrote. "It is high time that liberty be brought in, even if Spain has to be kicked out."[27] Building upon preexisting networks of communication as well as the bedrock of emancipatory internationalism, the Cuban solidarity movement grew rapidly. Soon after the Cooper Institute assembly, a mass meeting was held in Boston, and resolutions were passed "calling on the American people to urge the Administration to extend all legal aid to the patriots of Cuba in their struggle for freedom."[28]

Early in 1873, African Americans in Baltimore gathered at the historic Madison Street Colored Presbyterian Church to consider "adopting measures to petition the Congress of the United States to tender the powerful mediation of this great government towards ameliorating the sad condition of a half million of our brethren now held in slavery in the island of Cuba by Spain." The attendance was good, a number of those present being of "the gentler sex."[29] Samuel R. Scottron, a renowned inventor and cofounder of the Cuban Anti-Slavery Committee, was the keynote speaker. Scottron urged his audience to recall that "they had passed through the Egyptian bondage and through the sea of blood, and having become clothed in the habiliments of freedom, knew how to sympathize with the 500,000 of their own race bowed down in Cuba."

Black Baltimoreans, Scottron stated, should "petition the government of the United States to extend a liberal policy to the colored race in Cuba. The 800,000 votes of the colored people here would have their weight in that direction." A cadre of speakers reported on the resolutions being brought forward in the northeastern cities.[30] Toward the end of the evening's spirited gathering, Scottron returned to the speaker's podium in order to read the text of the national petition directed to President Grant:

> We, the petitioners, citizens of the United States, duly grateful for our own disenthrallment and enfranchisement, truly comprehending the genius of free government, and heartily sympathizing with the oppressed in every land, have the honor to call your attention to the existence of slavery in the island of Cuba, and the suffering condition of more than five hundred thousand of our race in consequence thereof. The repeated and flagrant violations of the most sacred treaty obligations and broken faith of the Spanish government in regard to slavery in Cuba, running through a period of more than twenty years, is sufficient evidence that slavery and the slave trade will be perpetually continued in event of the triumph of the Spanish arms in the war now going on in that island. We respectfully submit that we have the fullest assurances that in event of the triumph of the Cuban patriots the benefit of freedom will be secured to our enslaved brethren. We should therefore

pray that the government of the United States accord to
the Cuban patriots that favorable recognition to which a
four years' gallant struggle in the interest of freedom justly
entitles them.[31]

A half century earlier, Black Baltimoreans had assembled to make
a public statement connecting their aspirations for freedom with the
revolutionary works of Toussaint L'Ouverture and Simón Bolívar,
and the wars of independence in Latin America and the Caribbean.
Emancipatory internationalism had been born in the first stormy
years of the republic when African Americans and their allies recognized that slavery, racial capitalism, and imperialism were fatally
intertwined. Now, even as they were embroiled in struggles for land,
the right to vote, and protection from Ku Klux Klan terrorism, African Americans insisted that their emancipation was incomplete as
long as oppression existed elsewhere.

African Americans drew on their own experiences in making the
Civil War a war for freedom in order to build the Cuban solidarity
movement. The San Francisco *Elevator* argued,

> The Cuban struggle is not for national independence
> alone, although that was the original motive which induced
> the patriots to revolt against the power and tyranny of
> Spain; but finding national independence and personal
> slavery incompatible and incongruous ideas, and knowing
> that they could never achieve their object without the aid of
> the slaves, decreed emancipation on the same grounds that
> President Lincoln issued his Proclamation of Emancipation
> i.e., military necessity.[32]

A movement in support of the Cuban solidarity campaign blos-
somed in 1873. Organizing centers emerged in Charleston, South
Carolina; Key West, Florida; Washington, DC; and other regions
where Black Republicanism was strong.[33] The *New York Times*
announced, "The colored citizens of Columbia [Washington, DC]
will hold a mass-meeting on Thanksgiving Eve to give expression of
their sympathy for the Cuban cause. Frederick Douglass will be one
of the speakers."[34] Both the California State Colored Men's Convention and the National Civil Rights Convention, held in Washington,

DC, at the end of the year, passed strongly worded resolutions of support for the Cuban patriots.[35] Seeking to build the campaign's momentum, the Reverend W. H. Hillery, the keynote speaker at the fourth annual celebration of the passage of the Fifteenth Amendment, held in Chico, California, proclaimed, "Cuba, after more than five years of war and rapine, shouts forth to the world—Liberty or Death."[36] Leaders of the Cuban Anti-Slavery Committee met with Cuban insurgents in the United States to strategize; the committee also worked with white organizations that shared the same broad agenda and corresponded regularly with British antislavery organizations.[37]

Efforts to build international solidarity were not without tensions and contradictions. African American religious leaders' concerns for their counterparts in Africa, Latin America, and Cuba were often sprinkled with notions of paternalism and of Protestant uplift as antidotes to generations of slavery, colonialism, and Catholicism.[38] "What is the status of these Cuban and Puerto Rico freedmen?" asked the national organ of the African Methodist Episcopal church. "Their religious status, for they have no educational status. They can scarcely be called Christian. The majority of them fresh from Africa are still doubtless in a pagan state; or if they possess the least shadow of Christianity, it is of the lowest Catholic type."[39] Exuberance over their historic triumph over American slavery in 1865 led some African Americans to view their counterparts in the other regions as needing tutelage. Once the anticolonial struggle in Cuba gained momentum, however, African American paternalism was generally transformed into admiration for the Cuban people.

Black political leaders and state legislatures in the South played an important role in the Cuban solidarity movement by demonstrating that the international struggle had a mass base of African American voters. A giant of Louisiana politics, P. B. S. Pinchback, a Union Army veteran and the United States' first African American governor, was also a leader of the Cuban Anti-Slavery Committee. State Representative J. Henri Burch of Louisiana shepherded a resolution passed by the Louisiana legislature urging the United States Congress "to give its material assistance in the suppression of slavery in the Island of Cuba"; in the same session the legislature passed a civil rights bill.[40] For his efforts, the Cuban Junta named Senator Burch

"General Representative of the Republique of Cuba Abroad."[41] The 1873 Convention of Colored Men in Louisiana placed the cause of the "barbarous rule of Spanish authority in Cuba" alongside the effort to end electoral fraud and Ku Klux Klan violence in Louisiana.[42] The Louisiana Republican Party platform pledged to rebuild their war-torn state, improve race relations, advocate for a national civil rights bill, and remind the Republican Party "that we sympathize with the patriotic men in Cuba who fight for liberty, and that we urge upon the national Congress the early recognition of the independence of Cuba, and hereby instruct our Representatives in Congress to use their best efforts and influence to this end."[43]

South Carolina lieutenant governor A. G. Ranier presided over a Union League Hall meeting in Washington, DC, called in support of the Cuban patriots.[44] Ranier subsequently gave a rousing keynote address at the Maryland Union Republican Association meeting that included speeches by Governor Pinchback and African American congressman John R. Lynch of Mississippi. Ranier "concluded by saying that the Republican party in Congress could not afford to not pass financial measures, a recognition of Cuba and the Civil Rights bill."[45] In Florida, Congressman Josiah T. Walls, a Union Army veteran, helped lead a deliberative process that resulted in a joint resolution from the state legislature calling upon the federal government to recognize the Cuban insurgency.[46] Walls subsequently gave a landmark speech in the US House of Representatives in support of the Cuban insurgents. The Florida congressman reviewed the history of the Latin American independence struggles of the early nineteenth century and insisted that his resolution in support of Cuba be framed "in obedience to what I understand as the prevailing sentiment which soars above the selfishness of traditional dynasties or the soulless ordinances of international law."[47] Here was a new vision of freedom made possible by a national movement organizing in the name of emancipation without borders.

By the spring of 1873, leaders of the Cuban Anti-Slavery Committee had demonstrated the existence of so much popular support for their campaign that they earned a personal audience with President Ulysses S. Grant. The Cuban solidarity movement had accomplished the tremendous feat of gathering hundreds of thousands of signatures—some estimated the count at five hundred thousand—to present to Grant.[48] The delegation included the most prominent African American leaders of the time including Rev. Garnet, J. M. Langston, and George T. Downing. The previous winter, President Grant had given the movement hope when, in his message to Congress, he urged Spain to declare emancipation of the slaves in Cuba.[49]

Nevertheless, even though Grant politely received Henry Garnet and the delegation of the Cuban Anti-Slavery Committee, the odds were not in their favor that he would officially recognize the Cuban liberation struggle. Secretary of State Hamilton Fish viewed Cubans as racially inferior.[50] The historian Richard H. Bradford notes, "As a businessman Fish favored the interests of Americans who had invested in sugar and slaves and perhaps stood to lose if the revolution succeeded. . . . The 'hard-money elite' of upper-class Northeasterners in both parties" opposed formal recognition of the Cuban patriots.[51] Congressman Nathaniel P. Banks of Massachusetts, writing in 1873, explained why the United States ultimately betrayed the Cuban insurgents. Banks believed that the pursuit of overseas profits enshrined as imperial policy placed the United States on the side of Spanish plantation agriculture in Cuba. Congressman Banks was unsparing in his criticism of his government's rejection of the petition and demands of the Cuban solidarity movement:

> But the obstacle in the way was the position of the United States Government. It was the American Government which obstructed the way of progress and reform in the waters and islands of Cuba. . . . The trouble was that the people of the United States were wild, if not insane, in the pursuit of wealth, and sacrificed every consideration of right and public duty to that purpose and end alone.[52]

The imperatives of racial capitalism had once again trumped humanity and human rights.

African American organizers regrouped after being rebuffed by their nation and continued to build support for international solidarity with the Cuban patriots. As the presidency of Rutherford B. Hayes loomed, the *Savannah Tribune* wrote, "CUBA. The revolution in this island, has continued eight years, and has probably cost Spain nearly a billion dollars, and over a hundred thousand lives, many of them the flower of Castilian chivalry and the gem of the Antilles is still unconquered. We hope one of the first acts of President Hayes's administration [will] be to acknowledge the belligerency of Cuba."[53] At a mass meeting held in Philadelphia the following year, Henry Highland Garnet continued to expound on the theme that the work of abolishing slavery was incomplete, stating,

> If the veteran abolitionists of the United States had not mustered themselves out of service, I believe that there would not now have been a single slave in the Island of Cuba. . . . We sympathize with the patriots of Cuba, not simply because they are Republicans, but because their triumph will be the destruction of slavery in that land. All Europe now frowns upon Spain, because of her attitude toward human bondage. We must take our place on the broad platform of universal human rights, and plead for the brotherhood of the entire human race.[54]

After hearing addresses in Spanish and in English, participants formed the American Foreign Anti-Slavery Society to address the crisis in Cuba. The respect that Cuban revolutionaries held for Garnet was reflected when the Cuban patriot General José Antonio Maceó visited New York the following year and requested a private audience with the senior leader of the Cuban solidarity movement.

African American efforts to promote support for the anticolonial struggle continued. However, the momentum of the Cuban solidarity movement slowed as white supremacy, anti-Black violence, and voter suppression began to erode African American political power. The massacre of the Black electorate came in waves of violence and fraud—first in the form of the so-called First Mississippi Plan (Ku Klux Klan terrorism, lynching, and election corruption), and then in the Second Mississippi Plan (poll taxes, literacy tests, residential requirements).[55] Voter turnout in the South began a general decline, and the entire region began sinking into the venality of one-party rule.

The Cuban solidarity campaign launched by Black antislavery abolitionists in the heart of Reconstruction was one of the most remarkable social movements in American history. In placing the liberation of Cuba on the same platform with their desperate struggle for equal citizenship in the United States, African Americans from Key West to California created a new kind of freedom movement. The national petition campaign was built on the traditions of anti-imperial antebellum slavery abolitionism. Furthermore, the movement prefigured the Third World liberation and anti-apartheid struggles of the twentieth century. While Black organizers focused much of their energy on the question of race and slavery in Cuba, they also made it clear that they viewed the Ten Years' War as a multiracial anticolonial movement aimed at ending Spanish tyranny. In the eyes of the Cuban Anti-Slavery Committee, "white" Cuban rebels deserved support because they had abolished slavery for the same pragmatic reasons that Abraham Lincoln had issued the Emancipation Proclamation during the Civil War.

Henry Highland Garnet died on February 13, 1882. Having been appointed US minister to Liberia, the man who had once declared that he had no home other than the United States decided to spend the final weeks of his life in Africa. No one in the United States had fought more creatively for freedom in the Americas than Reverend Garnet. His call for a rising of the slaves in 1843 was a people's manifesto that maintained that it was up to the most oppressed to save the nation from complete destruction. Garnet grasped this most precious truth even before Frederick Douglass, who in turn glimpsed it long before Abraham Lincoln did. Garnet and his comrades proposed to heal the malignancies of the age with the balm of mass action. Garnet was the prophet of the Black general strike that won the American Civil War, as surely as he and his comrades in the Cuban Anti-Slavery Committee provided a new model of building international solidarity that echoed into the following century. The Cuban patriot José Martí provided a stirring eulogy to Garnet in *La Opinión Nacional*:

> He was Henry Garnet, who showed lazy, proud, and impatient men how, from a little Negro cabin boy—son of fugitive slaves who went naked through the snow and suffered hunger and cold in the woods—one could go on to become a pastor of a church, a teacher, a member of a Frankfurt congress, a mediator for free labor in England, a leader of his race, a representative upon foreign soil of a nation of fifty million subjects, an orator upon whose pure, proud

brow the serene and grandiose light of the Capitol played as if fond caresses. . . . He despised hatred. He deeply loved white men and Negroes alike. He died beloved.[56]

THE FREEST TOWN IN THE SOUTH

Even as powerful currents of white supremacy were sweeping the mainland, African Americans, exiled Cubans, Bahamians, and dissident Southern whites were building an enclave of freedom in Key West, Florida. Establishing this sanctuary was no easy task. When the island's Black community attempted to celebrate emancipation during the Civil War they were violently attacked by Confederate sympathizers. In 1865, there was a breakthrough: the *National Anti-Slavery Standard* reported, "Yesterday was the first time that the colored people of the Island have been allowed without violence and molestation to celebrate the anniversary of their emancipation."[57] There was a good reason that saboteurs were unable to disrupt the 1865 celebration. The participants were "escorted through the principal streets of the city by the Second Regiment U.S. Colored Infantry, with banners flying and to the sound of martial music, these happy and peaceful people met and rejoiced over the good fortune which had befallen them." Armed self-help in the defense of democracy would become a foundation of Key West politics.

Key West became an important site of the resurgence of the Cuban solidarity movement in the 1880s. The island's vibrant political culture attracted individuals such as J. Willis Menard, a prominent Black New Orleans politician who subsequently founded the *Key West News*.[58]

When former President Grant visited Key West in 1880, he was greeted by "the almighty public, where whites, negroes, Cubans and Chinese mingled in one enthusiastic and curious mass." Grant received delegations of African Americans and Cubans who still viewed him in a positive light as supportive of Cuban independence, against the Eastern establishment.[59] Cuban patriots and military leaders, including General José Antonio Maceó and Máximo Gómez, visited Key West in 1884 and were received with great enthusiasm by tobacco workers and the general population. "The city of Key West emerged triumphant from its early trials," José Martí observed. "In Yankee hands it was no more than sand and shacks, but now it can point proudly to factories that in their continual thought and study are like academies of learning; schools where the hand that rolls the tobacco leaf by day lifts a book and teaches by night."[60]

Black power built via interracial coalitions with Cuban émigré socialists and Knights of Labor union assemblies pointed the way toward a new kind of democratic politics in South Florida and the Gulf. Key West also became a critical movement center for the Independent Party of Florida, a statewide interracial political party.[61] Working-class self-activity was the foundation in the building of Key West's political culture. The nation's still-liberal voting laws for new immigrants were another important factor. The enfranchisement of African American men in Reconstruction led to the adoption of measures making it easier for immigrants to vote in the South. Cuban refugees to Key West found a relatively easy pathway to the ballot box via "declarant alien voting," which was passed by Florida's Reconstruction legislature in 1868 ("declarant aliens" were resident aliens who declared their intent to naturalize).[62] According to Article 14 of the 1868 Florida constitution, a man who swore to defend the laws of the land and to eventually become a citizen could vote.[63] The insurgent Knights of Labor gave the island's workers linkages to a potent national labor organization, and unionists in Key West organized at least two local assemblies and one district assembly of the Knights of Labor.[64] Local trade union publications included the *Equator* and the Spanish-language *El Jornalero*, both of which were listed in British government reports as "chief working class papers in America."[65]

L. W. Livingston, writing from Key West as a special correspondent for T. Thomas Fortune's *New York Age*, reported that Republican Party strength on the key was tied to its unique location in the international economy.[66] After the Civil War, Key West stood at the intersection of a brisk shipping trade in a variety of commodities, none more important over time than tobacco and cigars.[67] "We are on a little island here," Livingston reported, "cut off from the rest of the world, both civilized and uncivilized, and absolutely dependent upon Havana, New Orleans, Tampa and New York, especially the last named place."[68] Migration from these ports brought together a diverse working class: "There is such a conglomeration of American colored and white folks, Cubans, colored immigrants from Nassau and Conchs [white Bahamians], and such an admixture of them all that it is impossible to determine where the line begins and where it ends."[69]

The Republican Party forged a multinational, multiracial, and cross-class coalition in Key West that weathered the crisis of disenfranchisement then sweeping through the South and kept the Democratic Party at bay in that community. Republican meetings in Key West were boisterous and bilingual. As J. Willis Menard, the founder of the *Key West News*, told Joseph E. Lee, an African American leader of Black Republicanism, "Clubs of Laboring men" consisting of whites and Afro-Cubans, as well as African Americans, made up the rank and file of the Republican Party on the island.[70] "The Cubans are with us to a man," exulted William Artrell, an African American leader and former Key West alderman.[71] "There is generally at least one speech in Spanish and at a Republican meeting I attended recently a Cuban delivered two speeches," noted Livingston, "one in English and one in Spanish."[72] He marveled, "The idea I wish to convey is, that colored men here speak and act their sentiments, with none to molest or make them afraid, and there is nothing cowardly and servile about them." White Key West residents found themselves having to participate as equals in the public sphere, and did not always appreciate the novelty of the island's political climate.

In 1888, Key West voters elected James Dean to a judgeship—the first African American judge elected in the South since the end of Reconstruction a decade earlier—as well as an African American sheriff, Charles F. Dupont. Both candidates enjoyed strong support in the Cuban émigré community,[73] and Dean advocated slavery reparations in order to fund Florida's abysmal public education system.[74] Livingston captured the pageantry and joy of the celebrations that swept the island in the wake of this great victory: "Talking about enthusiasm, why the way the colored and white Republican Cubans, the colored Americans and Baham[ians] and the American white Republicans celebrated the election of the National Republican ticket here as well as their own county ticket, was enough to make old Zach Chandler turn in his grave." A great procession of "torchlights, brass bands, Cuban queens, Chinese lanterns, barbecues, cards marked 'free trade' and attached to the caudal appendages of horses, endless exclamations in Spanish and English—these are some of the manifestations of Key West enthusiasm."[75]

Livingston called Key West the "freest town in the South."[76] The political tensions that endangered this enclave of Black political power did not escape the reporter's attention.[77] But Livingston also wanted his readers in the North to understand what lay at the bottom of the Republican coalition's success in Key West: the ability of Black Floridians on the island to defend themselves from white incursions. Livingston observed that African Americans in Key West were "well equipped with the means of offensive and defensive warfare, as conducted in times of peace, with a good sprinkling of old soldiers among them, and the beauty . . . is that they are not the only ones that knows their power and invincibleness." Livingston was referring to Black veterans of the American Civil War as well as immigrant veterans of the Ten Years' War in Cuba.[78]

On the Florida mainland, African American workers were also making progress. In 1887, African American guano-fertilizer factory operatives in Pensacola formed an alliance with white railroad workers through the Knights of Labor and carried out a successful strike for higher wages. During the business downturn caused by the 1888 yellow fever epidemic, Black labor in Jacksonville organized an unemployed movement that successfully pressed municipal authorities to create a public works program that would provide jobs.[79] In addition, African Americans throughout Florida were taking part in the creation of a public education system that for the first time in Southern history served the children of poor and rich alike. These actions were animated by the knowledge that "Southern industry is but another name for colored industry, or the industry of colored people of the South, notably as this relates to cotton, rice and sugar. Subtract what the colored people produce and the remainder would scarcely be worth the mentioning. . . . And yet the laboring people of this section of the country are among the poorest of the nation."[80]

Albion W. Tourgeé, a former Union Army soldier who was the chief counsel in *Plessy v. Ferguson*, described a few of the major achievements of African Americans in the first years after the end of the Civil War:

> They instituted a public school system in a realm where public schools had been unknown. They opened the ballot-box and jury box to thousands of white men who had been debarred from them by a lack of earthly possessions. They introduced home rule in the South. They abolished the whipping post, and branding iron, the stocks and other barbarous forms of punishment which up to that time prevailed. They reduced capital felonies from about twenty to two or three. In an age of extravagance, they were extravagant in the sums appropriated for public works. In all that time no man's rights of person were invaded under the forms of laws.[81]

WHITE BUSINESS SUPREMACY STRIKES BACK

Moneyed interests in the South had no plans to share their power with workers, nor were they interested in building a public infrastructure to develop an educated working class. In 1889, Florida state legislators revoked the city charter of Jacksonville, an act that empowered the governor to replace pro-labor elected officials with a white regime controlled by the state. The Florida *Times-Union* described the new cabal taking charge of Jacksonville: "Everybody favors the bill: lawyers, merchants, and businessmen."[82] According to the pro-business *Times-Union*, the overthrow of elected government in Jacksonville would guarantee race *and* class domination: "If the present bill to amend the Jacksonville charter should fail, this city will get no relief whatever. Capitalists will not lend money to a municipality that can be bought for fifty dollars. At our next city election Jacksonville will be completely Africanized."[83]

Deep South leaders in politics and business skillfully replicated their system of voter suppression, low wages, and inequality across most of the Sunbelt states. The Florida state legislature provides a case study in the making of Jim Crow/Juan Crow segregation.[84] In 1889, Tallahassee legislators revoked the municipality of Key

West's charter, and Governor Francis Fleming deposed Judge James Dean for allegedly presiding over an interracial marriage involving a light-skinned African American man and an Afro-Cuban woman. Fleming used the state's miscegenation statute to remove a leader who had played an integral role in building multiracial alliances.[85] The state also revoked the charter of the city of Pensacola. Next, it imposed puppet regimes friendly to elite interests in all three of Florida's largest cities where active labor movements, interracial and internationalist, posed a threat to white business supremacy.[86] State seizure of local government was carried out in the interests of individuals whom the *Pensacola Commercial* celebrated as the "intelligent, enterprising, business men."[87]

In subsequent decades, more than a dozen states skillfully used Jim Crow segregation laws, as well as voter restrictions, to crush interracial alliances and curtail the rights of new immigrants to vote. Florida abolished declarant alien voting in the constitutional revision of 1895 as part of the state's move to disenfranchise both African Americans and immigrants.

Whites also engaged in political terror to intimidate African Americans from even attempting to vote. Lynchings were frequent throughout the South, and between the 1880s and World War II, Black Floridians generally suffered the highest per capita lynching rates in the United States.[88] "Too late to talk about the 'suppressed vote' now," a Black Floridian cried out in 1887. "We are in the hands of the devil."[89]

If corporations, planters, and banks needed a reminder of how dangerous a fully enfranchised working class was to their power, they only needed to look to the Colored Farmers Alliance, which, by May 1889, had "an estimated membership of 125,000 and 3,100 lodges." Working in tandem with the white-majority Southern Farmers' Alliance, "African American alliances advocated the order's overall economic program of building cooperatives, fighting the banks and 'trusts' as well as democratizing the nation's money supply."[90] In efforts to build an interracial political party that could confront the power of what William H. Skaggs called "the southern oligarchy," T. Thomas Fortune held lectures where he explained to white farmers that they were "systematically victimized by legislators, corporations and syndicates" and that "poverty and misfortune make no invidious distinctions of 'race, color or previous condition,' but that wealth unduly centralized oppresses all alike."[91]

Voter suppression in the United States was designed to ensure that the insights of Thomas Fortune and the Southern Farmers' Alliance were never translated into public policies. Voting restrictions against African Americans in the South, Mexicans in the Southwest, and Chinese and Indians in California were justified by business leaders who argued "that the voting poor constituted a threat to property."[92] Charles Francis Adams Jr., the grandson of John Quincy Adams, raised the alarm against the possibility of a multiracial democracy taking root in the United States: "Universal suffrage can only mean in plain English, the government of ignorance and vice:—it means a European, and especially Celtic, proletariat on the Atlantic coast; an African proletariat on the shores of the Gulf, and a Chinese proletariat on the Pacific."[93]

Voter suppression was the linchpin of a system in which the working class was bereft of real political and economic power. In 1884, a leading Democratic official in Florida explained that restricting the right to vote was the key to enforcing the republic of cheap labor:

> We are going to have a Constitutional Convention in less than eight months; that convention will be controlled by white men; no one but white men will be allowed a vote there; the angel Gabriel himself will not be allowed a vote; and don't you forget that the status of the nigger as a factor in the politics of this State will then be fixed. Then we want them to come. There are thousands of niggers in Georgia and Alabama who are working from 25 to 50 cents per day, while, in South Florida especially, we are being compelled to pay from one dollar and a quarter to two dollars a day.[94]

While the violence and fraud associated with the initiative to restrict suffrage was most intense in the South—and aimed most virulently against African Americans—voter suppression was a national phenomenon promoted by the most powerful interests in industrial America.[95] No other domestic policy in the coming decades would be pursued with more ingenuity by America's elites at all levels than the effort to restrict the voting franchise.

THE MAKING OF JIM CROW SEGREGATION

Southern spokesmen mounted a pro-segregation offensive using a discourse that their Northern peers could support. They pointed out that the South was economically undeveloped. White business supremacists contended that Southern economic development depended on the complete removal of black workers from politics. Daniel G. Fowle, the Princeton-educated governor of North Carolina, explained to the *New York Herald* that segregation enhanced America's competitiveness in the global economy:

> In social and political life the negro is subordinate in North Carolina as well as in New York. . . . In the stern realities of life as we find them, the white man is superior, and it is impossible for him to live under the domination of an inferior race. All sections of the country must agree with us in that. . . . Labor is so cheap with us that we can hire negroes for fifty cents a day, and our cotton fields can compete successfully with the world in the common grades of cloths.[96]

White leaders actually marketed segregation, voter suppression, and economic development on their terms as a package deal. To rationalize the separate and unequal world of Jim Crow capitalism, businessmen and academics vilified public education and depicted African Americans as lazy and unfit for politics. Robert Winston, president of the Durham, North Carolina, Chamber of Commerce argued that whites were tired of paying for public education. He commented,

> It is now becoming popular to teach that when you educate a negro you spoil a good farm hand. In fact, the average Southern negro has lost to a certain extent his Southern white friend. Why this change of feeling towards the negro? It is found in the fact that the modern negro by his idleness and worthlessness, as a laborer, has rendered the average Southern farm unfit to live upon, and has endangered the industrial basis of the average Southern home.[97]

Dr. George T. Winston, president of the College of Agriculture and Mechanic Arts in North Carolina, told the American Academy of Political and Social Science in Philadelphia that black people's progress "depends absolutely upon restoration of friendly relations with the whites. . . . Two things are requisite: 1. The Withdrawal of the negro from politics. 2. His increased efficiency as a laborer."[98]

"A TRAGEDY THAT BEGGARED THE GREEK"

W. E. B. Du Bois characterized Reconstruction as "the finest effort to achieve democracy for the working millions which this world had ever seen."[99] The subsequent defeat of Reconstruction "was a tragedy that beggared the Greek; it was an upheaval of humanity like the Reformation and the French Revolution." The decimation of Black ballots held cataclysmic consequences for all workers, and, as Du Bois pointed out, working-class people all over the world felt the shockwaves. In 1935, Du Bois concluded, "Imperialism, the exploitation of colored labor throughout the world, thrives upon the approval of the United States, and the United States gives that approval because of the South. World war waits on and supports imperial aggression and international jealousy. This was too great a price to pay for anything which the South gained."[100]

Voter suppression was designed to undermine the kind of democratic politics that the Cuban solidarity movement brought into being. Disenfranchisement removed the largest potential block of anti-imperial voters from the nation's voting rolls. African Americans recognized only too well that their country had descended into what William Appleman Williams called "the tragedy of American diplomacy," a system of expansion undertaken in the name of "freedom" that denied freedom to others. Black citizens were expelled from the body politic at the very moment when their voices were most desperately needed to challenge an imperial system that embroiled the hemisphere.[101]

Disenfranchisement, however, did not extinguish Black internationalism. African Americans drew inspiration from new anticolonial struggles in Latin America and used Latin American opposition to US hegemony to build a new movement to regain their own political rights.

CHAPTER 5

WAGING WAR ON THE GOVERNMENT OF AMERICAN BANKS IN THE GLOBAL SOUTH, 1890s TO 1920s

The paths of José Martí and Ida B. Wells-Barnett crossed at least twice in the course of their respective struggles for justice. Exiled from his native Cuba by the Spanish government, Martí traveled in the United States to build support for the Cuban liberation movement, as well as to write about its social conditions for Latin American readers. Wells-Barnett was an African American journalist who publicized the lynching of African Americans in a quest to build a campaign against lynching, voter suppression, and Jim Crow.[1] Martí and Wells-Barnett separately reported on the 1892 lynching of Ed Coy in Texarkana, Texas. According to the *New York Times*, Coy was burned at the stake for raping a white woman, Julia Jewell.[2] The *Times* silenced Coy's voice at the moment of his execution, choosing not to print his last utterance. In contrast, José Martí made sure that his *El Partido Liberal* readers in Mexico City knew that the doomed man cried out, "I offered Mrs. Jewell no offense! You're going to kill me, but I offered her no offense!"[3] Subsequently, Wells-Barnett proved that Coy had been falsely accused of rape.[4]

Martí reported stories of anti-Black violence, the repression of labor unions, and the power of banks in his campaign to warn his readers in the Americas that Yankee imperialism imperiled them all. Martí admired figures such as the Reverend Henry Highland Garnet and Walt Whitman, as well as members of the nation's embattled labor movement. However, he was alarmed at the tendency of US leaders to advocate the domination of Latin American affairs. In 1894, in "The Truth About the United States," Martí critiqued "this greedy, authoritarian republic, and the growing lustfulness of the United States." He wrote about US schemes to annex northern Mexico, as well as the efforts of US bankers to control the currency of the Americas. Now, Martí warned,

> an honorable man cannot help but observe that not only have the elements of diverse origin and tendency from which the United States was created failed, in three centuries of shared life and one century of political control, to merge, but their forced coexistence is exacerbating and accentuating their primary differences and transforming the unnatural federation into a harsh state of violent conquest. . . . The truth about the United States must be made known to our America.[5]

Wells-Barnett and Martí taught the absurdity of trusting the US government with defending their people's safety. After citing cases where African Americans had stopped lynch mobs dead in their tracks, Wells-Barnett observed:

> The lesson this teaches and which every Afro-American should ponder well, is that a Winchester rifle should have a place of honor in every black home, and it should be used for that protection which the law refuses to give. When the white man who is always the aggressor knows he runs as great risk of biting the dust every time his Afro-American victim does, he will have greater respect for Afro-American life. The more the Afro-American yields and cringes and begs, the more he has to do so, the more he is insulted, outraged and lynched.[6]

The second traumatic event that brought Wells-Barnett and Martí together was the death of General José Antonio Maceó in 1896. A brilliant tactician who enlarged the latest Cuban liberation war against Spain, Maceó's passing deeply impacted Martí, who said of the Afro-Cuban general, "His support will be himself, never his dagger. He shall serve his troops with his ideas even more than with his courage. Strength and greatness are natural to him."[7] Wells-Barnett and many African Americans mourned alongside Martí in spirit, and she was the keynote speaker at a Cuba Libre rally in Chicago's Bethel AME (African Methodist Episcopal) Church shortly after Maceó fell. The Indianapolis *Freeman* reported, "The meeting was held under the auspices of the members of the church, and 500 colored persons [who] attended demanded freedom of Cuba and bemoan[ed] the death of Maceo."[8] Wells-Barnett was on the speaker's platform when participants unanimously adopted the following resolutions: "Resolved, That the Afro-American citizens in Chicago in mass meeting assemble and express their deep sympathy with Cubans and deplore the untimely death of that matchless military leader, Antonio Maceo, and if killed by a disregard of the time honored and sacred law of a flag of truce, Spain is thereby placed beyond the pale of civilization."[9]

The Chicago ceremony was one of scores of events organized by African Americans across the country to commemorate the life of the man whom they had adopted as their beloved general. "The decease of Maceo comes to us as a personal affliction," the Indianapolis *Freeman* mourned. "We colored Americans need the inspiration of Maceo's memory. In these degenerate days when the gods of our land are silver and gold instead of liberty and freedom, we need the remembrance of some former deeds of such a hero."[10] A mass meeting held in Little Rock was reported in the *Cleveland Gazette*: "Prominent Afro-Americans from all sections of Arkansas met in mass meeting in this city Monday night and adopted a memorial to congress, urging action favorable to Cubans in their struggle for liberty. Stirring resolutions were also adopted condemning the brutal warfare of the Spaniards and calling for liberty-loving people to render all possible aid."[11] At the Emancipation Day commemoration in Kinston, North Carolina, the Reverend C. Dillard celebrated "the plumed knight of the Island, General Antonio Maceo, who baffled the skill of all Spain by his remarkable and almost phenomenal ability in chasing 20,000 well-armed and well-fed Spaniards with only 6,000 men."[12] Edward A. Johnson, a former slave who became a noted educator, wrote, "At a public gathering in New York, where [Maceó's] picture was exhibited, the audience went wild with applause—the waving of handkerchiefs and the wild hurrahs were long and continued."[13]

African Americans' tributes to Maceó transcended the Black-white racial binary frame that has long plagued efforts to think expansively about race in the United States.[14] Black writers celebrated what they perceived to be Maceó's racial hybridity and his ability to outsmart his Spanish adversaries. While Theodore Roosevelt and his eugenicist acolytes were preaching the doctrine of white racial purity, African Americans referred warmly to "Maceo, the mulatto," noting that the general's strength came from his combined African, Indigenous, and European ancestry.[15] The newspaper *Fair Play*, published in Fort Scott, Kansas, wrote that Maceó hailed from the north coast of eastern Cuba, "where all the people have Indian blood in their veins."[16] The Indianapolis *Freeman* celebrated Maceó's mixed racial lineage as a forte of his character: "Indian blood courses in the veins of its inhabitants—the Indians of whom Jesus Rabi, a prominent Cuban general, is so striking a representative."[17] African Americans imagined a new kind of identity that combined African, Indigenous, and European heritages with the struggle for national liberation as the central unifier of an individual's character.

Representations of Maceó demonstrate that African Americans did not believe that Cubans had to be saved by the United States; Cubans possessed the ability to achieve their own independence.[18] This contrasted with the white media's depiction of a helpless Cuban populace terrorized by the Spanish.[19] The historian Louis A. Pérez Jr. has explained how US political leaders and scholars erased the decades-long struggle of the Cuban people to expel the Spanish in favor of a self-serving Spanish-American War narrative crediting the United States with bringing about the island's independence. White nationalist leaders adopted the central idea put forth in Rudyard Kipling's essay "The White Man's Burden," published in *McClure's Magazine* in 1899, as poetic complement to the Roosevelt Corollary, an addition to the Monroe Doctrine that claimed "international police power" for the United States and reaffirmed the right of the United States to interfere in the affairs of Caribbean and Latin America nations.[20] Continuing in the anti-egalitarian tradition established by John Adams and his cohort, the nation's elites argued that people of African or Latin American descent were mentally deficient and were doomed to being permanent second-class citizens—even in their own countries.

The Reverend Lena Mason would have none of this racial paternalism. She admired Maceó and other Cuban resistance leaders for their creativity, intelligence, and common sense in recruiting women to their revolutionary columns. Mason, a renowned AME traveling minister, observed, "It is the history of all countries that the females are the bitterest partisans, the first to urge force of arms when prudence would dictate longer forbearance and the last to give up the grudge long after the hatchet is buried."[21] Mason noted that women played leading roles in the Cuban War of Independence: "Antonio Maceo also had more than a hundred females in his regiment—not coarse and shameless amazons, who chose the wild life for love of adventure, but mostly wives and mothers of standing and dignity. They dress[ed] in masculine attire, carried Mauser rifles, machetes, marched with men, endured all the hardships of camp and field and made as intrepid and uncomplaining soldiers as any."[22] Women partisan fighters played a major role in General Maceó's invasion of the Pinar del Río province, a turning point of the war. Mason related, "The women of San Juan Martinez took no small part in the rebellion. When Spanish troops under Cornell were on their way to that city the citizenry, men and women, met and took a vote as to what course they should pursue. They decided to burn their town to ashes, rather than have it destroyed by Spanish soldiers." Mason wanted her readers to understand the sacrifices that Cuban women were making to further the war of independence:

> So while the men took all the horses and hurried to the field, the women set their own homes on fire and then with their children in their arms walked to Guane, twelve miles distant. The Spaniards[,] enraged at finding themselves baffled, started in hot pursuit. Hearing of their approach the women fired Guane and walked to the next town, Moutezuma[,] and so they kept up the merry chase, burning village after village, until they reached the insurgent army.[23]

Like Maceó, Martí felt a grave sense of urgency in expelling the Spanish from Cuba and declaring Cuban independence before the United States could seize control of the island. On the day before he was killed in battle, Martí began composing a letter to his friend Manuel Mercado, in Mexico, explaining his fears of US imperialism. It was a prophetic rumination:

> Every day now I am in danger of giving my life for my country and my duty—since I understand it and have the spirit to carry it out—in order to prevent, by the timely independence of Cuba, the United States from extending its hold across the Antilles and falling with all the greater force on the lands of our America. All I have done up to now and all I will do is for that. . . . I lived in the monster, and I know its entrails—and my sling is the sling of David.[24]

When the United States launched the war against Spain in Cuba, Puerto Rico, and the Philippines in 1898, Martí's worst fears were realized. Although most African Americans supported the expulsion of the Spanish, African American writers generally doubted that the United States would treat the new nations as equals. The premise of the Cuban solidarity movement had been that the recognition of the legitimacy of the Cuban resistance—not a US military invasion—would have allowed Cuban patriots to receive international assistance allowing them to establish an autonomous republic on their own terms. How could the United States aid the cause of liberty anywhere when it was building elaborate structures of oppression against African Americans and Latinx people in the United States? The Black press reacted with outrage when General Maceó's son, a lieutenant volunteering for service against the Spanish in the Philippines, was refused admission to a public dining room in Spokane, Washington, because of his race.[25]

In a letter to one Black newspaper, the writer J. H. Wheaton shared his reservations about a US invasion of Cuba:

> I was recently approached by an old acquaintance, as to the reason I had not said more upon the question of Cuban Independence. There are many reasons, but my primary one is this: Should the United States recognize the independence of Cuba the chances are that she would establish a protectorate over the island. In the Spanish nations, color is no barrier to the progress a man may make in any of the

avocations of life. He rises according to his energy and ability. His capabilities are not shackled by his color, nor his progress hampered by race.[26]

Though Wheaton elided centuries of racism in the Spanish empire, his skepticism about US intentions was confirmed at the end of the Spanish-American War.[27] American occupation authorities exported the Jim Crow architecture of expropriation and inequality to the Philippines, Puerto Rico, and Cuba. US military officers paid no mind to the fact that Filipinos had waged a valiant struggle against Spanish imperialism for decades; occupation officials were obsessed with crushing the movement for independence in the Philippines.[28] When T. Thomas Fortune explored the possibility of bringing Black workers to the Philippines he was met with hostility by US authorities, who felt that African Americans would demand decent wages and build labor coalitions with Filipino workers: "The plea was that the Negro and the Filipino got along too well together and thus endangered the well-being of the government," Fortune remarked.[29]

The United States exported its weaponized labor relations to Puerto Rico, where big sugar growers counted on police power to crush strikes.[30] In 1925, the *Negro World* published a scathing critique of the conduct of US corporations in newly occupied nations, headlining its report in bold type: "American Capitalists Gaining Control of Industries in Porto Rico, Haiti, San Domingo and Reducing Natives to Peons." The report hammered American imperialism, stating, "Puerto Rico is superficially prosperous, but the masses of the people are wretched. They are landless in an agricultural country. Some of them are allowed a minute patch of ground on a plantation. In return they are expected to work on the plantation for a small wage. This is locally called peonage."[31] Dr. Gilberto Concepción summarized the "stark and tragic" consequences of US corporate control of Puerto Rico for the *Chicago Defender*:

U.S. controlled sugar interests—Fajardo company, South Puerto Rico Associates, and Guanica Central company—built a one-crop economy, controlling all fertile land except a few hundred acres unfit for sugar growing. Absenteeism prevails, profits going to absent owners in the U.S., who spend not one cent—not even taxes—beyond poor wages for sugar workers, for development of [the] Puerto Rican economy. U.S. laws governing the Island have hurt rather than helped.[32]

Puerto Rico became, in the words of journalist Juan Gonzalez, "the richest colony in American history," hugely profitable to US corporations, yet mired in poverty after generations of exploitation by the United States.[33] An impoverished working class began a decades-long exodus to the United States in search of economic security.[34]

In the United States, women's clubs, labor unions, churches, and secret societies sustained organizing traditions that served as platforms for the recreation of internationalist movement culture. This tradition infused a public manifesto issued by the Niagara Movement, a national civil rights organization founded in 1905 by W. E. B. Du Bois and the journalist William Monroe Trotter. The manifesto explained that racism and class oppression were intertwined in the United States and abroad:

> That black men are inherently inferior to white men is a widespread lie which science flatly contradicts, and the attempt to submerge the colored races is one of the world's old efforts of the wily to exploit the weak. We must therefore make common cause with the oppressed and downtrodden of all race[s] and peoples, with our kindred of South Africa and West Indies, with our fellows in Mexico, India and Russia and with the cause of working classes everywhere.[35]

In 1912, the National Negro Independent League announced at its fifth annual meeting, in Philadelphia, "We desire to ally ourselves with all those who are laboring for equal rights and opportunities for all the oppressed people of this world." The league used its critique of Jim Crow as a foundation to attack US imperialism abroad. Members of the league protested US control of the Philippines as well as the bloody suppression of the Cuban Partido Independiente de Color by the government of José Miguel Gómez in 1912. The league issued a declaration: "We commend the colored Cuban patriots for their manly resistance against a denial of full rights. Color prejudice has grown there by the invasion of people of the United States. We call upon Congress to prevent the sending of United States warships to Cuba to interfere against these Cubans fighting for their rights and liberties."[36]

Du Bois, one of the founders of the National Association for the Advancement of Colored People (NAACP), used that organization's publication, the *Crisis*, to expose imperialism's inner workings. In "The African Roots of War," an essay published in 1915, Du Bois argued that the origins of the war that he could see approaching could be traced to the European competition over the spoils of colonialism in Africa.[37] Black publications frequently showed how racial capitalism and imperialism worked together as a dual engine of expropriation. The *Washington Bee* argued that the invasion of Haiti in 1915 and the occupation of the Dominican Republic the following year were done "at the hands of the National City Bank group of New York City, aided and abetted by our Department of State, which in turn has been aided by our Navy Department." The Navy Department was led by Josephus Daniels, a leader of the 1898 white supremacist insurrection and coup in Wilmington, North Carolina, that led to the Wilmington Massacre. The *Bee* wrote: "It is superfluous to note that the Haitians are colored people and that the Democratic administration responsible for this deviltry is almost synonymous with the Solid South. The Solid South, which raised its vicious rebellion to perpetuate slavery in the United States! The Solid South, which has never repented its desire for race degradation and enforced labor!"[38]

African Americans debated within their churches, labor unions, and political organizations how best to confront racial imperialism. Should African Americans participate in the international conflict that came to be called the Great War (a strategy advocated by Du Bois) or should they refuse to fight? Should they place their hopes in the League of Nations or reject it as a prop for continued European colonialism? African American troops had fought heroically before without gaining anything from it. Did this not prove the futility of "working within the system" for change? After World War I, in 1920, members of St. Paul's AME church in Wichita, Kansas, gathered to hear an NAACP activist, Neval Thomas, speak on the League of Nations: "The League of Nations is a war-breeding pact to enslave the darker race of the world. . . . Wilson signed this pact which means that our black boys will be called at any time from the Jim-crow car, the city ghetto, and the menial service to which America's caste system has condemned them, to go overseas to maintain England's domination over nearly four hundred million of dark-skinned people."[39]

THE RESURGENCE OF EMANCIPATORY INTERNATIONALISM

W. E. B. Du Bois insisted that the struggle to regain the vote must be joined with anti-imperialism. To the audience at the 1928 NAACP convention in Los Angeles, Du Bois explained that the "disfranchisement of the Negro in Southern States has brought about such distortion of political power in the United States, that a small white oligarchy in the South is the dictator of the Nation."[40] To change this, he said, "The American ballot must be re-established on a real basis of intelligence and character." The stakes were high:

> Only in such way can this nation face the tremendous problems before it: the problem of free speech, an unsubsidized press and civil liberty for all people; the problem of imperialism and the emancipation of Haiti, Nicaragua, Cuba, the Philippines and Hawaii from the government of American banks; the overshadowing problem of peace among the nations and of decent and intelligent co-operation in the real advancement of the natives of Africa and Asia, together with freedom for China, India and Egypt.[41]

In linking the fight against "the government of American banks" with the crusade to regain the ballot, Du Bois channeled venerable currents of the Black radical tradition and directed these ideas toward a new generation of organizers who were fighting Jim Crow imperialism. The *Pittsburgh Courier*, a newspaper published by George Schuyler, approvingly quoted Senator John J. Blaine of Wisconsin, who excoriated "dollar diplomacy" and the US invasion of "14 out of 20 republics to the South," including Nicaragua and Haiti. "It is under the banner of bonds and bullets," Blaine argued, "that all the forces of privilege march and demand that our government guarantee their questionable and usurious loans and unconscionable exploitation of weaker people."[42] The Oakland-based Black newspaper *Western Outlook* pointed out that "North American officials were directing the financial policies" of several nations in Central America and the Caribbean and that "in six of them armed forces of the United States were backing up financial agents."[43] Responding to US officials who were surprised at the hostility they faced at the 1928 Pan American Conference in Cuba, the *Western Outlook* reported, "At the present time, parliamentary government is still suspended in Haiti, and the American high commissioner virtually runs the government. Our marines, sent to Nicaragua to preserve the peace pending an election[,] are killing and being killed by Nicaraguan insurgents who do not relish the arrangement. It there any wonder that these conditions breed discontent and hostility toward this country?"

Critiques of slave owners and manifest destiny gave way to condemnations of banks, military intervention, and racism as destructive forces. These critics rejected the idea that the United States had a mission to spread democracy abroad and insisted that people in the Global South had the right to determine their own destinies.[44] The resiliency of this political tendency served as precursor to the rise of organizations in the twentieth century such as the Universal Negro Improvement Association, the African Blood Brotherhood, and the Black leftist organizations of the New Deal era.[45] By stressing the connections between freedom, labor power, and national liberation, the practitioners of emancipatory internationalism unveiled the workings of racial capitalism while deepening democratic resistance to it.[46]

Anti-imperialism found thriving expression in the Black press in the 1920s. In criticizing US foreign policy vis-à-vis Mexico and Nicaragua, the *Pittsburgh Courier* explained that President Calvin Coolidge's aggressive policies in Latin America were pursued in the interests of Wall Street corporations:

> The reason why Coolidge and [Secretary of State] Kellogg
> are rattling the sabre now toward Mexico and Nicaragua
> is because the former wants to keep the natural resources

of the country for the Mexicans instead of the Americans, while [Juan Bautista] Sacasa, the legal President of Nicaragua[,] is being kept out of his office by American Marines as a penalty for his friendliness to the Labor Government of Mexico, which is leading the fight against the financial imperialism of the Yankee ruling class. This is the situation minus the flimsy excuses of "our" government and its apologists.[47]

The *Negro World* exposed the role of the United Fruit Company in promoting economic oppression in Honduras, while the *Philadelphia Tribune*, a Black newspaper, wrote of the situation in Haiti, "The [Woodrow] Wilson administration of affairs in Haiti is founded on two propositions, one being that the Haitians being colored men they have no rights which any white man, and especially any 'Southern gentleman,' is bound to respect, and secondly, that the negroes must be taught to obey every mandate from President Wilson, whether they like it or not."[48] The *Tribune* drew on the work of the Patriotic Union of Haiti to explain to its readers that the military occupation of the island was effected on behalf of New York bankers, who took control of the Haitian national debt, as well as corporations, which seized arable lands, forcing Haitian farmers to migrate to Cuba.[49] The *Tribune* printed an exposé of the US occupation of Haiti: "By a secret and unlawful agreement, the period of American control over Haiti has been increased from 10 to 20 years in order to assure the $40,000,000 Haitian loan floated by American banking institutions."[50] The *Negro World* reported: "In Cuba, the murderous regime of Machado, tool of the National City Bank, has slaughtered trade union leaders and members until their blood has attracted even the attention of [the labor journalist] Chester Wright."[51]

Just as the general strike against slavery prepared the way for the expansive thinking that produced the Cuban solidarity movement of the 1870s, Black resistance to Jim Crow generated creative possibilities of a revived anti-imperialism in the early twentieth century.[52] African American communities launched sustained boycotts of segregated streetcars and other mass transit in the South, took up arms to defend their communities against lynching, and agitated for a return of the ballot.[53] Community organizers built vital new institutions such as the Universal Negro Improvement Association (UNIA) as well as the NAACP, which launched national campaigns against debt peonage and voter suppression. Of course these campaigns took place on a profoundly unequal terrain that placed Black citizens in direct conflict with federal and state authorities, corporations that profited from their labor, and local white civilians and businessmen. Indeed, this insider knowledge of capitalism was what gave Black critics of US economic imperialism their special force. The Black journalist William Jones mounted an attack on US State Department interference with land reforms in Mexico, observing, "Those who have studied the Mexican problem will be inclined to believe that the whole sudden outburst on the part of the State Department was inspired by that group of capitalists in this country who have been for some time displeased with recently passed Mexican agrarian laws."[54] Jones accused the United States of falsely claiming that American citizens' lives were endangered in Mexico with the actual agenda of abrogating revolutionary land reform measures, which he said

> were so framed as to make it possible for actual toilers on the soil to compel foreign owners to dispose of their hold-ings. Americans call this confiscation when practiced in Mexico, but patriotism when exacted as California did against the Japs. But some human beings will always seek a way to keep other human beings toiling for them. You wonder why, with so much untilled land in this country[,] with our farmers begging for capital, and industry lagging, we have so much money to invest in Mexican farms.[55]

Decades of the abysmal economics of Jim Crow demonstrated that white employers would do everything possible to ensure that workers remained mired in poverty. Why should it be otherwise when these employers invested outside the United States? Jones asked why Washington opposed land reforms in Latin America, and answered his question:

> The answer is that in Mexico, it is still possible to grind out toilers for nearly nothing and "capital" always goes where it can squeeze the most out of the toiler. American farming

demands too much when it comes to dividing time, to suit capital, hence our [J. P.] Morgans aided and abetted by our Government sends it [capital] off to Mexico, to France, and other nations. While the American system of exploitation in such lands as Mexico, Haiti, Cuba and the Philippines differ[s] somewhat from that of English control of Africa, India and her other dominions, we may expect the same protest as these people rise in the spirit of nationalism and develop higher standards of living.[56]

THE UNIVERSAL NEGRO IMPROVEMENT ASSOCIATION AND GLOBAL STRUGGLE

The newest expression of emancipatory internationalism was informed by a vision of the past that imagined the Black freedom struggle as uniting people across the globe. With millions of members spread throughout at least forty countries, and chapters in many states and countries, the Universal Negro Improvement Association (UNIA) and African Communities League taught history without borders. UNIA's primary organ, the *Negro World*, a weekly founded by Marcus Garvey and his wife, Amy Jacques Garvey, in 1918, was published in New York. The paper featured reports on the activities of chapters in Central America, Africa, the Caribbean, and the United States, in Spanish, French, and other languages. The *Negro World*'s vibrancy was a reflection of a globally insurgent readership.[57] Theodora Holly, the French-language editor of the *World*, published essays on Haitian life that brought together Indigenous, African, Latin American, and European histories. She paid homage to the Indigenous people of the island of Hispaniola, the Caribs; the accomplishments of the Haitian Revolution; and the critical role that Haitians played in helping the "American colonies to achieve independence."[58] Holly emphasized the resourcefulness of the Haitian people, who toiled for more than a century under the weight of the indemnities levied by France against Haiti for abolishing slavery—penalties supported by other colonial powers as a tool to prevent the "contagion of liberty" in the Caribbean from spreading.[59] In "Heroic Women of Haiti," Holly again honored the Carib

Indians and the women who played a critical role in fighting the Spaniards in the 1490s while reminding her audience that Haitian women had served in combat against the French army in the great war of liberation.[60]

The December 20, 1924, edition of the *Negro World* celebrated Simón Bolívar, and joined Peruvians in observing the hundredth anniversary of the Battle of Ayacucho, one of the final struggles of the Latin American wars of independence. In the nineteenth century, Black newspapers had promoted the stories of South American freedom fighters, yet now, the *Negro World* lamented, US citizens were ignorant of this history.[61] Rejoicing in the fact that Bolívar's and General José de San Martín's armies had contained a mix of "Spaniards, Scots, Irishmen, Negroes and Indians," the *World* pointed out that "Anglo-Saxons, who boast of tenacity and courage as if these qualities were peculiar to Nordics[,] should read of the achievements of such men as Bolívar and San Martin. Then they might understand why their arrogant attitude has roused such resentment in the Latin American Republic[s]."[62]

The UNIA promoted a vision of Pan-Africanism moving in concert with anticolonial movements. With a distribution approaching five hundred thousand, the *Negro World* was more than the mouthpiece of UNIA's leader, the Jamaican-born Marcus Garvey.[63] (After Garvey's arrest for federal mail fraud in 1923, Amy Garvey took over leadership of both the *Negro World* and UNIA.)[64] The UNIA chapter reports pouring in from all over the colonized world allowed readers to join in a community of international struggle. "UNIA Continues to Sweep Cuba," read the headline over a summary of a bilingual meeting in Cuba. "The president of the division . . . gave a wonderful address on the aims and objects of the U.N.I.A. . . . While the band was playing the *Himno Bayames*; [and, subsequently] Master Elpidio Morales and Miss Memima James lifted the Cuban flag and Master Morales recited, 'Cuba Libre y Africa sera libre,' [Free Cuba and Africa will be free], then the tricolor was raised amidst great applause, while the U.N.I.A. anthem was sung."[65] (The national anthem of Cuba was "El Himno de Bayamo.")

The *Negro World* shared stories about Chinese workers' strikes in British-occupied China, anticolonial resistance in India, and the struggle against US imperialism in Puerto Rico, Nicaragua, and the Philippines.[66] The paper republished stories from white newspapers, including the investigation conducted by the labor journalist Chester Wright on the murders of Cuban trade union organizers in 1927 by "the murderous regime of [Gerardo] Machado, tool of the National City Bank."[67] The *Negro World* led with headlines such as "Race and Class Struggle Fierce in South Africa," and it emphasized that "the majority of workers of the world are non-European."[68] The *World* reprinted pieces from the *Johannesburg International Communist Organ*; one such story was headlined "Capitalists Exploit European White and Native Black Worker Alike."[69] In 1925, the *World* published the proceedings of the radical Industrial and Commercial Workers' Union in South Africa, approvingly quoting the keynote lecture of the Black leader Clements Kadalie, who advocated major labor reform.[70] Alongside Kadalie's speech, the *World* published an editorial titled "Our Labor Troubles Are World-Embracing and Perplexing" and lauded the work of the insurgent South African labor union: "They are going about it in a way to get what they want. We shall get a measure of it everywhere if we go about it with the like spirit."[71] In essence, the newspaper's tireless editors reminded their readers that they were engaged in a worldwide struggle against economic exploitation. In one example, the editors linked the migration of Black workers out of the American South, declining domestic cotton production, and Egyptian anticolonial insurgencies against British authorities seeking to export cotton to the United States.[72] A global community of readers united in anticolonialism made a global analysis of capitalism possible.

Domestically, the *Negro World* reported on numerous dimensions of Jim Crow in the United States, including anti-Black violence, employment discrimination, and educational inequalities. It also published cases of Jim Crow policies in Spanish-language columns in an effort to educate its international readership about "*procedimientos inhumanos*" (inhuman procedures), as one article on police torture in Washington, DC, called police actions.[73] Letters to the *Negro World* expressed excitement at the sense of being part of a worldwide movement against racial oppression. "Dear Editor of the Negro World," one letter from a member of a Cuban UNIA chapter began, "We rejoice at the fine support that American Negroes are giving the Universal Improvement Association. It encourages the oppressed members of our race in other countries to learn of what you are doing in America. Many members of our race in Cuba are just as interested and enthusiastic as those in other parts of the world, but we are not always able to do as much financially as we want to do."[74]

Black commentators warned that increasing US investment in the Global South would mean peonage, sexual violence, and political repression.[75] An editorial in the *Afro-American* observed, "In Central America, especially in Panama, since the United States commenced to build the Panama Canal, American prejudice has made its appearance until conditions are almost as bad there as in some parts of the United States although the larger part of the people are of dark skin."[76] Joseph Mirault, a leader of the Patriotic Union of Haiti, informed the readers of the *Negro World* that in the wake of the US invasion of Haiti in 1915, US occupation troops were censoring the mails, incarcerating dissenters, and murdering Haitians.[77] Black newspapers featured interviews with distinguished organizers such as Trinidad's George Padmore, who wrote, "Negroes have nothing to gain in imperialistic wars. Their place is by the side of the workers and the oppressed colonial people."[78]

The author James Weldon Johnson's 1920 exposé of the American occupation of Haiti, published in the NAACP's *Crisis* as well as in the *Nation*, used its audience's familiarity with Jim Crow in the United States to attack American imperialism abroad. Black audiences analyzed Johnson's shocking findings in Haiti by using the interpretive lenses they used to judge the United States. When Johnson gave a talk on US military atrocities in Haiti to a Cleveland-area audience, the Black press framed American war crimes in Haiti as "3,250 lynch murders."[79] Johnson began his published written report by arguing that in order to understand why "some three thousand Haitian men, women, and children have been shot down by American rifles and machine guns, it is necessary, among other things, to know that the National City Bank of New York is very much interested in Haiti. It is necessary to know that the National City Bank controls the National Bank of Haiti and is the depository for all of the Haitian national funds that are being collected by American officials."[80]

IN THE INTERESTS OF AMERICAN BANKERS

African Americans cheered the Nicaraguan resistance against the United States invasion of that country in the 1920s. Black media exposed the ugly reality that the US Marines were in Nicaragua to defend the profits of the United Fruit Company, Brown Brothers, J. & W. Seligman, and other entities with a monetary interest in exploiting the region. According to the *Pittsburgh Courier*, the United States sought to destroy labor and land reform in Latin America:

> Casting the last bit of pretense and hypocrisy aside, the United States Government has grabbed little Nicaragua. For years a detachment of American Marines was kept at the capital of the country as a warning to the politicians to work steadily in the interest of American business as represented by the mahogany and fruit companies. Alarmed by the success of the Labor government in Mexico which had taken over the land and given it to the peons and anxious to protect the investments of Yankees in Latin American countries from possibly a similar fate, the United States Government stepped into the picture recently when Sacasa, the Liberal leader, friendly to Mexico, was about to gain the Presidency of Nicaragua. The marines proceeded to make Nicaragua safe for Wall Street, as they helped to make the world safe for it ten years ago. Thousands of soldiers of the sea were piled into the country to "protect" the handful of Americans there.[81]

The *Courier* predicted a grim outcome for the Nicaraguans in the case of a successful US invasion, included the granting of apparent independence to leaders who actually served at the pleasure of their Yankee bosses. If the United States triumphed in Nicaragua it would mean that its nation's citizens would be subjected to the twentieth-century slavery imposed by the United States and its corporations:

> In reality she [Nicaragua] takes her place alongside of Haiti, which belongs to the National City Bank, and of Cuba, which is a satrapy of the Sugar Trust. Henceforth,

under the lash of "efficiency" and "improved methods" the dark-skinned workers of Nicaragua, formerly pawns in the frequent revolutions financed by alien schemers and headed by rival generals, will sweat to pay off money "lent" to them by their American masters. So, the American Empire follows its star of destiny.[82]

African Americans organized workshops and educational forums to learn about Haitian and Nicaraguan resistance movements. Harlem became a vital site of emancipatory internationalism and home to the Virgin Islands Committee, the Haitian Patriotic Union, the American Anti-Imperialist League, and other organizations led by immigrants from the Caribbean.[83] Harlem's Black churches hosted interracial meetings where organizations of different political tendencies met together to create strategies to combat US and European imperialism. Harlem's Grace Memorial Church was the site of a "monster mass meeting" in 1924 where the Black socialists A. Philip Randolph and Frank R. Crosswaith, as well as the Virgin Islands labor leader Rothschild Francis, joined with the American Civil Liberties Union, the American Federation of Labor, and a representative of the New York City Mayor's Office to protest US economic control of the Virgin Islands. Randolph stated, "The problem of the Virgin Islander, is one phase of the universal struggle on the part of the world's lowly, a place in the sun."[84] He pointed out the need for American Blacks to join with Blacks everywhere and present a solid front against the imperialists of every land. Touching on the point of constructive propaganda, Randolph said it was necessary "to interest the entire press of this nation in the affairs of the down-trodden peoples of the Virgin Islands." The Virgin Islands Committee used these meetings to create a campaign to pressure the federal government to guarantee "a permanent form of civil government" and a "bill of rights" for Virgin Islanders.[85]

The African American press celebrated the exploits of Nicaraguan revolutionary Augusto Sandino, who led the resistance struggle against the US invasion of Nicaragua in the 1920s. The *Pittsburgh Courier* wrote, "It is assumed that the Nicaraguan patriots who are following Sandino are illiterate. Illiterate they may be, but certainly they are as surely patriots as the ragged hosts that cast their fortune with George Washington in 1776. Mention of the Negroes brings to mind the fact that in the State of *Neuva Segovia,* in Northwest Nicaragua, there are close to 10,000 Negroes, and many of them are fighting in the Army of Sandino."[86] The *New York Times* depicted Sandino as a criminal and called him a "small-time Cesar." A rejoinder came from the *Amsterdam News*: "Sandino has been called a bandit, but his words are not those of a bandit; they would have fitted the mouth of George Washington when he was fighting the British. The worst feature of the business is the curtailing of Latin American freedom of speech by American military power. In Nicaragua, the [US] marines seem to be repeating their record in Haiti and the Virgin Islands."[87] The *Norfolk Journal and Guide* editorialized: "The victory of our fighting forces over the Nicaraguan rebels may have been a fine achievement for the military, but it is nothing to reflect credit upon our country's Latin-American policy. In fact, it is rather a discredit, indeed a disgrace."[88]

When citizens of the Dominican Republic rallied against the US occupation of their country, the *Cleveland Gazette* ran the headline "Rah! For The Dominicans! They Demand the Unconditional Withdrawal of U. S. Marines and It Ought to Be Done."[89] The *Pittsburgh Courier* railed against the exploitation of African workers; its Views and Reviews section pointedly noted in 1928,

> What has happened in Liberia is precisely what has happened in Nicaragua, Haiti, Santo Domingo, Bolivia, Venezuela, Colombia, Costa Rica, Porto Rico, Honduras, Guatemala, Panama, Ecuador, and Peru, and what will someday happen in Mexico, i.e., the country is now irretrievably in the claws of the American bankers. The country is having a new day, all right, but the profits will hereafter go almost entirely to the Firestone Company and the National City Bank.[90]

In a review of W. E. B. Du Bois's *The Gift of Black Folk: The Negroes in the Making of America,* Schuyler referred in deprecating terms to the "Mexican land grab" and noted that African Americans, who had served in every other war, "should be proud" that they had not been involved in the Mexican-American War.[91] In 1943, the *Courier* formulated a powerful argument in favor of reparations for slavery and debt peonage by unifying the suffering of African Americans as "among the earliest victims of white aggression" with that of Mexican Americans who had been "murdered and enslaved" and of Native Americans and the victims of French and Belgian imperialism in Africa. Reparations from the imperial powers were only fair: "Since [US president Franklin] Roosevelt and Co. are so enthusiastic about this sort of thing [compensation] for others, I think the United States should wholeheartedly subscribe to this program of recompensing the victims of robbery and aggression."[92]

African Americans drew courage from the resistance of Latin American freedom fighters and they brought anti-imperialism as a way of life into the twentieth century. They built a movement culture around identifying with oppressed people facing US military aggression in Latin America and the Caribbean—a culture with which their counterparts in the Cuban solidarity movement of the 1870s and their earlier ancestors in the radical abolitionist movement would immediately have identified. By defining the core of US imperial culture as "the government of American banks," Black critics identified the newest phase of American imperialism, its origins, and its financial imperatives. The rising power of Wall Street to determine US foreign policy was exposed at its roots. Such an incisive analysis would bear fruit as Black internationalism flowered once again after World War II.[93]

During the 1928 presidential election campaign, the Baltimore *Afro-American* sent Herbert Hoover a public questionnaire asking, "Where does Hoover stand on the withdrawal of Marines from Nicaragua and Haiti[?]"[94] Unsatisfied with Hoover's evasive response, the *Afro-American* editorialized:

> Mr. Hoover may be only a secretary of commerce now, but he is asking the people of this country to elect him to the presidency. For this reason, the people have a right to ask him—Mr. Hoover, where do you stand on the Haiti and Nicaragua question. Will you continue the Coolidge policy of imposing on these small countries because they

cannot fight back, or will you treat them like you'd treat England and France or Japan, the great nations who are able to match you bullet for bullet and man for man?

The editorial concluded by tying the fate of African Americans to that of the individuals fighting imperialism in the Americas: "Mr. Hoover, if elected to the presidency would you continue [to] be the bully with the big stick or would you be the big brother to these weaker nations of Central America? . . . If you cannot be depended upon to give a square deal to the weak white man in Nicaragua, how can we expect you to give justice to the weak black man at home?"[95]

The *Washington Bee* evaluated the US's commitment to democracy thusly: "What really counts—the acid test—is what we shall do to little Haiti, the one country which, by a curious irony, made a really substantial contribution to the cause of Bolivar and South American freedom, while we stood aloof."[96] If this internationalist vision of social justice had been allowed real political expression, the subsequent history of US-sponsored violence in the Americas might have been avoided. Again, however, the pall hanging over the prospects for challenging US imperialism was voter suppression.[97] White business supremacy kept Black people away from the ballot box, where they would have been able to join their votes to their voices. Latin America suffered from US interventions made possible by Jim Crow.

Like José Martí a generation earlier, Bernardo Ruiz Suarez left his native Cuba in the early twentieth century to write about the United States. Suarez observed, "The white race is haughty and domineering everywhere. In those countries where religion, education and other influences have softened the hearts of men, the sentiment of brotherhood tends to level the inequalities and barriers of race and to give reality to that form of society which in Political Science is called Democracy."[98] Suarez warned that the United States lacked the "sentiment of brotherhood" altogether: "But the race which colonized and still forms the majority of the people of the United States, with its historical antecedents and its degrading record of bloodshed, cannot be classified, in the opinion of an impartial observer, as a democratic race."

The refusal of people in Haiti, Nicaragua, Mexico, and other nations to submit quietly to US power inspired African Americans trying to ward off racial capitalism's blows in the United States throughout the twentieth century. Veterans of the war on the government of American banks would have taken exception to a later generation of scholars who characterized the United States as either "isolationist" or democratic. The insurgent citizenry of the Americas who faced the "colossus of the North" would have scoffed at the idea that the United States was not an empire. The opponents of the US military invasions of the early twentieth century demanded that the United States be held accountable for its overseas depredations. Instead, historians shrouded the country's history in a veil of innocence and exceptionalism, which has undermined the nation's ability to reform itself to this day. It cannot be said that scholars lacked sources that could have guided them to the truth. Suarez, whose nation had dealt with US power for decades, spoke for many in the Global South in 1922 when he concluded, "No matter what is said to the contrary, and there is much truth that may be said, the United States of America have by no means lived up to their professed abhorrence of autocracy and aggressive imperialism in their international affairs."[99]

CHAPTER 6

FORGOTTEN WORKERS OF AMERICA
RACIAL CAPITALISM AND THE WAR ON
THE WORKING CLASS, 1890s TO 1940s

Between the Gilded Age of the 1890s, which saw an eruption of
capitalist wealth in the United States, and the Great Depression,
workers in the United States endured the bloodiest labor conflicts in the history of the industrializing world. Centuries of violent labor relations in slavery became generalized throughout the
nation.[1] Strikers were massacred by officers of the state. Fortified
armories were built in city centers, and troops were called out to
crush walkouts. Republican as well as Democratic presidents issued
sweeping injunctions to undermine national labor organizing efforts.
Employers hired private militias and engaged armed detectives to
break union campaigns. In self-defense, working-class communities engaged in mass strikes, boycotted firms, torched buildings,
destroyed hundreds of miles of railroad tracks, and, in fits of self-
destructive rage, turned on each other. Class conflict was a pervasive fact of American life. The railway strike of 1877 (known as the
Great Upheaval), the massacre of Chinese workers in Rock Springs,
Wyoming (1885), the Haymarket Square Riot (1886), the Thibodaux
Massacre (1887), the Apalachicola general strike (1890), the Homestead lockout (1892), the Pullman strike and boycott (1894), the
Colorado labor wars of 1903–4, the Triangle Shirtwaist Factory fire
(1911), the Ludlow Massacre (1914), the Everett Massacre (1916),
and the Elaine Massacre (1919)—these were just a few of the better-
known conflagrations.[2] By the start of World War I, in 1914, the
idea of the United States as a "classless society" was finished.

The power that employers wielded in the state legislatures and in the courts meant that struggles for shorter work hours and better wages often had to be decided by workers' direct action.[3] The legal historian Karen Orren observes that workplace relations in the United States were governed more by the ancient feudal law of master and servant than by the Bill of Rights.[4] Police and vigilante homicides of independent-minded workers were excused as a necessary aspect of establishing capital's authority in industrializing America. The victims of the police attack that culminated in the massacre of striking steelworkers in Chicago in 1937 were denigrated by the corporate media as "Bolsheviks and Mexicans."[5] Interracial union organizing that challenged the availability of the nation's cheap labor was especially dangerous. In Bogalusa, Louisiana, white union organizers were assassinated, and Black union members were terrorized by the Loyalty League, an organization created by timber companies to destroy unionizing in the state.[6] In 1917, Mexican members of the Industrial Workers of the World (IWW) were violently deported by state and vigilante forces from Bisbee, Arizona, during a strike of copper miners.[7] Lucy Gonzalez Parsons, an anarchist of African, Mexican, and Indigenous descent, admonished workers in Chicago to fight back with every means at their disposal: "The voice of dynamite is the voice of force, the only voice which tyranny has ever been able to understand."[8]

In a nation of many ethnicities the only common language appeared to be subjugation of the working classes. One Mississippi plantation owner stated, "I will be glad when free schools are abolished. Our tenants don't need them and we can get along without them."[9] Science was enlisted by capital to prove the foolishness of upsetting social hierarchies by compassionate social policies and education, and Social Darwinism was used "as an evolutionary rationale for the inevitability of poverty."[10] The Progressive Era was a time when corporations and employers consolidated their power vis-à-vis the rest of society. Working-class resistance to corporate rule was not tolerated. The pro-business *Florida Times-Union* wrote, "When the soldier represses disorder he serves labor first, though he shoot strikers and bayonet brethren of his own craft—all must be taught to obey the law or the weak will go to the wall, and labor is the weakest of all the factors that now uphold society."[11] The *Times-Union* warned African American workers that Black lives only mattered insofar as they made themselves useful to capitalism: "In the South, the negro in politics is not tolerated—in other sections he must obediently follow. There are lynchings so nearly everywhere that the rule is established, but the South does not forbid the black man to earn a living as do our neighbors. If the negro be wise he will respect the limits set for him as does the elephant and the tiger and the other who accept rules and make no pretense to reason."[12]

According to the American Social History Project, "By 1910, the United States was the world's greatest industrial power."[13] Inequality underwrote dramatic economic growth; racism reinforced class oppression; and voter suppression was an integral part of capital's national toolkit of labor repression. "The new disfranchisement is in the main a master stroke of concentrated capital against labour," W. E. B. Du Bois noted, "and an attempt under the cover of racial prejudice to take a backward step in the organization of labour such as no modern nation would dare to take in the broad daylight of present economic thought."[14] After the nation's leaders oversaw the suppression of Black voting, first-generation immigrant workers were next in line to lose meaningful access to the ballot.[15] The erosion of voting rights and the consolidation of corporate power meant that many Eastern European immigrants had a harrowing experience in the workplace. Russian workers in Pennsylvania referred to the region's steel towns as Little Siberias while Italian laborers who worked for Jones & Laughlin Steel in Aliquippa, Pennsylvania, in the 1930s compared the governance of their town with their experiences in Fascist Italy.[16] The historian Gabriela F. Arredondo notes that many Mexican American factory operatives in Chicago declined to become US citizens even when they were eligible to do so. As one Mexican worker noted, "Even if we do become citizens here, we always remain Mexicans."[17]

The reconfiguration of racial capitalism in the early twentieth century hinged upon the exploitation of agricultural workers who were fired, deported, or driven into cities when they tried to organize in defense of their interests. Local governments, growers, and vigilantes in the Sunbelt counties stretching from Orange County, Florida, to Orange County, California, put the hammer down on agricultural laborers seeking to achieve independence.[18] Employers and their enforcers ruthlessly suppressed Mexican, Chinese, Sikh, Japanese, Indian, Italian, white, and African American farmworkers seeking to organize.[19] In 1908, a group of armed white citizens marched into a camp of farmworkers of Indian extraction in Live Oak, California, and "burned it to the ground, beat and terrorized a hundred or more Hindus in the camp, drove them out of the community, and, in doing so, robbed them of about $2,500."[20] For decades, politicians in California used anti-Chinese racism as bluntly as the Democratic Party used anti-Black hatred in the South to consolidate power.[21] Leading growers in Jim Crow Florida urged their industry to look to California for a solution to the "labor problem" in agriculture.[22]

The birth of modern agribusiness in the United States is a chronicle of dispossession. The Texas Rangers and other law enforcement agents played a key role in the bloody process of expropriating lands belonging to Mexican and Native American people. The historian Robert Perkinson writes, "From the beginning, the territory's pioneering lawmen did less to suppress crime in any conventional sense than to force open lands for Anglo American settlement."[23] Mexican victims of the Texas Rangers' furious attacks were quite often landowners with extensive holdings: "Title challenges and outright theft led to a loss of more than 187,000 acres of land for Tejanos in the lower Rio Grande Valley from 1900 to 1910." The historian Zaragosa Vargas notes, "The eventual violent collapse of Tejano ranching society took place in the early twentieth century, when the Texas Rangers, intermediaries in the transition to capitalism, cleaned out the remaining Tejano landowners, summarily executing more than three hundred 'suspected Mexicans.'"[24] Over time, the pace of land theft quickened. Native Americans suffered most grievously, losing approximately ninety million acres of land in the decades after the implementation of the Dawes Act in 1887.[25]

Agribusiness in the Sunbelt was marked by an authoritarian pattern of social control whereby racism, patriarchy, and rule by force overwhelmed democratic institutions. Writing in 1928, the Trinidadian American sociologist Oliver Cromwell Cox noted, "The Southern leadership, because of its success in disenfranchising its colored labor force, has remained a turbulent, primitive group of capitalists. It has been relatively untouched by the democratic restraints operative in other sections of the country. It can be depended upon, therefore, to throw its vast weight against organized labor and to obstruct movements to implement the democratic gains of the people as a whole."[26] When one extends Cox's thesis to the entire Sunbelt, it is apparent that the disenfranchisement of farm labor lent an antidemocratic thrust to rural American politics with regressive implications for democracy that can be felt up to the present day.

In 1915, inspired by the land reforms of the Mexican Revolution, insurgent Tejanos and Mexicans promulgated the Plan de San Diego, which called for the reclaiming of land in southern Texas for Mexican people and Native Americans as well as an independent state for African Americans.[27] The insurgents launched bloody attacks on white ranchers under banners reading "Equality and Independence," but they were defeated, and a new reign of Ranger-led violence was initiated. It resulted in the murder of hundreds of Tejanos and "the forced displacement of thousands of Mexicans who fled for their lives across the border."[28]

The US Border Patrol was created in 1924, ostensibly to provide border security. However, as the historian Kelly Lytle Hernández observes, officers of the agency quickly understood immigration enforcement as labor control. Hernández quotes one Texas farmer as saying, "We tell the immigration officers if our Mexicans try to get away to the interior, and they stop them and send them back to Mexico. Then in a few days they are back here and we have good workers for another year."[29] Mexican laborers who regularly crossed the border between Mexico and the United States to work in Texas—for example, from Ciudad Juarez to El Paso—were sprayed with DDT, Zyklon B, and other carcinogenic chemicals by US health inspectors who used these Mexicans as unwilling subjects in experiments with different delousing treatments.[30] Jose Burciaga, who worked as a janitor in El Paso, recalled, "At the customs bath by the bridge . . . they would spray some stuff on you. It was white and would run down your body. How horrible! And then I remember something else about it: they would shave everyone's head . . . men, women, everybody. . . . The substance was very strong."[31] On January 28, 1917, Carmelita Torres, a domestic worker, organized Latinas who refused to be deloused: they shut down traffic in El Paso and protested the racial stereotype of Mexicans as disease carriers.

Employers and politicians invoked racialized stereotypes of Mexican workers to justify poverty wages and the denial of citizenship. Dr. George P. Clements, manager of the Agriculture Department of the Los Angeles Chamber of Commerce during the 1920s, denigrated the Mexican American worker: "He is ignorant of values; he knows nothing of time; he knows nothing of our laws; he is as primitive as we were 2,500 years ago. He does not know our language, the result being that he becomes a petty criminal through ignorant violations. . . . He rarely if ever takes out his citizenship, mixes in politics, or labor squabbles unless directed by some American group. He is the most tractable individual ever came to serve us."[32] Ralph H. Taylor, the executive secretary of the California Agricultural Legislative Committee, claimed, "The Mexican has no political ambitions; he does not aspire to dominate the political affairs of the community in which he lives."[33] Growers and state officials repeatedly emphasized that Mexican workers were preferable to any other form of labor because if they demanded rights or citizenship they could easily be deported.[34]

The respect for individual improvement that supposedly characterized American culture was not tolerated when it was expressed by African Americans and Latinx people. In 1895, when Thomas A. Harris ignored Ku Klux Klan warnings against practicing law in Tuskegee, Alabama, he was shot and fled to sanctuary in Mexico.[35] Du Bois noted that when Black farmers made gains in land ownership, white merchants responded with complaints "of labor scarcity, and they began systematically to scheme for some method by which Negro ambition could be kept from soaring too high, and by which the black man could be kept from benefiting from the new economic development in the South."[36] Black farmers had difficulty accessing federal farm loan programs "because they are excluded from white agricultural associations that qualify for these kind of loans."[37] In March 1925, the *Negro World* noted, with heavy irony, "Negroes could greatly improve the fine relation between the white people and themselves by their giving up business, quitting the professions, discarding land ownership and home building, deserting the school and renouncing the ballot, and by all making a mad rush for the first saw-mill that bids for labor. Suppose we agree on this step for the sake of our best friends."[38]

Forced labor was an integral part of the South's modernization program, with Northern-owned firms profiting from unfree labor in the region's mines, blast furnaces, textile industry, and road-building.[39] In parts of Texas and Louisiana, employers and sheriff's departments cooperated to operate large-scale virtual slave markets of Negro and Mexican cotton pickers, using vagrancy statutes to kidnap workers "to work under armed guard, and without being tried."[40] In other cases, labor agents "await Negroes and Mexicans on the highways and offer them a bonus and free transportation to go with them to some fictitious place to pick cotton. The cotton pickers having accepted the terms are taken to some distant point outside of a town and there go into camp. The would-be employer leaves them under guard and finds farmers who need cotton pickers."[41]

The Department of Justice, the Mexican government, and the NAACP launched investigations into the abuses of workers, but none of these inquiries curbed employers' appetites for cheap labor supplied by the state. The Black press published an exposé of the plight of Puerto Rican workers who were lured to Arizona by the promise of high wages in 1926. Instead, the Puerto Ricans discovered to their horror that they were being used by the Cotton Growers Association of Arizona to "batter down the prevailing starvation labor wage now being paid the American Negro and Mexican cotton field laborers."[42] When nearly six hundred Puerto Ricans struck over their living and working conditions, they were arrested and herded into an open-air concentration camp near Phoenix. After strikes, protests, and investigations into their mistreatment, most Puerto Rican workers left Arizona.[43]

Law enforcement officials profited from vagrancy statutes, and counties filled their coffers from the proceeds of forced labor. African American union members and homeowners in Florida were abducted by Broward County sheriff's deputies and charged with vagrancy to discipline them. Morris Milgram, a social reformer writing in the 1940s, described how, in central Florida, "a series of arrests on charges of vagrancy, aimed at forcing workers to pick oranges against their will, occurred in picturesque Lake County early in 1945."[44] Lake County's Sheriff Willis McCall acquired a reputation of beating workers who tried to bargain for better wages from their employers. In response to a Black worker who protested this state of affairs, the Leesburg chief of police, Frank Morgan, stated, "Well, I guess they had a right to arrest him and knock him on the head if he wouldn't work." Brutality against Black workers was the cornerstone of the Jim Crow social order.[45]

Stocks and futures of the commodities produced by workers trapped in the convict lease system—including coal, cotton, phosphate, and naval stores (articles used in shipping)—were publicly traded for lucrative profits on New York, Chicago, and other exchanges. A Jacksonville reporter, writing in the *Florida Metropolis*, candidly noted that vagrancy laws and convict labor were needed to keep the turpentine, timber, and phosphate industries profitable in Florida.[46] "Three young, hearty and strong negroes go to State prison for life," the *Florida Metropolis* exulted in 1906, "and they will make excellent naval stores laborers, in fact, we understand that one of the three is an expert in that line of business."[47] In the same year, a Tampa councilman admitted that African Americans were the sole targets of that city's vagrancy laws.[48] The beneficiaries of the South's draconian vagrancy laws were just as likely to be found on Wall Street as in a local sheriff's headquarters.

The triumph of white business supremacy relegated African American and Latinx workers to the bottom of the occupational ladder, and this meant they had to work for less than their white counterparts. The author Mario Barrera found that, in the first half of the twentieth century, Chicana/o workers in the Southwest were systematically paid lower wages than whites in agriculture, mining, railroad, transportation, construction, and other industries.[49] Likewise, African Americans were shunted into the most menial jobs and were paid less for their work. In 1930, there was not a single African American railroad conductor or banker in Memphis, Tennessee. Black women were often paid half of what their white male counterparts were paid in Virginia's major industries on the eve of the Great Depression.[50] One of racial capitalism's grimmest achievements was voter suppression and the weaponized labor relations that transformed the Sunbelt into a haven for cheap labor.

Capital employed a dual-wages system (different pay according to race and gender) in the United States and South Africa to divide and conquer the working class. Unfortunately, most white-dominated labor unions played right along. Wage differentials gave even poorly

paid white workers what historian George Lipsitz calls a "possessive investment in whiteness," and they served as one of the most
visible wedges between white workers and workers of color.[51] When
Mexican workers went on strike at the Pacific Electric Railway company in Los Angeles in 1903, they fought for an equalization of
wages and solidarity with Anglos.[52] In an effort to preserve the race-
based wage disparity, white coworkers responded by siding with
employers—repudiating a broader class alliance. Barrera notes that
craft unions often barred Latinx workers from membership, hence
from well-paying occupations.[53] These color bars to many trades
froze Mexican, Puerto Rican, and African American workers out of
skilled employment.[54] Such job discrimination deepened rifts within
the working class and made union organizing far more difficult.[55]

Divisions within the working class impoverished African Americans and Latinx workers and created the spectacle whereby society's
laborers—even whites—found themselves begging employers and
distant politicians to address economic issues that the nation's leaders had no incentive to deal with. The same leaders perpetuated policies in trade, immigration, and housing that kept workers at each
other's throats while spouting pieties about being the "workingman's friend." Howard Kester, a cofounder of the Southern Tenant
Farmers' Union, trenchantly observed:

> Inter-racialists of the Atlanta School take particular pains
> to point out the ancient hatred which has existed between
> the poor white man and the Negro. At the same time, they
> take great delight in attempting to show that the rich man
> with his vast benevolence and paternalism is the Negro's
> best friend, conveniently forgetting that if the poor white
> man is the Negro's worst enemy it is the members of the
> so-called "best families" who force these equally exploited
> groups to struggle against each other.[56]

While Progressive Era reformers lamented sanitation conditions
in the nation's burgeoning working-class slums, the *Afro-American*
responded incredulously: "Here in Baltimore there are men who are
getting and using $200 per day for the proper support and care of
their families and there are other men who must struggle along on
$2 and even less. Take any family of five human beings, even from

the most highly developed section of the city, and place it on a $2 daily allowance with the present cost of commodities and they will finally be shoved into a congested block."[57]

Ultimately, driving down the living conditions of African Americans negatively impacted whites as well, as the *Afro-American* journal noted: "Down in the hill country of Tennessee, we have seen proud Anglo-Saxon stock of blue blood degenerate into feudists, into ignorant weaklings under the strain of barren and unproductive soil even when they had all the fresh air and health of the highlands. Proper food, shelter and cultural contact can only be bought with money and since the money source of the majority of colored city dwellers come in wages, it is thru wages and honesty in distribution of jobs that salvation must come."

Intergenerational economic inequality had a devastating cumulative effect on Black and Latinx families because it meant that they would not be able to pass down meaningful amounts of wealth to their children. The economic historian Carol Shammas writes, "The bulk of household wealth in America, perhaps as much as 80 percent of it, is derived from inheritance, not labor force participation."[58] Both Jim Crow and Juan Crow ensured that working-class Latinx and African American families had far less of a financial legacy to leave to future generations.

RACE RIOTS AND REPATRIATION

In the final months of World War I and in the aftermath of the Armistice in 1918, oppressed people throughout the colonized world, as well as in Europe, struck for their freedom. Ten million war deaths and the carnage of four years of trench warfare initiated by the "civilized" powers exposed a global economic and political system in decay. The institutions that propped up that system—imperialism, white rule, and Western capitalism—were called into question as never before. While tens of thousands of African Americans were escaping the repressive South and forming insurgent chapters of the Universal Negro Improvement Association, their counterparts in Latin America and the Caribbean were challenging colonial rule with mass strikes and demands for self-government.[59] Workers in

Eastern Europe and Germany took inspiration from the rise of the Russian Revolution and fomented their own revolution in the streets. W. E. B. Du Bois, A. Philip Randolph, and other African American leaders believed that the social forces unleashed by the Great War would help Blacks challenge the system of white supremacy in the United States. Industrial labor union organizing committees undertook major unionizing campaigns in Chicago, Birmingham, and other urban areas.[60] The most powerful unions had traditionally operated with color bars that excluded African Americans, Chinese, and others. Black workers, however, responded with guarded optimism to organizers' efforts to build interracial locals.

It was not long, though, before the forces of reaction regained the upper hand. In the United States, a right-wing political backlash termed the "Red Scare" was designed to undermine immigrant working-class and Black militancy. This reactionary movement was led by future FBI director J. Edgar Hoover, Attorney General A. Mitchell Palmer, and others who used their authority to order the arrest, the detention, and, ultimately, the expulsion of thousands of "alien" political activists. As "law and order" types such as Hoover gained ascendancy, spaces for social and economic justice organizing diminished rapidly. State and federal authorities used powers gained through the Espionage and Sedition Acts of 1917–1918 to disrupt legitimate protest groups while ignoring real crimes that exacerbated racial tensions. For example, in the two years leading up to the Chicago race riot of 1919, scores of African American homes were bombed, and yet state authorities conducted no meaningful investigations nor were any of the perpetrators ever found. When similar bombing attacks rocked black homes in Miami, Florida, undercover federal agents appeared more interested in spying on African Americans than in catching the guilty parties.[61]

The anti-Black race riots of 1917–23 and the forced "repatriation" to Mexico of Mexican Americans during the Great Depression demonstrate one political function of racism in a society that seeks out scapegoats to hide the fact that it cannot serve the needs of its citizenry. Federal malfeasance was a major factor in the racial explosions that rocked the nation. The government largely turned a blind eye to the rebirth of the Ku Klux Klan in the South and to the escalation of violence against African Americans who had moved to the North during and after World War I to fill the needs of wartime production and burgeoning industries in Northern cities.

Instead of investigating the illegal suppression of Black voting in the South, in 1917, US attorney general Thomas Gregory launched an investigation into alleged illegal Black voting in the Midwest at the same time that he ordered the Justice Department to suppress the IWW.[62] Members of President Woodrow Wilson's administration even claimed that African American migration to the North had been motivated by "sinister forces" bent on undermining the nation's political system. Black aspirations for economic betterment were defined as incendiary.[63] As Department of Justice investigators interrogated African Americans in Chicago and East St. Louis about their allegedly menacing reasons for coming north, the mass media encouraged the broader public to view Black people as subversives. Newspaper readers saw hysterical headlines such as "Negroes Flock in from South to Evade Draft" (*St. Louis Times*), "North Does Not Welcome Influx of South's Negroes" (*Chicago Herald*), "Negro Migration: Is It a Menace?" (*Philadelphia Record*), and "Negro Influx On, Plan to Dam It" (*Newark News*).[64]

A newly rising tide of racism was a response to the fact that Black people were waging increasingly effective struggles against white supremacy. The writer James Weldon Johnson, who also headed the NAACP, sensed a revived spirit of hope among African Americans during the Great Migration:

> I was impressed with the fact that everywhere there was a rise in the level of the Negro's morale. The exodus of Negroes to the North . . . was in full motion; the tremors of the war in Europe were shaking America with increasing intensity; circumstances were combining to put a higher premium on Negro muscle, Negro hands, and Negro brains than ever before; all these forces had a quickening effect that was running through the entire mass of the race.[65]

The NAACP had scored a major victory in 1915 with the Supreme Court's *Guinn v. United States* decision, which outlawed the Grandfather Clause, legislation that allowed white voters to circumvent the barriers put on Black voters. The *Guinn* decision encouraged African Americans to undertake new initiatives to register to vote. By the time Black World War I veterans returned from France demanding their civil rights, the Universal Negro Improvement Association was already a mass movement and the NAACP was organizing hundreds of new branches in the South and Midwest. Black Floridians organized a statewide movement to destroy Jim Crow, and Black voters began to participate in municipal elections in the North. Perceiving this trend, the *Miami Herald* published a warning to its white readers on the eve of the 1920 presidential election:

WHITE VOTERS, REMEMBER!

WHITE SUPREMACY IS BEING ASSAULTED IN OUR MIDST,
AND THE MOST SACRED INSTITUTIONS OF THE SOUTH
ARE BEING UNDERMINED BY THE ENEMY FROM WITHIN[66]

The organized race riots of the era and the practice of so-called repatriation of Mexicans—actually forced deportation—demonstrate the linkages between racism, labor oppression, and inequality. Anti-Black race riots were organized by whites in Chicago, Philadelphia, Charleston, and Washington, DC, among other places. In 1919, in the course of these riots, eleven African American men were burned at the stake. In that same year, other lynch mobs murdered sixty-nine Black people, including ten who were World War I veterans. White perpetrators enjoyed an almost universal immunity from prosecution, whereas their Black victims were often incarcerated for defending their homes and neighborhoods. Whites who rioted were motivated by political, economic, and social factors. The East St. Louis race riot in 1917 was aimed in part at keeping African Americans from moving up the occupational ladder. In Western Orange County, Florida, the 1920 Election Day massacre of African Americans who attempted to vote enforced voter suppression. Whites who organized the Tulsa race riot of 1921 destroyed a thriving Black business district, and, as the historian John Hope Franklin notes, expropriated Black property.[67] Mabel Little spent years building a successful hairdressing practice in Tulsa and lost it all in a day: "At the time of the riot, we had ten different business places for rent. Today, I pay rent."[68]

Expropriation of black property and wealth was the order of the day. The riots often became racial pogroms and allowed white developers to take control of Black property for drastically reduced prices or for nothing at all.[69] When African American sharecroppers in the Arkansas Delta in 1919 began organizing a union to demand higher wages, employers responded by launching a violent attack on the organization. Scores of workers were murdered in the Elaine, Arkansas, massacre of 1919, which drove cotton wages back down. When African Americans in Longview, Texas, began experimenting with cooperative purchasing and marketing of farm produce—thus bypassing creditors and merchants—whites in the area launched a murderous assault on the Black community.[70]

African American landowners in Florida were subjected to a campaign of violence that coincided with the state's land boom of the 1920s. "Our daily newspapers tell us now of outrages in Florida," the *Pittsburgh Courier* noted. "We have just read an account of a Florida mob visiting a Negro farmer and setting fire to his place to run him away from some rich Florida soil. Another farm was visited, and the owner of rich lands warned to get out of these parts at once. Of course, the sheriff of the county got busy—after the house was burned to ashes."[71] An armed column of white citizens burned office buildings and Black-owned residences in northwestern Tampa, driving off policemen who tried to stop them.[72]

The police investigations in these cases usually amounted to nothing. Too much profit was at stake, as the *Chicago Defender* noted: "According to information from reliable sources, a plan is on foot to obtain by threat all valuable property owned by our people for promotional purposes among the whites since the Florida realty boom began months ago. Northern capital has thus far squeezed out southern interest in the most choice subdivisions in white sections, reaping a harvest of gold, and what remains now for speculation is largely held by members of the Race."[73]

THE GREAT DEPRESSION

Government leaders in President Herbert Hoover's cabinet whipped up anti-Mexican sentiments to direct popular anger away from the failure of the federal government to deal with economic suffering and high unemployment.[74] In 1929, the US Congress passed the Immigration Act, which enabled the US to target Mexicans for deportation. The avowed mission of the American Federation of Labor was to organize the unorganized, yet it failed abjectly to fulfill this mission when it reproached Mexican workers for taking jobs away from "real Americans."[75] Facing high unemployment, some Mexican workers voluntarily left the United States, but most who left, citizens and noncitizens alike, were forcibly deported by local officials as well as by agents from the US Labor Department, the US Immigration Bureau, and the Border Patrol.[76] Habeas corpus was effectively suspended, and many workers were searched and seized without arrest warrants or any semblance of due process during the so-called repatriation. Indeed, as Zaragosa Vargas notes, "As an added insult, many American-born Mexican adults and children lacking proper identification but having dark skin and Spanish surnames were apprehended and removed to Mexico."[77] Ironically, employers periodically intervened to stop repatriation to assure their continued access to low-wage and terrorized labor. Still, by 1935, more than 350,000 Mexican and Mexican American workers had been deported to Mexico.

As Oliver Cromwell Cox observed, "Race prejudice is a social attitude propagated among the public by an exploiting class for the purpose of stigmatizing some group as inferior so that the exploitation of either the group itself or its resources or both may be justified"[78] Race riots and repatriation were two tools to exploit Black and Latinx workers for their labor, steal their property, and expel them when convenient.

The great labor historian Carey McWilliams published his classic text on California farm labor, *Factories in the Field*, in 1935—the same year that John Steinbeck's *The Grapes of Wrath* appeared. McWilliams found that growers routinely engineered terror campaigns to prevent "unionization of farm labor on any basis," as both Mexican and white workers organized a record number of agricultural strikes in 1934. McWilliams uncovered the existence of a concentration camp near Salinas that was built to imprison farmworker union activists—although one grower claimed that the camp was constructed "to hold strikers, but of course we won't put white men in it, just Filipinos."[79] McWilliams characterized the authority that agribusiness exerted in California as "farm fascism."[80]

The Associated Farmers of California, organized in 1934, set maximum wage levels and continued the state's tradition of bloody labor relations by organizing private armies of men to destroy farmworker organizing efforts.[81] Along with their counterparts in the Deep South, California growers routinely garnered tens of millions of dollars in federal subsidies while their tenants, sharecroppers, and day laborers were kept in destitution.[82] The Associated Farmers were backed by urban-based corporations that exerted enormous power in the California state legislature. McWilliams demonstrated that banks, railroads, food storage firms, paper companies, utilities, and all kinds of other firms garnered terrific wealth from California agriculture. The entities that financed the AFC's antilabor activities included the Bank of America, the San Joaquin Cotton Oil Company, Hunt Bros. Packing Company, and other powerful firms. "The gentlemen who sit in their offices in San Francisco and Oakland and write checks to the Associated Farmers are not the men who, wearing the armbands of the group, organize mobs to browbeat and coerce agricultural workers," McWilliams explained. "They have cleverly stimulated the farmers and townspeople to act as their storm troopers."[83] In addition, wrote McWilliams, the corporate backers of the AFC displaced the growers' anger at the farm revenue lost to shipping firms, banks, and railroads onto the backs of farmworkers: "The 'allied industrial interests' are naturally friendly to any movement or organization that will direct farm unrest, not against them, but against labor. They are willing, therefore, to finance vigilantism; to goad the farmer into fury about labor."[84]

From the perspective of African Americans and Latinx people, the Great Depression meant that the majority of the American population now felt something akin to the harshness of living conditions that they had been subjected to all along. William Jones used his helm at the *Afro-American* to demand public relief in Baltimore: "There was a time when a community could wash its hands of the evils of badly managed industry which brought hard times, but the new idea in governmental efficiency now supposes that those who manage industry and also municipalities should see to it that when hard times come, the resources of the community, private and public, should be pooled to provide work and industrial opportunities for every good citizen."[85] Jones ridiculed President Herbert Hoover's plan to give millions of dollars directly to bankers to solve the nation's economic problems: "Somebody ought to tell Herbert Hoover that millions of harassed, worried, and in some cases, despondent voters, have looked far enough into this depression to know that it has been the selfish, shortsighted and greedy leadership of the bankers and captains of industry in America and throughout the world who got us into this muddle and who are unwilling to admit that it is time to make a radical change in our system of economy."[86] This was powerful rhetoric. But it would fall to working-class people to challenge the inertia that seized government at all levels.

THE FORGOTTEN NEW DEAL

One Saturday morning in August 1933, hundreds of African American women workers at the Charleston (South Carolina) Bagging and Manufacturing Company organized an occupation strike that completely shut down their textile bagging factory, idling eight hundred workers. The strike began on August 26, at 7 a.m. in the weaving room, where 130 women worked. "After the work had ceased there," the *Charleston News and Courier* reported, "the agitators went into the spinning room, where a like number of workers had begun their day's work." The newspaper alleged that the women workers "threatened violence to those who would not cease work and at this time Samuel E. Stauffer, general manager, ordered the power turned off and the machinery stopped and called the police."[87] When the Charleston police arrived, however, they quickly found themselves on the defensive as the women defended their occupation strike with bobbins and knives. The women formed picket lines and sang improvised spirituals such as "I Ain't Gonna Work No More" and other, more traditional gospel songs. The Charleston police called for reinforcements. The regional newspapers published stories aimed at robbing the insurgency of any political meaning and invoked insulting Hollywood racist stereotypes to denigrate the strikers. For example, the *News and Courier* claimed that the strike "resembled a jungle scene shown in the motion pictures."[88] Newspapers ran headlines such as "Spirit of Jungle Animates Negroes in Strange Strike at Charleston Bagging Mill."[89]

Antilabor media coverage obscured the fact that these women timed their strike to the very moment that representatives of Franklin Delano Roosevelt's administration and owners of bagging companies across the country were meeting to create new wage and hours guidelines in the bagging industry.[90] These guidelines, or codes, fell under the jurisdiction of the New Deal's National Recovery Administration. The NRA was designed to lift the country out of the Great Depression via industrial recovery; among other things, it provided for minimum wages and maximum hours.[91] African American women in Charleston were excluded from giving testimony at the high-level NRA hearings on the wages and working conditions in their industry, which were being held in Washington, DC. Nevertheless, the women fought to make their voices heard through courageous direct action, demanding a minimum wage of twelve dollars a week, exactly the same "blanket wage" recently negotiated in the textile and tobacco industries under the NRA.[92] Black women's fight in Charleston for a uniform minimum wage affirms their roles as pioneers of the resurgence of radical labor activism that birthed industrial unionism as well as paving the way for the formation of the Congress of Industrial Organizations (CIO) in 1935. The African American women at Charleston Bagging and Manufacturing were not merely waging a wildcat strike; they were struggling to expand the scope and scale of the New Deal to their workplaces and communities.[93]

They were part of what would become a mass movement of African American women across the country calling for federal intervention in the economy. Three days after the bagging strike broke out, domestic workers in nearby Edisto Island began insisting their employers pay the NRA's minimum industrial wage of thirty cents an hour, despite the fact that domestic workers were excluded from the codes. One African American woman reportedly told a prospective employer: "You ain't gonna git a cook less you pay her thirty cents by the hour, no mam! Uncle Sam done set the wage at that and you can't ride over what he say."[94] African American women in Kingstree, South Carolina, told their bosses that the NRA required them to increase wages, and in rural Williamsburg County, the *News and Courier* reported, "There are some who have been working for years in the same place who either demand more pay or shorter hours. And from farms come reports that negroes who have been content to work for a dollar a day cording wood and other jobs now openly state they will have their 'thirty cent a hour like de guv'mint pay.'"[95]

African American and Latinx women in St. Louis, Philadelphia, and Tampa would join their sisters in Charleston in major strikes that challenged the government's wages and hours codes. In March 1934, Black female laundry and cafeteria workers in Birmingham led wildcat strikes for better wages and working conditions under NRA code agreements.[96] In the wake of the Birmingham upheavals, Black women domestic workers in New Hope, Alabama, launched the first recorded strike in the city's history. Like their counterparts in Edisto, the New Hope women demanded a minimum wage scale that would cover all domestic workers.[97] Black and white women farmworkers at Seabrook Farms in New Jersey stood up to tear gas and police beatings to demand NRA wages in their industry.[98]

Black women organizers expanded the normal scope of labor politics by demanding that their unions confront racism and anti-Black violence. Moranda Smith, a union leader at the R. J. Reynolds plant in Winston-Salem, North Carolina, and a member of the Communist Party, told the national convention of the Food, Tobacco, Agricultural and Allied Workers, "We want to stop lynching in the South. We want people to walk the picket lines free and unafraid and know that they are working for their freedom and their liberty."[99]

The meaning of the New Deal was at stake. At the time of the Charleston Bagging and Manufacturing Company strike, white South Carolinians were hotly debating the causes of the Great Depression. State senator J. C. Long told a large Charleston gathering, "The depression was caused, in the final analysis, by the lack of people spending money"; he argued for the need to raise taxes in order to create public works projects.[100] Full-page newspaper advertisements criticized the low wages and prices that seemed to be dragging the country deeper into depression. Charleston businesses promised to raise wages. On the day of the strike by bagging workers, the *News and Courier* ran an ad featuring a white woman lamenting, "I am a stenographer. I have been making only $10.00 a week and had to care for my mother and younger brother."[101] The message of the ad, endorsed by twenty-one major Charleston businesses, seemed to be that low wages were a scourge on society.

Black women workers at Charleston Bagging and Manufacturing

were working fifty-four-hour weeks and making an average of eight dollars a week. They knew that they were being excluded from the debate when the *News and Courier* supported the aspirations of fictitious white female stenographers and ignored the plight of real Black workers. Charleston businesses supported the idea that white workers should enjoy higher wages in order to get the economy going again, but they rejected similar aspirations among Black workers. The *News and Courier* took a hectoring tone when it wrote, "As usual they [Black workers] have interpreted the news [of the NRA codes] to suit themselves, and have managed to get hold of a mass of misinformation."[102] The paper also quoted supposed economic experts in the South who argued that if the federal government raised industrial wages, then Black farmworkers would refuse to work for white farmers.[103]

The one-sided debate in the press reveals the ways that the New Deal marginalized and excluded many workers in the name of economic progress.[104] Workers were aware of these exclusions. In the fall of 1933, African Americans in Birmingham organized the Forgotten Workers of America (FWA), whose purpose was to democratize Franklin Roosevelt's industrial policies. "Our name comes from President Roosevelt's phrase, 'the forgotten man,'" James "Doc" Mason, an FWA leader, wryly noted. "There are four types of workers the National Recovery Administration forgot," Mason continued. "They are the domestic, agricultural, educational and governmental employees. What we are trying to do is to obtain for these workers' recognition, better working conditions, and higher wages."[105] By the spring of 1934, the FWA had organized six local chapters.

The Charleston bagging workers strike was defeated by police force. Bobbins were no match for guns, and by the evening of Saturday, August 26, Charleston police had driven the women out of the factory. From this point onward, police deployed in force whenever African Americans tried to picket or even gather near the plant.[106] The city also suppressed the annual Colored Labor Day march. The excuse was "possible communistic influences"—but Black workers didn't need Marxists to explain the labor theory of value to them.[107] With roots in the nineteenth century, Colored Labor Day was an event where African American unionists from Charleston and the Sea Islands gathered to celebrate the role their labor had played in building the nation.[108] A day after the elimination of Colored Labor Day, the *News and Courier* wrote, "Charleston celebrated with the nation yesterday the first Labor day under the new deal, and celebrated it quietly."[109] Yet it was a quiet only achieved by police suppression. The following week, the city of Charleston sponsored a gala parade celebrating the achievements of the National Recovery Administration.[110] African Americans were not invited. Racial capitalists in Charleston helped transform the New Deal into a White Deal.

Throughout the nation, Latinx workers were at the forefront of the birth of industrial unionism and the Congress of Industrial Organizations (CIO) at its inception in 1935. The CIO organized workers in steel, rubber, food processing, textiles, and other major industries. The historian Vicki L. Ruiz found that Mexican American cannery workers in the Southwest drew on strong kinship networks in their communities to create a vibrant, democratic unionism in their workplaces from the Great Depression into the 1940s.[111] Latinx and African American workers were organizers and leaders in Communist-led unions such as the United Cannery, Agricultural, Packing and Allied Workers; the International Union of Mine, Mill & Smelter Workers; the Food, Tobacco, Agricultural and Allied Workers; and many others. Building on the work of Luisa Capetillo, her Latina predecessor in Florida, Luisa Moreno, a native Guatemalan, became one of the nation's most effective organizers. She helped tobacco workers, pecan shellers, and farmworkers build new unions across the country.[112] Moreno's Marxist background, her antiracism, and her commitment to building working-class power made her a tremendous force for social justice—workers composed ballads in her honor. Facing deportation hearings in 1949, Moreno, a regional director of the Food, Tobacco, Agricultural and Allied Workers in California, urged her CIO comrades to carry the movement forward: "From New York to Florida, from Florida to Texas and California, in several states in many cities and towns I became a part of the struggle to strengthen old AFL locals, to build and extend CIO locals—for better working conditions, for more pay, for improvements in the deplorable conditions of women workers, Negro workers, Mexican workers."[113]

Rank-and-file activists built their unions member by member, sacrifice by sacrifice. Leon Alexander, a coal miner and organizer for the United Mine Workers in Alabama's coal fields, inherited his union lineage from his father, who had been blacklisted along with all of his African American comrades in the bloody 1920 Alabama coal strike. Alexander credited the rise of the CIO to years of bitter African American struggles in Alabama's coal pits: "In Alabama Black folks was in the forefront of it, because the first ones that was organizing was only Blacks. Whites didn't have anything to do with it. They was afraid of being branded as a 'nigger lover' that's what they posted, put up posters all around, those white people who *finally* decided to help us organize District Twenty, they plastered up posters saying that *they* were nigger lovers."[114] Alexander credited a UMW organizer, Walter Jones, with convincing white workers to join the union: "He had a saying that when the company's kicking ass they don't look to see whether the ass is Black or white they just started kicking ass and if it happen to be a white ass he get kicked just like the Black one, and he convinced them and showed them that."

Max Guzmán was a leader of the Steel Workers Organizing Committee (SWOC) in Chicago. He began working at the Republic Steel Corporation in 1927. A decade later, Guzmán was one of hundreds of Mexican American factory operatives who formed the core of the Little Steel Strike in the spring of 1937. Historians have noted the important contribution of these workers: "According to an early president of the SWOC local at Inland, Mexican workers were crucial to the success of the picket lines at East Chicago's steel plants, contributing at times three-fourths of the demonstrators."[115] Guzmán carried an American flag during an outdoor SWOC mass meeting on May 30, 1937, that was attacked by Chicago police. He was brutally beaten by the police, who murdered ten workers during the Memorial Day Massacre.[116] The police arrested Guzmán, accused him of being a Communist, and threatened to deport him to Mexico "any time they felt like it."[117] Other courageous workers like Leon Alexander and Max Guzmán were integral to subsequent union victories in basic manufacturing in Chicago, Los Angeles, and Memphis.

Skillfully administered union contracts had the potential of bringing more equity onto the shop floor by breaking down generations of color bars, and abolishing the dual wage system.[118] However, the fight to overcome entrenched racism in unionized workplaces was an ongoing struggle made more complicated by generations of inequality. Leroy Boyd became an effective union shop steward in his cotton compress plant in Memphis in the 1940s. His first challenge, however, was in convincing white operatives to stay in the union:

> Well, at one time we had a little problem there with the white [workers]. The whites didn't want to be in the same union. The white wants to get more [pay] than the black. So you had a problem with the white and black sticking together. So as times went on and you got good union representatives, they point out to them, you know, at meetings that your only survival is to everybody unite together. There was a game that the company play is to play the white against the black and the black against the white. So they worked there. We had whites in the shop. In some of the shops we had whites try to get out of the union. Wanted to form another union. They didn't want to be in a union with Negroes.[119]

Interracial solidarity was in constant peril. Facing white intransigence in the early 1940s, an organizer in Alabama, Earl Brown, had to go outside the UMW contract and threaten a wildcat strike of fellow African American miners in order to equalize job opportunities in District 20's coal mines.[120] A United Auto Workers' representative, Ralph Thompson, recalled that into the 1970s, white unionists in Memphis's International Harvester Company plant silently cooperated with management—even to the point of sabotaging machinery and putting lives in jeopardy—in order to keep African American workers out of the skilled and higher-paying jobs.[121]

THE UNFULFILLED NEW DEAL

Industrial unions continued to make gains during World War II. In 1941, A. Philip Randolph and the Brotherhood of Sleeping Car Porters and Maids union threatened a mass march on Washington, DC, to protest employment discrimination in the nation's defense industries. Franklin Roosevelt responded by issuing an executive order to establish the Fair Employment Practices Committee (FEPC).[122] In the two-year period following World War II, approximately five million workers waged massive strikes—including several general strikes—which encouraged some to believe that a new day was dawning for the American working class as a whole.[123]

It was not to be. Capitalist powers regrouped and struck a number of counterblows, including the consolidation of its power in the Sunbelt against further unionization. The capstone antilabor achievement of the postwar period was Congress's passage of the Taft-Hartley Act of 1947, which severely undermined the power of labor unions to strike and enshrined the right of the federal government to intervene on the side of employers during labor disputes.[124] Equally important were federal and state government programs that enforced a steady supply of workers from other countries who lacked the power—or legal right—to bargain collectively with their employers. On a national level, agricultural employers used the Bracero Program, the federal program instituted to provide low-cost Mexican labor to agribusiness, to replace "native" US workers with workers from Mexico. The historian Rodolfo Acuña noted that "unionization [in agriculture] was futile while the Bracero Program remained."[125]

Organized labor also played a role in its own slow demise. As the Cold War gathered momentum, the CIO began purging left-led unions like Moranda Smith's and Leroy Boyd's Food, Tobacco, Agricultural and Allied Workers. Left-wing organizers such as Luisa Moreno were deported. The historian Michael Honey writes, "By 1949, any union with antiracist policies was at risk within the southern CIO."[126] The energy that labor needed to consolidate its fragile gains and to defeat Jim (and Juan) Crow was wasted in fighting a Cold War that enriched the same employers' organizations that worked assiduously to keep workers as powerless as possible. The continuing weakness of the working class in the Sunbelt made the region attractive to corporations. Often these corporations used the South as their first step to relocating permanently outside the United States.[127] The republic of cheap labor was the Achilles' heel of American democracy.

African American and Latinx workers' insurgencies helped set the stage for the rise of industrial unionism and the CIO. It was not coincidental that Congress ensured that millions of Black and Latinx workers were excluded from New Deal social legislation in order to placate business interests from South Carolina to California who fought to maintain white business supremacy.[128] Agricultural workers and domestic workers—two of the largest categories of Black and Brown workers—were barred from the core New Deal protections such as Social Security, the Fair Labor Standards Act, and the National Labor Relations Act, which gave workers the right to organize. These exclusions in turn exacerbated Black and Latinx poverty, and drove deeper wedges between sectors of the US working class to create cleavages that would never be resolved. Birmingham's Forgotten Workers of America understood at the outset that the New Deal fell grievously short of addressing the fundamental issues raised by working-class women and men of color in canneries, bagging plants, agriculture, and other sectors.

Racial capitalism produced cohorts of politicians and political institutions whose primary function was to keep wages low, to quash dissent, and to severely curtail the freedoms of African American and immigrant workers. Politicians who built their careers at the expense of Black and Brown labor became the leading political figures of the postwar period in Mississippi, Florida, and California. These guardians of inequality opposed every effort to reform the nation's labor and civil rights laws. Simultaneously, they and their acolytes were the proponents of the Cold War's military industrial complex, which drained the resources of the nation in a devastating new round of military interventions from Latin America to Southeast Asia. The republic that had spent much of its energy suppressing Black and Brown labor in the first one hundred twenty-five years of its existence carried forward the grim legacy of disenfranchisement into the twentieth century.

Regardless of these many setbacks, however, African American and Latinx workers continued striving to create a political and economic system that valued human rights and individual dignity above property rights and the power of employers' organizations. The organizers who built the social movements of the Great Depression would soon link up with a new generation of activists in the 1960s to generate a revived struggle for dignity and justice on all fronts. First, however, as World War II wound down, a remarkable international conference in Mexico brought new hope to the American working class.

CHAPTER 7

EMANCIPATORY INTERNATIONALISM VS. THE AMERICAN CENTURY, 1945 TO 1960s

The writer Carl Hansberry traveled to Mexico in the winter of 1945 for the *Pittsburgh Courier* to cover the Inter-American Conference on Problems of War and Peace, convened at Chapultepec, a historic suburb of Mexico City. Delegates from twenty independent nations of North America, Latin America, and the Caribbean met to forge "further cooperative measures for the prosecution of the war to complete victory."[1] The Chapultepec Conference, as it would come to be known, was tasked with creating a plan furthering "the maintenance of peace and collective security" in the hemisphere after the end of World War II. Participants were also charged with discussing the "consideration of methods to develop such cooperation for the improvement of economic and social conditions of the peoples of the Americas, with a view to raising their standard of living."[2] The Mexican muralist Diego Rivera sketched scenes from the conference's daily proceedings with a plan to create a series of murals on the subject of fostering hemispheric unity.[3]

The United States delegation steered the assembly to focus on security and trade matters.[4] However, nations such as Nicaragua, Mexico, and the Dominican Republic understood from decades of hard experience what the United States meant by "security." As if to confirm their suspicions, Senator Tom Connally of Texas, chair of the Senate Foreign Relations Committee, claimed that the assembly was creating a new Monroe Doctrine, backed by all the Americas instead of just the United States. Connally asserted that this new Monroe Doctrine would be "based on the president's war powers to order U.S. armed forced anywhere they may be needed to promote the United Nations war effort."[5]

Haiti dropped a bombshell on US plans to dominate the conference. The Haitian delegates submitted a resolution that said the security of the hemisphere hinged on the equality of nations as well as the equality of people *in* those nations. This resolution stunned the delegates, and it was not covered in any mainstream media outlet in the United States. Carl Hansberry excitedly shared the exact language of the Haitian resolution in full with his *Pittsburgh Courier* readers. It read:

> Whereas the practice of racial discrimination is not only contrary to the positive reports and conclusions of scientists, but is also in formal contradiction of the Christian doctrine on which our civilization is based;
>
> Whereas the Nazi doctrines that submerged humanity into the most terrible catastrophe of all time came for the most part from the Nazis' pernicious and pretended notions of the inequality of races;
>
> Whereas world peace cannot be established except on the valid idea that all men, regardless of their race, nationality or religion, be accepted with full equality;
>
> Therefore, the Conference on Problems of War and Peace resolves to recommend to the governments of the American Republics the complete abolition of all political regulations or actions which make possible discriminations against people, based upon race, religion or nationality.[6]

Haiti had once again struck a blow for liberty. Delegates built on Haiti's bold intervention to craft a more democratic vision of postwar possibilities. Ezequiel Padilla, Mexico's secretary of foreign affairs—who had been elected president of the Chapultepec Conference by acclamation—demanded an end to "race hatred" in the Americas. The *Cleveland Call and Post* reported that Mexico "presented the resolution suggesting the abolition by the American States of 'sex discrimination that may still exist' and proposed that each government allocate funds annually for 'the financing of the Inter-American Committee of Women in the same manner as it is being done for the other institutions of the Pan American Union.'"[7] African American newspapers reported that the United States was working behind the scenes to put a damper on discussions of global inequality. For example, the *Amsterdam News* wrote,

> It is significant that very little if anything has appeared in the newspapers of the United States in connection with the Haitian resolution against discrimination. What is more, *The Amsterdam News*, in an attempt to get an official view of the resolution and to find out what has been done with it, telegraphed Secretary of State Edward R. Stettinius, Jr., Nelson Rockefeller, Assistant Secretary of State, in charge of Latin-American affairs, and the redoubtable Tom Connally, chairman of the Senate Foreign Relations Committee, but up to press time, no replies had been received.[8]

Even though the conference's final declarations on human rights were not as strongly worded as the original Haitian offering (the final wording was "the equality of rights and opportunities for all men, regardless of race or religion"), the prominent African American writer Albert L. Hinton thought that "the Act of Chapultepec drawn up at the recent Inter-American Conference of Foreign Ministers held in Mexico City, is an historic document judged by any standards. But because it contains among other things, a declaration against racial discrimination and persecution of minority groups, it is destined to go down in history as one of the greatest international peace documents of all time."[9] To Hinton, the Act of Chapultepec signaled the death knell of Jim Crow: "The state of South Carolina could do much worse than study the Act of Chapultepec in the light of the Palmetto State's action a year ago in abolishing all of its primary laws with the avowed purpose of preventing Negro South Carolinians from voting."[10] Hinton argued that the act essentially outlawed recent efforts to bolster segregated education in Alabama, writing,

> And finally, Uncle Sam, who played such a major role in drafting the Act of Chapultepec, might scrutinize the Act more closely and then ask himself why it is that in this supposed land of plenty and opportunity there

are still four-million farm families ill-housed, 850,000 rural homes with no toilet facilities, many rural counties with only one physician for each 10,000 of its population, and 1,400 of America's 3070 counties, most of them rural, with no full-time health department. . . . The Act of Chapultepec document "which may conceivably become the great charter of equality and human freedom" for the black and brown peoples of the Western hemisphere, is international in character, but in a very real sense, powerfully implemented by the declaration against racial discrimination, it might very well serve as a charter or code of conduct for a certain section of the U.S.A.[11]

The Act of Chapultepec now carried with it the force of law in the United States.[12] Harold Preece, a Texan, a socialist, and a frequent contributor to African American newspapers, was jubilant. "I'm not going overboard when I agree with leading diplomats in Mexico City interpreting the Chapultepec declaration for inter-American cooperation and defense as 'the greatest joint document of democratic principles and hemispheric unity ever signed by the American nation.'"[13] Preece stated that Chapultepec "means that Negroid nations like Haiti, the Dominican Republic, Cuba and Brazil, stand on the same plane with predominantly white nations like the United States and Chile." Most important, Preece asserted, was that the Act of Chapultepec slammed the legal brakes on US military intervention in Latin America and threatened the power of government by American banks to control the people of the Global South:

It's also a freeze bath for people like Mr. Henry Luce, publisher of Time Magazine, who spout eyewash about "the American Century" and who see the United States using the big stick to build a big empire of blood and cash. For the big stick "rared up" and hit us in the face when we used it by sending marines to suppress the Negro peoples of Haiti and Santo Domingo and to chase the Negro-Indian Nicaraguan guerrillas who helped head off the American Century under the leadership of that Indian patriot of the Americas, General Sandino.

This time, the big stick is going to be wielded by the peoples of the Americas against all those who would disturb the peace and prosperity of the Americas.[14]

PUTTING CHAPULTEPEC TO WORK

African American, Latinx, and Jewish organizations seized on the domestic and foreign policy potential of the Act of Chapultepec. After a courageous group of Mexican American parents organized in Orange County, California, to challenge the inferior schooling their children were receiving, the American Jewish Congress filed a brief on behalf of the parents in the Supreme Court case, *Méndez v. Westminster*.[15] Counsel for the plaintiffs included Pauli Murray and Thurgood Marshall. The parents' attorneys argued that the Act of Chapultepec and the United Nations Charter—promulgated in 1945—required signatory nations to outlaw "not only discrimination but also its potential causes. This is certainly broad enough to cover segregation."[16] Katharine F. Lenroot, head of the Children's Bureau of the Department of Labor, concurred, and shared her analysis of the treaty with the National Congress of Colored Parents and Teachers, which was held in Washington, DC, also in 1945. Lenroot argued that "the Chapultepec Conference . . . reaffirmed the principle [of] equality of rights and opportunities for all men, regardless of race or religion, a principle recognized by all American states."[17]

Senator Dennis Chavez of New Mexico, the first Mexican American elected to the US Senate, used the Act of Chapultepec to advocate for the creation of a permanent Fair Employment Practices Commission to protect the civil rights of workers and to end discrimination on the job. The original Fair Employment Practices Commission was the fruit of the march on Washington threatened by Randolph's Brotherhood of Sleeping Car Porters and Maids in 1941. Now the FEPC was endangered especially by Southern Democrats, who looked to re-entrench Jim Crow labor relations at the end of the war. Working in tandem with the New York civil rights organizer Anna Arnold Hedgeman, Chavez argued that a permanent FEPC would demonstrate to the nations of the hemisphere that the United States was serious about democracy: "Our Latin neighbors have had every reason to question the motives of our Government, and the Chapultepec agreement goes a long way toward the cherished goal of honest inter-American relations."[18] With Hedgeman as secretary of the National Council for a Permanent FEPC, Chavez worked with some of the nation's best community organizers, including the Arkansas NAACP leaders Daisy Bates and her husband, L. C. Bates. However, the National Council also faced powerful opposition in Washington from what the Black press called the "Bilbo-Eastman filibusters," referring to Mississippi's senatorial guardians of Jim Crow, Theodore G. Bilbo and James Oliver Eastland.[19]

A legal team headed by Charles Hamilton Houston brought the Act of Chapultepec to the United States Supreme Court in 1948 during oral arguments in the *Shelley v. Kraemer* restrictive racial covenant cases. Earlier, in his capacity as vice president of the American Council of Race Relations, Houston had cited the Act of Chapultepec and the 1945 United Nations Charter as "international agreements [that] obligate our government to work to eliminate all racial discrimination."[20] At the *Shelley v. Kraemer* hearings, one of Houston's co-counsels, Herman Willer, argued that "the nation's treaties, the United Nations Charter and the Act of Chapultepec, have established a public policy of equal treatment for all and have made the covenants void."[21]

One pathway to the origins of the modern civil rights movement, as well as to the Chicano/a movement, runs straight through Chapultepec, Mexico. The impetus that Haitian delegates gave to civil rights and labor struggles in the United States at the Chapultepec Conference was immediately seized upon by African American and Mexican American organizers. These activists could exploit the democratic openings created at the Inter-American Conference on Problems of War and Peace because they recognized the centuries-old currents of freedom that flowed from nations such as Haiti and Mexico. While John Adams and generations of elite leaders in the United States had depicted the Haitian and Mexican people as backward, visionaries such as Dennis Chavez, Harold Preece, and Carl Hansberry were the inheritors of the traditions of emancipatory internationalism that had led them to look to the Global South for lessons on liberation.

Soon, however, these openings began narrowing. Even though

restrictive covenants and segregated schools for Mexican American schoolchildren were abolished in law (if not in actual practice), Chavez's multiracial FEPC crusade failed, destroyed by Sunbelt employers' advocates in Congress.[22] In 1946, soon after writing a piece critical of the Ku Klux Klan, Harold Preece was driven out of the South by white terrorists.[23] And, after years of fighting racial discrimination in Chicago, Carl Hansberry's experiences at Chapultepec convinced him that his family's future was in Mexico, but he died in 1946, before he could move his family there. His daughter, the celebrated playwright Lorraine Hansberry, stated: "American racism helped kill him." It is possible to glimpse a vision of her father's dreams in her 1959 play *A Raisin in the Sun*.[24]

The United States rejected Haiti's vision of the equality of nations and privileged its own definition of "national security," ultimately ensuring that chaos, violence, and genocide would become the fate of millions.[25] Militarism and political manipulation in the service of Washington-directed capitalism were the preferred tools of US foreign policy in Latin America in the twentieth century.[26]

In 1954, the *New York Times* warned hysterically that "Communists might ultimately take over Guatemala and use it as a base to infiltrate other Latin nations and the vital Panama Canal zone."[27] In the same year, the United States engineered a bloody coup against President Jacobo Árbenz, even as it flooded the region with arms shipments to US-friendly regimes in Honduras and Nicaragua.[28] In reality, the historian Greg Grandin writes, Guatemala's leaders "were trying to implement a New-Deal-style economic program to modernize and humanize Guatemala's brutal plantation economy."[29] Árbenz's only crime, writes Grandin, was "to expropriate, with full compensation, uncultivated United Fruit Company land and legalize the Communist Party—both unacceptable acts from Washington's early-1950s vantage point."[30] African Americans responded to the newest wave of US invasions in Latin America in much the same way that they had reacted to imperialism between the 1820s and 1920s.[31] In a letter to the *Pittsburgh Courier* that criticized the US-sponsored coup in Guatemala, Mack Nance of Nogales, Arizona, stated,

> For an individual or group of individuals to imply that we, the people of the USA[,] do not seek to dominate or

to extend our authority over others, is to ignore the very history of the country in which we reside, resulting in prevarication, evasiveness, or intentional falsehoods. From the very birth of our country, we have sought to extend our authority over others. For example, we need only point to our great Western states, snatched from the Indians; the Mexican War; Puerto Rico, the Hawaiian Islands, Guam, the Philippines, Nicaragua, and Guatemala.[32]

Ralph Matthews, a *Cleveland Call and Post* columnist, launched a devastatingly sarcastic attack on US crimes in Guatemala.

This new government, headed by a very wicked man by the name of Jacob Arbenz, set out to confiscate the land not being cultivated by the Boston people, and divided it up among the peons who had never owned a foot of earth in all their lives or the lives of their fathers before them. He compounded this rascality by offering to pay the Boston people not what the land was actually worth, but the value the owners themselves had place[d] upon it when paying taxes to the Guatemalan government. This was no way to treat the stockholders. By encouraging the formation of labor unions, [Arbenz] satanically and with malice aforethought, forced the bleeding company to pay excessive wages which increased things to the point where workers who formerly earned the tidy sum of around $185 a year were now carrying home as much as a thousand dollars per annum.[33]

Matthews observed that the United States government could not tolerate the specter of "workers who had never earned more than 85 cents a day . . . now carrying home as much as a buck and a half. This was communist infiltration pure and simple and threatened the peace of the Americas and the world. Anyone with a grain of sense could see that this evil state of affairs could not be tolerated in the Western hemisphere."[34]

African Americans would continue to express their dissent against coups and military interventions from Guatemala to Vietnam as well as the US-sponsored "dirty wars" in Central America in the 1980s. During her keynote address at the 1986 Black Women Writers in the Diaspora Conference, Black feminist Audre Lorde asked audience members to understand: "Sisterhood and Survival demands that I ask myself as an African American, what does it mean to be a citizen of the most powerful country on earth? And we are that. What does it mean to be a citizen of a country that stands upon the wrong side of every liberation struggle on this earth? Let that sink in for a moment."[35]

THE RISE OF THE FARMWORKER MOVEMENT

The experiences of most Brown and Black workers in American history do not square with the idea of the United States as a middle-class republic. Martin Luther King Jr. dismantled the myth of universal upward mobility in his final book, *Where Do We Go from Here: Chaos or Community?* King believed that the idea of the "middle-class Utopia" derailed comprehensive efforts to end poverty.[36] If US society was based on "fair play," as so many alleged and assumed, then obviously the poor only had themselves to blame for their poverty. In reality, however, the hardest-working members of the United States were consistently the poorest and least advantaged. King writes: "We must honestly admit that capitalism has often left a gulf between superfluous wealth and abject poverty [and] has created conditions permitting necessities to be taken from the many to give luxuries to the few, and has encouraged smallhearted men to become cold and conscienceless so that, like Dives before Lazarus, they are unmoved by suffering, poverty-stricken humanity."[37]

A 1969 study of working-class Mexican American communities in the Southwest strongly echoed King's observation on the intersections of class and race inequalities. Ernesto Galarza and his colleagues wrote: "As percentages of [the] poor, brown and black [populations] hold about equal shares of not having."[38] Throughout the Sunbelt, agribusiness depended on the federal government to provide them with a variety of "guest worker" programs that would produce a labor force unable to challenge the authority of their employers.[39] As a result, Galarza finds, "There is everywhere a large number of politically and culturally immobilized residents. . . .

Their separation from the functions of citizenship was total."[40] In districts containing such working families, the result was unpaved streets, impoverished schools, and lack of running water. "The non-citizen, whether he is a registered alien or a *bracero* or an illegal, can be nothing but a petitioner for services," writes Galarza.[41]

And yet, there was even then a silent revolution brewing in the region's barrios and agricultural valleys. In 1952, César Chávez, a WWII veteran and the son of migrant farmworkers, took a job in San Jose, California, as an organizer with the Community Service Organization.[42] Along with a cohort of remarkable activists that included Dolores Huerta and Gilbert Padilla, Chávez learned the skills of community organizing. A decade later, the group began organizing a labor union, and formed the National Farm Workers Association. The philosophy of the NFWA was rooted in asking new members to contribute whatever they had—dues, spare food, labor—to keep the organization running. Instead of dictating the answers from above, NFWA organizers urged workers to develop their own solutions to problems. The idea was to show people that they can begin to change their lives for the better. No problem was too big or too small to tackle: job discrimination, police harassment, difficulties getting loans—Huerta, Chávez, and a growing cadre of organizers worked with the farmworkers to solve these dilemmas. Bureaucrats at state employment offices were surprised when campesinos began demanding an end to discriminatory hiring practices. In the process, farmworkers began to discover that they had the ability to change their lives. When an action failed, members regrouped to talk to each other about what went wrong, and how to do better the next time.

Fred Ross, the founder of the Community Service Organization and Chávez's mentor in the pre-NFWA days, recalled that Chávez was adept at forming relationships of trust and encouraging people to develop their own leadership abilities:

> The Service Center, with César in command, was much more than your routine problem clinic; it was a sovereign restorative of human dignity and a means of drawing the people, whose lifestyle had been one of being pushed around by the authorities without a peep[. They] soon

learned to stand their ground, speak out, and get what they came after. In the agony of forcing themselves to do this, they suffered a sea change: they got organized.[43]

The NFWA's grassroots organizing style required months of house meetings, countless conversations, and arguments to unfold. The rewards were slow in coming. One month the group would sign up dozens of new members. The next month the new members quit. NFWA organizers never lost faith in the mission. Chávez recalled, "Of every hundred workers I talked to, one would say, 'It's time [to form a union].' Everybody said no one could organize farmworkers, that it couldn't be done. But we got a group of forty or fifty, and one by one, that's how we started."[44] After three years of these intensive face-to-face meetings the NFWA grew to twelve hundred members.

The federal Bracero Program ended in 1964. Hundreds of Filipino farmworkers, members of the Agricultural Workers Organizing Committee (AWOC), called a grape strike in California's Coachella Valley in the first week of September 1965. Picking grapes several miles away from the strike's epicenter, Philip Vera Cruz, a Filipino farmworker, was electrified by the news.[45] Vera Cruz had come to the United States in 1926 hoping to become a lawyer. Instead, he had joined the rest of the *Manong* generation of male Filipino migrants—the first wave of Filipino immigrants, in the 1920s and '30s, who worked in low-wage occupations and were forbidden by US immigration laws to bring their wives with them from the Philippines. Filipino farmworkers in California were subjected to harsh racism. Pete Velasco recalled, "When we walked the sidewalks in those early days, they shouted at us, 'Hey monkey, go home!'"[46]

Now, four decades after his arrival in the United States, Vera Cruz saw his opportunity to build an organization dedicated to justice and equality. "That's when I stopped picking grapes for the first time in over twenty years, and I never went back." The sixty-year-old farmworker became a strike leader. The NFWA was faced with a momentous decision: join their Filipino brothers and sisters on strike or watch from the sidelines. After Dolores Huerta, who had served as secretary-treasurer of AWOC, rushed to the picket line, the NFWA called a meeting to deliberate on the situation. By design, the leadership of the organization decided to hold the strike vote on September 16, Mexican Independence Day. At the meeting, approximately 2,700 NFWA members unanimously voted to support AWOC's strike against the Coachella grape growers. The die was cast for one of the most important labor struggles in modern American history.[47]

To win this strike, the farmworkers resurrected a venerable tool of the labor movement: the consumer boycott. In the summer of 1965, the NFWA and AWOC called a boycott on all California table grapes. To win the grape boycott, the union had to educate America about labor. If consumers did not understand who was responsible for tending and harvesting the food that graced their tables, then someone had to teach them. Chávez was blunt: "We need the help of all to add power to the poor."[48] Soon, students joined workers, clergy, and other supporters on boycott committees that were responsible for bringing the boycott to the attention of America and, finally, the world. Members of the Student Nonviolent Coordinating Committee (SNCC) and the Congress of Racial Equality (CORE) who had worked with the civil rights movement in the South played integral roles educating consumers about the grape boycott. The *Pittsburgh Courier* reported that both the Negro American Labor Council of New York City and the Mississippi Freedom Democratic Party were actively supporting the boycott. James Farmer, the director of CORE, demanded that Congress "place all agricultural workers under the protection of federal minimum wage and collective bargaining laws. Many Negroes, especially in the southern cotton belt, are not protected by such laws."[49] In the fall of 1968, an FBI agent observed an NAACP-supported parade in Pittsburgh, writing that "approximately 128 individuals composed of both blacks and whites marched from the Hill District to Point Park in downtown Pittsburgh."[50] The source further advised that the march was led by Albert Rojas, a representative of the United Farm Worker Organizing Committee, and was in support of the California grape pickers and their national boycott.

"Who can say 'no' to the simple cry for help from the grape pickers in Delano, California?" Charlotte Chase wrote in a letter to the editor in the Baltimore *Afro-American*. "Their plea is for the right to live and work in dignity as human beings. The indignities they suffer . . . are of such a nature that news articles and handbills only hint at them."[51] Dolores Huerta, speaking in Washington, DC, noted that growers resorted to the well-known tactic of divide and conquer to undermine the union. The *Pittsburgh Courier* reported her speech: "Mrs. Huerta pointed out that 'most of the field workers are Mexican-American, Filipino, Negro and Puerto Rican.' The growers she said, 'try to . . . play one race against the other . . . and actually perpetuate race prejudice. . . . It is not just a question of wages. It is a question of human dignity, of equality,' she asserted."[52]

Careful observers of the grape boycott understood what was at stake. In March 1968, Martin Luther King Jr. sent a telegram to Chávez: "My colleagues and I commend you for your bravery, salute you for your indefatigable work against poverty and injustice, and pray for your health and continuing service as one of the outstanding men of America. The plight of your people and ours is so grave that we all desperately need the inspiring example and effective leadership you have given."[53] King supported the boycott because he believed that it represented a two-pronged assault on racism and poverty. "Many white Americans of good will have never connected bigotry with economic exploitation," he explained. "They have deplored prejudice, but tolerated or ignored economic injustice."[54]

By 1970, the grape boycott had cut into growers' profits and had turned popular opinion against the table grapes industry. It was estimated that 17 percent of the American public supported the boycott.[55] In addition, the constant strikes, marches, and organizing in growers' fields undermined their claims that they knew what was best for "their" workers. On July 29, 1970, the United Farm Workers signed union contracts covering approximately thirty thousand workers in the grape industry. The labor historian Robert Gordon notes, "All of the newly signed contracts insured substantial wage increases, created a union hiring hall, and established strict regulations regarding the use of pesticides."[56]

THE ARC OF THE CIVIL RIGHTS MOVEMENT

African American insurgencies in the South beginning in the 1950s changed the trajectory of American politics and birthed numerous social movements throughout the nation. Each major victory in the

Black freedom struggle depended on the self-activity of working-class African Americans to carry the day, beginning with the Montgomery, Alabama, bus boycott of 1955. In his account of the boycott, *Stride Toward Freedom*, Martin Luther King Jr. noted, "The majority of the Negroes who took part in the year-long boycott of Montgomery's buses were poor and untutored; but they understood the essence of the Montgomery movement."[57]

While King's soaring "I Have a Dream" became the most-cited speech given at the 1963 March on Washington for Jobs and Freedom, A. Philip Randolph's address on the perils of job-killing automation, deindustrialization, and labor oppression was equally prophetic.[58] Randolph tried to build a universal conception of freedom that was rooted in his people's experience of slavery and racial capitalism: "For one thing, we must destroy the notion that Mrs. Murphy's property rights include the right to humiliate me because of the color of my skin. The sanctity of private property takes second place to the sanctity of the human personality. It falls to the Negro to reassert this proper priority of values because our ancestors were transformed from human personalities into private property." Randolph argued that Americans should support "a free democratic society" with "new forms of social planning, to create full employment, and to put automation at the service of human needs, not at the service of profits." Randolph drew upon African American history to articulate a socialist vision of the future.[59]

SNCC discovered that it needed the creative energy of the most oppressed people of the Mississippi Delta to challenge the power of Mississippi's segregationist leaders. Lawrence Guyot, cofounder of the Mississippi Freedom Democratic Party, noted that the MFDP, organized in 1964, was composed primarily of working-class people, "sharecroppers, barbers, and maids" who were able to "take on the most powerful political party in the country."[60] Local people like Bolivar County's Margaret Block introduced SNCC activists to the traditions of armed self-help in the Deep South, as organizers defended Northern volunteers from Klan violence.[61] The MFDP grew so powerful, and produced such a brilliant leader in the person of Fannie Lou Hamer, a former plantation worker, that the president of the United States, Lyndon B. Johnson, was forced to intervene in an effort to derail the MFDP's national impact during

Hamer's address to the 1964 Democratic National Convention in Atlantic City.[62]

African American communities in the North were also rebelling against decades of residential segregation, economic oppression, and police brutality. The Watts rebellion in the summer of 1965 was sparked by a confrontation between Los Angeles Police Department (LAPD) officers and a Black motorist. In reality, though, it was decades in the making, a response to the habitual police violence against African Americans and Mexican Americans. The author Gerald Horne writes, "Some officers randomly and arbitrarily beat and tortured black men, even those who were not suspected of anything." Horne quotes a former LAPD officer who remembered: "'Bending fingers back, twisting ears, tightening handcuffs into medieval torture devices, slamming the victim's head into the door while placing him in a vehicle,' were some of their milder techniques."[63] A municipal judge in San Bernardino, California, told investigators after the riot, "When I review a person's criminal record for any purposes, I give no weight whatsoever to a Los Angeles felony arrest unless it is followed by a conviction, since in my opinion, it frequently means merely that the defendant was in the wrong place at the wrong time."[64] The LAPD were rarely questioned or disciplined in any way for their attacks on civilians. Horne notes that in the three years preceding the Watts riot, "There were sixty-five inquests involving homicide by officers during that time, and only one ended with a verdict other than justifiable homicide, a case in which two officers 'playing cops and robbers' in a Long Beach Police Station shot a newspaperman."[65]

Generations of inferior job opportunities, residential segregation, and Mayor Sam Yorty's blocking the flow of federal antipoverty funds into Los Angeles also fueled anger. When the riot broke out, insurgents and police alike invoked the specter of the war in Southeast Asia. "If I've got to die, I ain't dying in Vietnam, I'm going to die here," said one rioter, and many others echoed these sentiments.[66] As his precinct stations were deluged with calls and false alarms designed to confuse police dispatchers, LAPD Chief William Parker stated, "This situation is very much like fighting the Viet Cong." The commission that studied the aftermath of the riots rejected Governor Edmund Brown's idea of creating a major job-creation program to address Black unemployment in Los Angeles, stating, "Obviously such a program is bound to encounter tough sledding in Washington, especially as the Vietnam costs escalate."[67]

Martin Luther King's meetings with the "desperate, rejected, and angry young men" in cities boiling over with violence pushed him to oppose the Vietnam War. King explained to his audience in a speech at Riverside Church on April 4, 1967, that he had urged nonviolence as a tool of social change to youth in

> the ghettos of the North over the last three years, especially the last three summers. But they asked, and rightly so, "What about Vietnam?" They asked if our own nation wasn't using massive doses of violence to solve its problems, to bring about the changes it wanted. Their questions hit home, and I knew that I could never again raise my voice against the violence of the oppressed in the ghettos without having first spoken clearly to the greatest purveyor of violence in the world today: my own government.[68]

King compared his nation's attack on Vietnamese peasants to its brutal treatment of poor people at home, many of whom were being sent to fight the war. He noted that the war abroad had destroyed the War on Poverty:

> It seemed as if there was a real promise of hope for the poor, both black and white, through the poverty program. There were experiments, hopes, new beginnings. Then came the buildup in Vietnam, and I watched this program broken and eviscerated as if it were some idle political plaything of a society gone mad on war. And I knew that America would never invest the necessary funds or energies in rehabilitation of its poor so long as adventures like Vietnam continued to draw men and skills and money like some demonic, destructive suction tube. So I was increasingly compelled to see the war as an enemy of the poor and to attack it as such.

King and the Southern Christian Leadership Conference began mapping out plans for a massive Poor People's Campaign.[69] The crusade would unite the poor of all races into a nationwide movement that would descend on Washington and stay there until the highest officials in the land agreed to formulate a plan to abolish poverty. "Something is wrong with capitalism as it now stands in the United States," King observed near the end of 1967. "We are not interested in being integrated into *this* value structure. Power must be relocated; a radical redistribution of power must take place."[70]

Before the Southern Christian Leadership Conference could initiate the Poor People's Campaign, municipal sanitation workers in Memphis went out on strike on February 12, 1968, to demand higher wages and union recognition from the city government. As the city's worst-paid public employees, the sanitation workers— "garbage men"—had to carry leaky, fifty-pound garbage pails full of maggoty foul matter from the backyards of affluent Memphians. Most full-time sanitation workers were paid so little that they qualified for welfare. The city did not provide work clothing or gloves, and at the end of the day, the men's clothing was so drenched with filth that they had to strip outside their houses rather bring the toxic muck into their homes.

The strike captured King's imagination; he instantly realized that by attempting to unionize, Memphis garbage workers were engaging in the most efficient form of antipoverty activism possible. King rushed to Memphis on March 18 to stand in solidarity with the garbage men. He was assassinated on April 4, 1968—exactly one year to the day after his antiwar address. A week later, the Memphis sanitation workers successfully unionized as members of American Federation of State, County and Municipal Employees Local 1733.

RAINBOW COALITIONS

King's death robbed the United States of its greatest champion in the battle against race and class oppression. Yet the Freedom Movement that had propelled King to the heights of radical leadership in 1968 endured well after his passing. African Americans and Latinx people organized the Black Panther Party for Self-Defense, the Young Lords, the Chicano Moratorium, the United Construction Workers Association, and hundreds of organizations that drew from the organizing traditions of emancipatory internationalism to confront capitalism and imperialism while making common cause with struggling movements in the Global South.[71] In 1969, the Chicago Black Panther Party created the original Rainbow Coalition, composed of the Puerto Rican Young Lords and the Young Patriots, a group of revolutionary white activists.[72] Carlton Yearwood, a Panther organizer, explained the multiracial coalition: "We believe that racism comes out of a class struggle, it's just part of the divide-and-conquer tactics of the Establishment and a product of capitalism. When we provide free breakfasts for poor kids, we provide them for poor whites and poor blacks."[73]

Organizers consciously adopted what the historian Jakobi Williams calls a "universal identity politics."[74] The United Construction Workers in Seattle, Washington, founded by an electrician, Tyree Scott, fought to tear down "racially exclusionary hiring practices in Seattle's construction unions in the fall of 1969."[75] Composed primarily of African Americans, the United Construction Workers adopted a politics based on "the struggles of Third World, poor, and working women and men to obtain our rights."[76] The UCWA's newsletter, *No Separate Peace*, celebrated the "flowering of many communities, cultures, and movements: National groupings: Black, Chicano, Asian, Native American, Latino; Sexual groupings—women, gay people; as well as workers, young people, soldiers, prisoners, and even neighborhood groupings." The United Construction Workers applauded the radical potential of these diverse communities, but did not expect them to organize in the same space: "Therefore, we will emphasize the art and poetry and culture of the various communities in our area, while educating people to struggle against the divisiveness of racism, sexism, and imperialism."[77] *No Separate Peace* honored distinctive cultures while emphasizing the importance of solidarity: "And the question of whether or not it's the Chicanos versus the Blacks is bullshit. And the only way you're going to get caught up in that question is not knowing who your enemy is."

Piri Thomas's memoir, *Down These Mean Streets*, first published in 1967, presented a new vision of racial identity. Coming of age in Spanish Harlem in the Great Depression as the son of Puerto Rican and Cuban immigrants, Thomas was the darkest-skin member of his family.[78] He wrote about feeling constantly out of place in an immigrant family that desperately wanted to hide its African roots—Thomas's parents and siblings explained to Piri that he owed his color solely to the "Indian" in their ancestry. Thomas's journey to find wholeness in a society that denigrated Blackness led him to establish an identity based on solidarity with the oppressed, and to declare that it was possible to be Black *and* Latinx. Supporting the Black freedom struggle, as well as the Nicaraguan battle against US military intervention in the 1980s, Thomas wrote, "'Tierra Libre o Morir' [Free Homeland or Death] is the cry of [Augusto] Sandino and the Nicaraguan patriots. 'Give me liberty or give me death' is the cry of Patrick Henry and the American Patriots. Tell me freedom lovers, what's the difference?"[79]

The multiracial coalitions of the 1960s joined the struggle to free South Africa of apartheid. The United Construction Workers' Tyree Scott traveled to Mozambique and South Africa in the 1970s to help build the anti-apartheid movement.[80] In 1985, Howard Jordan, New York assemblyman Jose Rivera, and Congressman Roberto Garcia founded Latinos for a Free South Africa. Growing apartheid repression in South Africa "mandates a collective response by the Latino community," Rivera was quoted as saying. "Our new organization represents the first endeavor to bring isolated initiatives together under one banner for freedom."[81] In a collective statement given to the press, the founders of Latinos for a Free South Africa stated, "Latinos who along with their African-American brothers have been the victims of discrimination and racism in this nation, are particularly repulsed by this South African system of apartheid where resources are allocated on the basis of color." Jordan stated, "We want to foster Black-Latino unity through an understanding of the relationship between the struggle in South Africa, Central and Latin America and the domestic situation affecting Blacks and Latinos in the US."[82] The organization engaged in direct action, legislative lobbying, and international diplomacy in tandem with other anti-apartheid organizations.[83]

The second Rainbow Coalition was part of a resurgence of emancipatory internationalism in the 1980s. Groups such as the Committee in Solidarity with the People of El Salvador, Witness for Peace, the US/Guatemala Labor Education Project, and Veterans for Peace organized to oppose imperialism in Latin America.[84] The Reverend Jesse Jackson initially formed the National Rainbow Coalition to support his 1984 presidential campaign. The coalition supported the Farm Labor Organizing Committee's (FLOC) eight-year boycott of the Campbell Soup Company, called to exert pressure for recognition of the farm labor union; Jackson used the 1984 Democratic National Convention as a platform to urge support for FLOC's unionization struggle.[85] The National Rainbow Coalition also supported the United Farm Workers of Washington State's eight-year boycott of Chateau Ste. Michelle Wines, which ended victoriously in a union contract in 1995, a rare success story in an era of dramatic union decline.[86] Ronald Walters remembers the sense of excitement during Jackson's presidential campaigns:

> No one else at that level was talking about environmental racism, "no first use" of nuclear weapons; antiapartheid (remember, the ANC was a "terrorist organization"); the Arab-Israeli situation. No other candidate had an economic policy based on major investment and cuts in the military, a program Bill Clinton would run on in 1992 (though abandon forthwith). None advocated extension of the Congressional health plan to all Americans. None regarded gay rights as inherent in a larger moral claim and not simply something to be pandered to. None twinned race and class so naturally.[87]

A perennial dynamic in US history is that advances made by African Americans and Latinx people always elicit counterattacks from state and private interests. J. Edgar Hoover's Federal Bureau of Investigation developed the Counter-Intelligence Program (COINTELPRO) to undermine and destroy individuals such as Martin Luther King Jr. and organizations such as the Black Panther Party and the Young Lords. California governor Ronald Reagan, as well as other politicians, availed themselves of COINTELPRO's resources to sabatoge antiwar activism on college campuses and consolidate their hold on power.[88] Given the power and diversity of the movements for justice on all fronts in the 1960s and '70s, it is no surprise that the following three decades would witness one of the most extensive backlashes against social progress in American history.

CHAPTER 8

EL GRAN PARO ESTADOUNIDENSE
THE REBIRTH OF THE AMERICAN WORKING CLASS,
1970s TO THE PRESENT

On May 1, 2006, International Workers' Day, Latinx workers initiated the largest general strike in the history of the Americas. Known as *el gran paro Estadounidense*, the Great American Strike, this mass action breathed new life into a labor movement that had been in disarray for decades. The general strike impacted every aspect of American life. Approximately 70 to 90 percent of students in Chicago skipped school to show the country what "a day without immigrants" looked like.[1] The strike lent momentum to the immigration rights movement and helped to birth a new effort to pass national legislation for a living wage. Latinx workers and their organizations also contributed mightily to the election of Barack Obama, the nation's first African American president. Less than a decade after the big strike, workers chanting, "Fight for fifteen [dollars] and a union!" had joined forces with a reinvigorated Black freedom movement to demand an end to labor exploitation, police violence, and US imperialism.

The general strike was launched in the era of neoliberalism, a political philosophy marked by fiscal austerity, privatization, mass incarceration, and militarism. Seeking to counter the social movements and national labor strikes of the Vietnam War era, corporate-funded Republicans and so-called "New Democrats" destroyed unions, downsized social welfare, cut taxes on the rich, and unleashed the power of banks and corporations through deregulation in order to discipline an insurgent citizenry.[2] After consulting with leading figures from both political parties, the Federal

Reserve chairman, Paul A. Volcker, declared in 1979, "The standard of living of the average American has to decline. I don't think you can escape that."[3] One of neoliberalism's preeminent spokesmen, Thomas Friedman, warned in March 1999 that this experiment in social engineering would require military muscle: "The hidden hand of the market will never work without a hidden fist. McDonald's cannot flourish without McDonnell Douglas, the designer of the F-15. And the hidden fist that keeps the world safe for Silicon Valley's technologies to flourish is called the US Army, Air Force, Navy and Marine Corps."[4] According to the grim tribunes of neoliberalism's ruling class, all claims of equal justice must now be submitted to the grand jury of capitalism.[5]

When the Democratic Leadership Council (DLC) was formed in 1985 it moved the Democratic Party away from African American, Latinx, and working-class constituencies and toward big donors and military-industrial corporations. DLC members in Congress spearheaded punishing domestic and foreign policy measures, including the North American Free Trade Agreement and the Violent Crime Control and Law Enforcement Act, both in 1994, as well as the US invasions of Iraq, in 1990 and 2003.[6] NAFTA increased the pace of deindustrialization in the United States, and neoliberal trade policies hit Latinx and Black workers particularly hard. Yolanda Navarra, a Watsonville, California, cannery worker, observed, "We lost our work here so that these giant companies can go and exploit those of us who remained in Mexico."[7] NAFTA also had a destructive impact on small farmers in Mexico. Texas Fair Trade Coalition organizer Bob Cash notes, "What NAFTA actually did in Mexico was throw 2 million farm families off their farms, many of them forced to come to the U.S. to find work to feed their families."[8]

In the 1990s, agricultural workers on the West Coast were fighting for the rights that many thought had been earned decades earlier. In 1994, Gerard Rios, a Chateau Ste. Michelle vineyard worker, testified before the Washington State Liquor Board using words that could have been spoken generations earlier: "We [farmworkers] have made, through our sweat and sacrifice of our health, the agricultural industry the best in the world. Why don't you come and eat in the fields where I eat and drink the contaminated water that the company gives us?"[9]

The 2000 presidential election, which ended with the Supreme Court choosing the president, demonstrated the linkage between neoliberalism's contempt for democracy and racial injustice. According to the election study conducted by the US Civil Rights Commission, chaired by Mary Frances Berry,

> During the three days of hearings, numerous witnesses delivered heartrending accounts of the frustrations they experienced at the polls. Potential voters confronted inexperienced poll workers, antiquated machinery, inaccessible polling locations, and other barriers to being able to exercise their right to vote. The Commission's findings make one thing clear: widespread voter disenfranchisement—not the dead-heat contest—was the extraordinary feature in the Florida election.[10]

The report emphasized that Haitian American and Latinx voters encountered significant barriers to voting alongside African Americans. In a shocking disregard for the impact of voter suppression on the nation's institutions, the Supreme Court and the Congress gave the election a clean bill of health and placed George W. Bush in office. Disenfranchisement and the demobilization of much of the electorate enabled policies that starved cities such as New Orleans, Detroit, and Flint, Michigan.[11]

The US government's response to Hurricane Katrina in 2005 stunned the world and served as a case study of neoliberalism in action. Federal and state authorities—not to mention the corporate media—depicted working-class people, particularly African Americans and immigrants, as alien outcasts, prone to criminality and depravity.[12] During the crisis, the governor of Louisiana issued shoot-to-kill orders to National Guardsmen, even though soldiers on the ground stated that stories of civilian violence in the New Orleans Superdome and on the streets were grotesquely exaggerated by the media. Regarding the rumors of mass murder and rape in the wake of the hurricane, Sergeant First Class Jason Lachney, who played a key role in security and humanitarian work inside the Dome, where many residents had taken shelter, said, "I think ninety-nine percent of it [media reports] is [expletive]. Don't get me wrong—bad things happened. But I didn't see any killing and raping and cutting of throats or anything. . . . Ninety-nine percent of the people in the Dome were very well-behaved."[13]

Corporations and private investors were the big winners in the wake of the disaster in New Orleans. The state quickly replaced the city's public school system with charter schools. Immigrant workers from Latin America and India were held in debt peonage or saw their wages stolen by employers while hotel and construction firms raked in huge profits from the disaster.[14] Many workers were brought in to New Orleans after the hurricane. One Latina immigrant hotel worker in New Orleans testified, "Every one of us took out a loan to come here. We had planned to pay back our debt with our job here. They told us we would have overtime, that we could get paid for holidays, that we would have a place to live at low cost, and it was all a lie."[15] Because this worker and her Latina coworkers had signed contracts that bound her to one employer they risked forfeiting thousands of dollars if they quit their jobs. "I felt like an animal without claws—defenseless. It is the same as slavery."

A lawyer with the New Orleans–based Loyola Law School Legal Clinic noted, "Since the hurricane we've really seen a meltdown of wage and hour laws, OSHA [the US Occupational Safety and Health Administration] laws, and practically every other standard that exists for work in this country." Luz Molina, another participant in the Loyola legal advocacy program, observed, "The money is going to the big corporations and not to the workers. There is no quality control and no oversight of who they are contracting with."[16]

THE CONTEXT OF HURRICANE KATRINA

"Experts" claimed that Hurricane Katrina had forced the nation's leaders to once again pay attention to race in America; however, that's all they had been doing the previous three decades.[17] Public policies were formulated more on the basis of enhancing the race and class privileges of the few than delivering the greatest good to the many. The nation's policy makers oversaw the resegregation of public education, the shrinking of municipal services, and the wholesale destruction of African American, Puerto Rican, and Mexican American neighborhoods from New York to Arizona in the name of "urban renewal," "slum clearance," and the "planned shrinkage" of minority neighborhoods.[18] The destruction of these neighborhoods was part of a broader counteroffensive against Black and Brown community organizing. This included the murderous withdrawal of fire protection from the South Bronx in an effort to clear city streets for lucrative property development.[19] When city officials in Arlington, Texas, wanted to move working-class Mexican Americans out of the way for a professional football stadium, they declared the neighborhood "blighted" and invoked eminent domain in order to destroy it.[20] The resulting multibillion-dollar Dallas Cowboys' stadium, subsidized with public dollars, symbolizes who contemporary municipal governments work for in the United States—and who they work against.

Simultaneously, the United States built a prison industrial complex that incarcerated more citizens than any other penal system in modern history. The prison population is disproportionately African American and Latinx people. Ostensibly in the prosecution of the War on Drugs, New York and other cities implemented policing practices that fueled the incarceration boom. The historian Carol Anderson notes, "In 1999, blacks and Hispanics, who made up 50 percent of New York City's population, accounted for 84 percent of those stopped and frisked by the NYPD; while the majority of illegal drugs and weapons were found on the relatively small number of whites detained by the police."[21] In 1972, America's correctional facilities held some 333,000 prisoners. By 2000, the inmate population had soared to 1,890,000. As the sociologist Jordan Camp has demonstrated, mass incarceration is in part a corporate and state response to crush insurgencies from below, as well as a mechanism to defend an economic system based on inequality, noting, "Structural unemployment, concentrated urban poverty, and mass homelessness have accordingly become permanent features of the political economy."[22] The United States has literally decided to "incarcerate the crisis" ushered in by neoliberalism. Writes Camp, "Increased spending on incarceration has occurred alongside the reduction of expenditures for public education, transportation, health care, and public-sector employment. Prison expansion has coincided with a shift in the racial composition of prisoners from majority white to almost 70 percent people of color."[23]

The funneling of educational resources toward well-to-do school districts doomed many working-class youth to lives of poverty. In New York, state outlays to local school systems approached a 14:1 ratio in favor of wealthy, predominantly white districts. [24] In 1987, a *New York Post* report revealed that "money earmarked for fighting drug abuse and illiteracy in ghetto schools was funneled instead to schools in wealthy areas."[25] In Hartford, Connecticut, one study found that 93 percent of the schoolchildren in the public schools are either Latino or African American, and "more than two-thirds of the city's students live in poverty. Six minutes away on the highway are affluent, nearly all white suburban, high-achieving school districts that seem a world away."[26] According to the business journalist Eduardo Porter, "The United States is one of few advanced nations where schools serving better-off children usually have more educational resources than those serving poor students."[27]

The nation's policy makers turned to the politics of deception to deal with these grotesque inequalities. Media pundits, foundation leaders, and "think tank" commentators claimed that the nation's greatest fiscal enemies were union workers, Black single mothers, and "illegal immigrants." During the same time period, taxpayers were shaken down to pay for public bailouts of savings and loans institutions, banks, investment firms, and a Pentagon budget so large it could no longer effectively account for how its resources were spent.[28] Between 1981 and 1984, military-industrial firms such as Boeing received $285 million in tax *refunds*. As high-tech firms such as Apple and Microsoft mastered the art of tax avoidance, ordinary people's Medicare and Social Security payroll taxes increased markedly, 22 percent between 1997 and 1999 alone.[29] Ronald Reagan deftly played on the racial animosities of white Americans. He deflected anger from the bitter fruits of trickle-down economics and deindustrialization by promoting the story of an African American woman from "the south side of Chicago." According to Reagan, this conniving "welfare queen" picked up her government checks in a Cadillac. A subsequent investigation by a Pulitzer Prize–winning journalist found that this "welfare queen" was a myth that Reagan had invented on the campaign trail. The woman he described did not exist.[30]

Poverty was racialized, even though the great majority of people living in poverty were—and are—white.[31] Franklin D. Gilliam found that "sixty-two percent of poverty stories that appeared in *Time, Newsweek*, and *US News and World Report* featured African Americans," and "sixty-five percent of network television news stories about welfare featured African Americans."[32] This incessant media barrage had a powerful impact on public perceptions of Blacks. A National Opinion Research Report in 1990 found that a majority of whites believed that African Americans were "innately lazy and less intelligent and patriotic than whites," and preferred welfare to work.[33] After Blacks and other nonwhites had been subjected to three centuries of slavery and nearly a century of Jim Crow labor oppression, this result has to be seen as possibly the most remarkable propaganda coup in American history. It helps to explain why there were no serious efforts to address poverty or to increase wages in the wake of Hurricane Katrina, an event that demonstrated in a startling manner the cost of inequality.

During the civil rights era of the 1960s, Martin Luther King Jr. urged that the lack of economic opportunity be addressed as a collective issue, one to be solved by creating policies to lift millions out of poverty at once.[34] In the era of neoliberalism, by contrast, Americans were trained to see poverty as a behavioral issue primarily concerning minorities, the "underclass," individuals with low IQ, and single mothers.[35] In the 1990s, the *New York Times*, the *New Republic*, and other publications routinely launched attacks on African Americans, and incorrectly claimed that affirmative action benefited minorities when in fact the policy's main beneficiaries have been white women.[36] The relentless anti-Black disinformation campaign reached a new low in 1989 with the hysterical media frame-up of five African American youths—known as the Central Park Five—in the rape of a white woman in New York City's Central Park. Liberals and conservatives joined hands to indict the teenagers without a modicum of evidence. New York businessman Donald Trump built his political career by whipping up public sentiment against the youths. Subsequently, it was revealed that police had coerced the confessions of the teenagers, and they were exonerated in 2002, after serving their prison sentences.[37]

PRELUDE TO A GENERAL STRIKE

In 2005, members of Congress, led by Wisconsin Republican Jim Sensenbrenner, began crafting the Border Protection, Anti-Terrorism, and Illegal Immigration Act, whose result would have been to turn undocumented workers and those who assisted them into felons. The lives of immigrant laborers, including Latinx workers, were precarious to begin with. "Aside from South Africa's pass system," Elizabeth "Betita" Martinez noted, "it is hard to imagine any mechanism in modern times so well designed to control, humiliate, and disempower vast numbers of workers than the [US-Mexico] border and its requirements."[38] Going back to first causes, the desperate conditions created by US-sponsored coups and civil wars in Latin America forced many people to flee from the region making them all the more vulnerable to exploitation when they arrived in the United States.[39]

Immigrants often pay labor contractors thousands of dollars to work in seasonal and unstable occupations in agriculture, construction, and service industries. When these workers arrive in the United States, they find themselves in debt and victimized by firms who sometimes force them to work for little or no wages.[40] They are virtually enslaved. Lucas Benitez of the Coalition of Immokalee Workers in South Florida explained that farm laborers were caught in a terrible trap: "It's a fundamental problem in Immokalee that the workers get no respect from the growers," Benitez noted. "The growers think they have peons, not employees."[41] The Anti-Slavery International bestowed the 2007 Anti-Slavery Award on the Coalition of Immokalee Workers for its work in exposing slavery in Florida agriculture.[42]

Latinx workers in the United States were anything but passive. Workers in the meat- and poultry-processing industries were especially active in fighting to improve their working conditions. Latinx workers at the four-thousand-worker Smithfield Foods plant in Tarheel, North Carolina, tried to unionize for well over a decade.[43] High processing and packaging line speeds in these factories translated into very high levels of laceration of workers' hands, repetitive motion, and cumulative trauma injuries.[44] Workers who are injured on the job are often pressured by supervisors to hide their injuries in order to save their firms money. Historically, poultry and meat processing were unionized and paid well. Now, however, according to a Human Rights Watch exposé of the poultry and meat processing industries, "many workers who try to form trade unions and bargain collectively are spied on, harassed, pressured, threatened, suspended, fired, deported or otherwise victimized for their exercise of the right to freedom of association."[45]

North Carolina, a state where more than three hundred thousand Latinx people moved to in the 1990s, was a hotbed of movement organizing. One example of Black-Brown coalition building occurred during the 2001 Juneteenth celebration in Raleigh, jointly organized by the Farm Labor Organizing Committee, Black Workers for Justice, and United Electrical Workers Local 150. FLOC was in the midst of a difficult organizing campaign that led to the union's calling a boycott of the Mt. Olive Pickle Company.[46] African Americans had traditionally celebrated Juneteenth to commemorate the abolition of slavery in Texas. The 2001 event was organized "in the spirit of the freed Texas slaves" and was intended to "celebrate the end of chattel slavery, and celebrate unity of Black and Latino workers in the new movement for justice in the South."[47] The organizers' joint statement argued that immigrant workers had been "forced by unjust global economic policies to leave their homes and endure slave-like conditions." The event organizers formulated a list of demands that spoke to the historic struggles of the working class:

> The Juneteenth celebration will focus on the following issues:
>
> An end to racial profiling;
> Amnesty for undocumented workers;
> The rights of workers to organize into unions (including support for the Mt. Olive Pickles boycott and support for organizing efforts by public employees);
> A living wage for all workers;
> Language and culture rights; and
> Reparations for African Americans, Black Farmers, and Mexican Braceros.[48]

Meanwhile, Guatemalan immigrant workers at the Case Farms poultry plant in Morganton, North Carolina, engaged in a broad range of protests against low wages and substandard working conditions, including petitions, strikes, and union organizing. In the summer of 2005, Case Farm employees struck and began to organize a new union after management refused to slow production lines and issue appropriate safety equipment.[49] This struggle followed years of in-plant organizing by Latinx workers that achieved union recognition votes, raises, and safer working conditions in the plant. Most of the original cohort of employees at Case Farms were Highland Mayans who had skills in administering cooperatives, community committees (*comités cívicos*), and leadership committees (*directivas*) in Guatemala.[50] These immigrants came to the United States with the knowledge and experience that collective organization paid dividends. The union organizer Luz Rodriguez stated, "We have to stand up for ourselves. We must defend our rights."[51]

THE GREAT AMERICAN STRIKE

When migrant laborers, Nuyoricans, Chicana/os, Afro-Cubanos, Guatemaltecos, and immigrants from every part of earth united on May Day in 2006, they protested immigration restriction measures that threatened their families, their livelihoods, and their dignity. The testimonials featured on picket signs, in interviews, and on the Internet and other venues opened a window into the resurgence of working-class political culture. The demonstrators vigorously expressed their opposition to US House Resolution 4437.[52] Latinx workers restored the age-old faith that racial capitalism had tried to drown out, that labor was the true source of the nation's wealth. Yolanda Lopez, a custodian and union organizer in California, stated, "We consider that as workers without faces, we are the ghosts who clean but never have any type of recognition. So I think that this is a very good fight we have now, which is to try to gain equality and respect." Lopez and her *compañeras* were fighting for better wages and working conditions, but they were also looking for recognition of their humanity as women and as immigrant workers: "With equality we will get a more just salary. And with respect we feel more honored as a human being. We are here. I have a face, I have a name, and I am here."[53]

Millions marched down main streets across the country shouting "*¡Sí, se puede!*"—Yes, we can!—and carried signs proclaiming, "You Might Hate Us/But You Need Us," "Primo de Mayo, a Day Without a Mexican," and "This Land Is Your Land, This Land Is Our Land." In New York City, Latinx workers were joined by thousands of African Americans as well as Jamaican, Irish, and Chinese immigrants who added their voices to the protests.[54] Reflecting on her experience marching in Los Angeles, Sonja Marie Diaz reflected, "To me, May Day is an extension of transnational social movements; something that transcends borders and embodies the experience of people of color everywhere." Diaz, the daughter of United Farm Worker parents who had been activists in the 1960s, stressed the continuity of struggle that May Day represented for her: "Growing up in Los Angeles as a third-generation Chicana, protesting was part of my history. From the displacement of my grandparents due to unfair land laws and zoning, to discrimination in schools, and illegal labor treatment in the fields, my family was on the front lines advocating for their survival and justice for all."[55] Maria Padilla, a university dining hall employee and union organizer at the University of California, Santa Cruz, talked about the importance of students and workers coming together in an internationalist endeavor:

> I think the most positive thing today, for me, was to see the unity between workers and students. To see that united we have the strength and will be heard. . . . And I am not only here fighting for the workers who are here in this country. I think of those who are [in Mexico] who are in the maquiladoras, in the fields, and in the factories. Where they are mistreated and only get paid twenty-five cents an hour, and they are forced to work for long hours. I am also fighting for them here.[56]

The Great American Strike shut down meat packing, garment manufacturing, port transportation, trucking, and food service in many parts of the country.[57] Several days in advance of the gigantic protest, dubbed by some organizers as "A Day Without Immigrants," the companies Cargill, Tyson Foods, and the Seaboard Corporation announced that they would be closing their operations due to a lack of personnel.[58] Customers of fast-food franchises in California were turned away by apologetic managers who explained that "Mexican truckers" had refused to deliver bread. The May Day protests followed an earlier wave of walkouts that occurred in March and April. These incipient strikes were led in many cases by agricultural and construction workers seeking to boost their wages and to escape poverty conditions.[59] "In South Florida and Immokalee, [harvesting] pretty much ground to a halt," said G. Ellis Hunt Jr., president of Hunt Bros., a Florida grower and packinghouse owner with more than five thousand grove acres split equally between Polk and Immokalee counties.[60]

In the weeks leading up to International Workers' Day, the union organizer Jorge Rodriguez vowed, "There will be 2 to 3 million people hitting the streets in Los Angeles [on May 1] alone. We're going to close down Los Angeles, Chicago, New York, Tucson, Phoenix, Fresno. . . . We want full amnesty, full legalization for anybody who is here. That is the message that is going to be played out across the country on May 1."[61] Latinx workers organized the demonstrations through the social institutions that had helped sustain their communities, including *comités cívicos* from their home countries, workers' centers, labor unions, Catholic Church social justice committees, sports clubs, and civil rights organizations. Many of the regions that witnessed high turnouts of Latinx workers in the May Day protests had long histories of Latinx economic and social justice organizing.[62]

One of the most popular picket signs on May Day vowed *"Hoy Marchamos, Mañana Votamos"*—"Today We March, Tomorrow We Vote." The historian Ruth Milkman notes, "Soon after the marches, the We Are America Alliance and many other organizations launched naturalization and voter registration drives. These efforts had already begun to yield fruit by the November 2006 [midterm] elections."[63] As Milkman observed, the general strike prepared the way for new kinds of political movements rooted in the everyday concerns of the working classes. María Elena Durazo used the momentum generated by the Great American Strike to call for a new living-wage movement.[64] Durazo was the daughter of migrant farmworkers, and she herself picked fruits and vegetables as a young girl in the 1960s. Like so many young Latinas of her generation she was inspired by the United Farm Workers to become a labor activist; she eventually rose to become the executive secretary–treasurer of the Los Angeles County Federation of Labor.

Magnifying the lessons of May Day, 2006, Durazo said, "We must build a movement with thousands of leaders and millions of supporters that can pressure elected officials and corporations to do the right thing. When we build a movement of the working poor, we will have the power to end poverty."[65] Subsequently Durazo was one of the first major Latina leaders in the United States to endorse Barack Obama during the Democratic primaries in 2008. Explaining her endorsement, Durazo said, "On a personal level [Obama] embodies the slogan we use a lot, Cesar Chavez's 'Sí, se puede.' He has proved it by the way he inspires voters."[66] The Illinois senator had actually learned his signature slogan from the farmworker movement, which the UFW cofounder Dolores Huerta pointedly reminded him of in 2008.[67]

International Workers' Day organizers began weaving together new alliances for social justice. "The diversity of organizations proved that May Day and fighting for immigrant rights was bigger than a 'Latino' fight," Danae Tapia, one of the student organizers of the strike movement in Central California, wrote. "We all tied the injustices that we faced with immigration, borders, war and an unfair education system. For example, Palestine and Mexico; undocumented students and undocumented workers; unequal access to education & unfair wages; war in the Middle East & wars around the world that force people to migrate, etc."[68] Tapia's coalition that prepared for May Day mobilizations included white unionists, longtime Chicano *movimiento* people, undocumented college students, socialists, and many more. This was an alliance that was sustained in subsequent union and immigration rights drives due to its breadth and depth. "Because of the diversity of organizations," Tapia observed, "our action was so much stronger and that's how we continued our marches and actions the years that followed because the injustices that we all faced were intertwined with each other. Our local fight is a global fight."[69] The Latinx-led labor insurrections of 2006 provided the first hints of the beginning of a sea change in American politics.

In the wake of the Great American Strike, the percentage of

workers joining unions increased for the first time in a generation. The Labor Council for Latin American Advancement reported, "Close to 30 percent of the growth is attributed to Latinos who added 120,000 members to the labor movement."[70] At the gigantic Smithfield Foods plant in Tarheel, North Carolina, Latinx workers walked off of the job with their African American and white counterparts on Martin Luther King Jr. Day in 2007. The union organizer Eduardo Peña told the media, "We've got Latino workers here ready to walk out for the holiday. I hear them saying things like, 'People assume that we don't know who King was—his struggle was the same struggle we're going through now.'"[71] Subsequently, the United Food and Commercial Workers won a union representation election at the four-thousand-worker plant after sixteen years of trying.[72] These gains built on the increase in Latinx workers who had organized and joined unions in the preceding decade.[73]

Insurgency and organization were the new watchwords of the working class.[74] Less than a month after Obama's election, workers at the Bank of America–controlled Republic Windows and Doors in Chicago seized control of their factory after managers announced that they were unilaterally closing the plant. Even though Bank of America had recently received a $25 billion taxpayer bailout from the public, Republic employees were informed that they would receive no severance pay. What the bank did not count on, however, was the resolve of its 240 employees: "A mostly African-American and immigrant Latino workforce," Jerry Mead-Lucero noted, "they organized into [United Electrical Workers] Local 1110 four years ago after dumping a company union that had agreed to a wage freeze and had allowed dozens of workers to be fired with no protest." After shutting out the bosses, Republic Windows employees called on the community for support, and soon the plant was surrounded by hundreds of supporters for nearly a week. Faith-based organizations provided strike assistance. Jerry Mead-Lucero described how "supporters appeared at the factory's entrance bearing gifts of food, coffee, blankets, and sleeping bags. They signed posters that workers taped to the factory walls, with messages like 'Thanks for showing us all how to fight back' and 'You are an inspiration to us all.'"[75] The first sit-down strike waged by American workers in years earned the work force a severance package and public support from Barack Obama and served as an inspiration to others that organizing is worth it.[76]

THE ELECTION OF BARACK OBAMA

A significant amount of Barack Obama's election and reelection efforts in California and Florida—states with large populations of Latinx workers—hinged on the energy of local labor councils in canvassing, multilingual phone banking, and other outreach activities. Many of the activists in these labor councils, from all racial and ethnic backgrounds, had earned their organizers' stripes during the Great American Strike. Was Senator Barack Obama's 2008 election victory an example of postracial politics? Not according to the exit polls, which demonstrated the crucial role of race *and* class in the election.[77] Despite the claims of some in the corporate media that Latinx people would "never vote for a black man," black and Latinx support was crucial in Obama's victory in key states, including Nevada, Colorado, New Mexico, and Florida. Nationally, 55 percent of white Americans voted for Senator John McCain, with the white college graduate vote split nearly evenly for the two major contenders.[78] In contrast, 96 percent of African Americans, 67 percent of Latinx Americans, and 63 percent of Asian Americans voted for Obama. In Florida, Obama won a remarkably high percentage of the Hispanic vote, even though some conservative Cubanos in South Florida featured car bumper stickers that read "Cuba Voted for Change in 1959."[79] On the day after the election, the *Miami Herald* observed that Obama was the "first Democrat[ic] candidate to win Florida's Hispanic vote."[80] In South Florida, an epicenter of the strike, Latinx workers—even noncitizens—were a decisive part of Election Day 2012. According to Gihan Perera, "In Homestead [Florida] undocumented workers who couldn't even vote pitched in with a mariachi band and barbecue" to encourage thousands of African Americans, Latinos, and progressive whites to stay in line and cast their ballot.[81]

Intergenerational organizing was pivotal in Obama's election.

Many of the canvassers and door-to-door organizers in the vaunted "Obama Ground Game" in 2008 were veterans of the Student Non-violent Coordinating Committee, the United Farm Workers, the Chicano Moratorium, the Young Lords, the Black Panther Party for Self-Defense, and the National Rainbow Coalition.

In the months leading up to the 2012 presidential election, nearly three hundred thousand Latinos, African Americans, and Asian American workers organized and joined unions.[82] Workers' strike activity increased significantly around the time of the election. "The number of union-related work stoppages involving more than 1,000 workers, which reached an all-time low of just five in 2009, rose to 13 this year as of October. And unions aren't done yet," reported the *Los Angeles Times*.[83] Weathered by their experiences in fighting for immigration and living-wage and voter-protection laws, an increasing number of organizers linked social movement activism with electoral politics. On Election Day, African Americans and Latinx voters in Florida waited six to eight hours to vote in Orlando and Miami. "Voter suppression is not something that is new to our community and neither is our reaction," said the NAACP's Marvin Randolph. "If you look back to the civil rights movement, we passed the hat around and raised money to pay the poll taxes. And there were literacy tests. We educated our community to be able to say whatever you had to say to pass those literacy tests. Just as we did this time, we educated."[84] Nationally, Latinx voters chose Barack Obama by a 71 percent margin over the Republican contender, Mitt Romney.[85] "This poll makes clear what we've known for a long time," Eliseo Medina, secretary treasurer of the Service Employees International Union commented. "The Latino giant is wide awake, cranky, and it's taking names."[86]

BACKLASH

The reaction against African American and Latinx political and labor organizing has been relentless. The US Immigration and Customs Enforcement (ICE) has carried out so-called "immigration raids" in many workplaces where Latinx people were trying to organize unions.[87] These raids are ostensibly carried out to enforce immigration laws, but the labor journalist David Bacon sees them differently: "If anything, ICE seems intent on punishing undocumented workers who earn too much, or who become too visible by demanding higher wages and organizing unions."[88] During the Smithfield Foods organizing campaign, local government officials assisted the firm by distributing anti-union propaganda at the workplace. Subsequently, state investigators responded to workers' safety complaints by haranguing them about their union sympathies. The federal government later targeted this same factory complex for a raid on suspected illegal immigrants. The union activist Julio Vargas affirms that Latinx and African American workers believed that the government raided their plant "because people were getting organized."[89] Workers seeking to improve their economic conditions faced opposition from company management as well as local, state, and federal officials. A Human Rights Watch report on American workplaces concludes that "freedom of association is a right under severe, often buckling pressure when workers in the United States try to exercise it."[90] Until the right to organize is guaranteed, efforts to address inequality and poverty will be doomed to failure.

The Voting Rights Act of 1965, a key achievement of the civil rights movement, has been a continuous target of reactionary forces in American politics.[91] The act had helped to protect the voting rights of African Americans, Latinx people, Haitian immigrants, and many other groups that had been historically discriminated against and disenfranchised. Between 2010 and 2013, however, Republican-dominated legislatures in thirty-one states passed scores of bills designed to restrict voting rights in order to constrict democracy.[92] Recent advocates of voting restrictions claimed that Hispanic "illegal immigrants" in Florida and other states threatened to "decide the next presidential election."[93] The US Supreme Court lent its imprimatur to the restriction tidal wave by formally abrogating the Voting Rights Act in 2013.[94] "Chief Justice John Roberts Jr., writing for the majority, declared that the Voting Rights Act had done its job, and it was time to move on," wrote the *New York Times*' Jim Rutenberg. "Republican state legislators proceeded with a new round of even more restrictive voting laws."[95] In response, new as well as older grassroots liberation movements such as the Dream Defenders in Florida, the Mexican American Legal Defense

Fund, and the NAACP launched voter registration and protection efforts nationwide.[96]

Racial profiling in policing is part of the backlash to suppress working-class people and to boost dwindling tax revenues by turning low-income communities into cash cows to fund municipalities through the issuance of bench warrants, traffic tickets, and fines.[97] In one example of "broken windows" policing—based on the theory that prosecuting minor crimes will prevent major ones and which fueled mass incarceration in minority-majority neighborhoods—individuals in Pagedale, Missouri, were fined if their residences had chipped paint or mismatched curtains.[98] In 2010, Arizona moved to enhance the power of the police to detain immigrants. Crafted by the pro-corporate American Legislative Exchange Council and supported by firms that run for-profit prisons positioned to benefit from the detention of immigrants, Arizona's Senate Bill 1070 made racial profiling the de facto law of the state.[99] Racial profiling allows law enforcement authorities to target minorities for questioning and arrest. An investigative report conducted by the NAACP discovered that thirty states "have some form of racial profiling laws on the books," and that no state engaged in training or data collection to ensure that law enforcement officers did not racially profile individuals.[100] Bryan Stevenson, the founder of Equal Justice Initiative, observed, "We have a system that treats you much better if you're rich and guilty than if you're poor and innocent. Wealth, not culpability, shapes outcome."[101] Advocates of racial profiling invoked stereotypes enhanced by Hollywood films and television shows to argue that Latinx people, Arab Americans, and African Americans were criminals.[102]

African American critics of Arizona's SB 1070 pointed out that the law criminalizes Latinx people the way that Jim Crow criminalized African Americans. "To my . . . black brothers and sisters who think this is not your fight," said the Reverend Al Sharpton, "let me tell you something: after dark, we all look Mexican right now."[103] Legendary rapper Chuck D from Public Enemy reworked a song that once protested Arizona's opposition to the Martin Luther King Jr. holiday into an anthem against SB 1070 titled "Tear Down That Wall."[104] At the 2010 May Day Immigration Rally in Washington, DC, the Reverend Jesse Jackson compared Arizona today with repressive Selma in 1965 and urged a boycott of the state.[105] Congresswoman Barbara Lee called SB 1070 a "national disgrace," noting, "It harkens back to the era of Jim Crow or apartheid in South Africa."[106]

Concurrently, the passage of Arizona House Bill 2281 was part of a national move to roll back the efforts of schools to offer courses on the contributions of racial minorities in the development of the United States.[107] The bill targeted a Mexican American studies program based in Tucson's Unified School District that had markedly increased student success and graduation rates.[108] Considered together, SB 1070 and HB 2281 were efforts to erase the spirit of the nascent Latinx social movement that formed the base of the May Day protests.

Arizona's HB 2281 fueled a nationwide response by ethnic studies educators in K–12 schools, as well in communities that demanded that the school districts begin to include the stories of Chicanos, Koreans, Chinese, and African Americans in the building of the United States. In response to a grassroots petition campaign, the Los Angeles Unified School District made ethnic studies learning a requirement for high school graduation in 2014.[109] The State of California considered following suit.

THE FUTURE IN THE PAST

In 2013, Barack Obama traveled to Las Vegas—the most heavily unionized city in the United States—to make a signature speech on the need for comprehensive immigration reform. To understand why Obama traveled to Vegas at that moment reveals the distance that African American and Latinx workers have traveled in the United States. Las Vegas is home to one of the most powerful unions in the Americas, Culinary Workers Union Local 226, an organization built and led largely by working-class women of color who are maids, custodians, and food service workers on the Las Vegas Strip and beyond.[110] Local 226 was one of the first major unions in the West to endorse Obama during the presidential primary season of 2008.[111] During the election campaign, then Senator Obama openly endorsed two of the union's strikes, saying, "I have been on the picket line for years with workers in Illinois, and if workers in Nevada are forced to strike I will be standing on their side as well."[112]

The sixty thousand members of the Culinary Workers Union Local 226 hail from eighty-four different nations, and the local has been led by working-class women since the union's six-year Frontier Strike in the 1990s. Without their endorsement, it is quite likely that Obama would not have been elected to the White House. Herein lies the symbolic power of his speech on immigration as well as the transformations in American life that it reveals. In the 1990s, the Culinary Workers grew to prominence led by the African American unionist Hattie Canty, who migrated from rural Alabama in the late 1950s. In contrast to George Meany, the head of the AFL-CIO from 1955 to 1979, who bragged that he had never been on a picket line, Canty led a strike where not a single one of the hundreds of strikers crossed the picket line. "Coming from Alabama, [to me]," Canty observed, "this seemed like the civil rights struggle. . . . The labor movement and the civil rights movement, you cannot separate the two of them."[113] Whether they hail from Alabama, Thailand, Central America, or someplace else, the members of Local 226 represent the potential future promise of the Americas. At the end of the Frontier Strike, the bosses hired back all of the original strikers, and the owner of the chain "said he was happy to have the strikers back since they showed nerve and moxie throughout the 6½ year strike."[114]

The circumstances surrounding President Obama's Las Vegas speech encapsulates the existence of larger currents of protest that may yet create an expansion of democracy. True, the effort at comprehensive immigration reform in 2013 failed. However, the strikes, boycotts, and extensive organizing campaigns undertaken against the neoliberal backlash demonstrate that working-class politics is not dead. One thing is beyond dispute: African American and Latinx organizers are drawing on the lessons of history to build momentum for social justice struggles. Student immigrant DREAM activists achieved state and national victories, while service workers from Miami to Seattle engaged in rallies and civil disobedience in support of the goal "$15 and a union," a demand that seemed impossible only a decade earlier.[115] The first national conference of Fight for $15 organizers was held in Richmond, Virginia, the former capital of the Confederacy, "to highlight how racism and anti-union hostility combine to trap an estimated 64 million Americans in jobs that pay less than $15 an hour."[116] Invoking history in his keynote address to an energized audience, the Reverend William Barber II observed, "It took us 400 years from slavery to the present to reach $7.25, but we can't wait another 400 years."[117]

The Black Lives Matter movement, composed of scores of local and national organizations such as the Dream Defenders in Florida, emerged as a leading national force against inequality. Initially focused on police homicides of African Americans, Black Lives Matter quickly connected anti-Black violence to other forms of oppression. In 2013, the Florida Dream Defenders described the destructive power of the system they were battling:

> In every corner of our country, we find the cancer of an unchecked correctional system. It is ravaging our state and our black and brown communities in particular. . . . We are black, brown, poor and minority. A system that seeks to incarcerate us now invigorates our fight for freedom. We have dedicated our lives to battling the criminalization of our generation. A system that once divided us now unifies us. The Dream Defenders are that opposition.[118]

Black Lives Matter activists joined together economic justice, anti-imperial, and prison abolition concerns to draft a platform in 2016, titled "A Vision for Black Lives." This document was the foremost statement of emancipatory internationalism in the twenty-first century. It pointed out the terrible costs paid by people in the Global South for the United States' permanent War on Terror. "A Vision for Black Lives" criticized US imperialism in Latin America and misguided foreign policies that led to the oppression of others in the Global South.[119] Bakari Kitwana notes, "A public policy agenda hell-bent on elite wealth accumulation at the expense of the majority poor has, ironically, politicized a defiant generation whose brand of resistance insists that the criminal justice system will no longer have the last say."[120]

Donald Trump's 2016 presidential campaign gained traction by attacking Muslims, African Americans, and Latinx peoples as depraved and violence-prone. Blatantly ignoring two centuries of emancipatory internationalism in the United States, Trump vowed to build a wall to segregate the United States from Mexico and the rest of Latin America. James Brown, an African American probation officer in Lithonia, Georgia, took offense to Donald Trump's campaign slogan "Make America Great Again," because of the obliviousness to the true history of the United States that it displayed. In 1923, the Ku Klux Klan in Kissimmee, Florida, had mobilized to lynch Brown's great-grandfather, Oscar Mack. The KKK targeted Mack because he had accepted a well-paying US Postal Service job hitherto reserved for whites. After a gun battle in which he killed two of his attackers, Oscar Mack fled on foot to the North. For much of the rest of his life, Mack lived under an assumed name, on the run from white terrorists. Mack's great-grandson vowed to turn a family tragedy into a story of redemption and reconciliation:

> This means a lot to me. Not only for him, but for all of the other people who are lying in their graves who were never heard, who were treated not even as second class citizens in this country. Not only for Black people, but for Hispanics, for women, for any other minority group if you will. We had talked about the fact that our government is saying "Make America Great Again." I cannot see where she was ever great. The bare fact is that in this country over fifty million Native Americans were murdered, and Black people were enslaved, and other ethnic groups were disenfranchised. So it was never great, but I do believe now because of the stories that are surfacing, we can use these as a tool to bring people out of their ignorance.[121]

If American history serves as a guide, not even the president of the United States can stem the tide of grassroots freedom movements and the ability of people throughout the hemisphere to draw inspiration from each other's struggles. An African American and Latinx history of the United States teaches us that the self-activity of the most oppressed is the key to liberty in the future of the Americas.

EPILOGUE

A NEW ORIGIN NARRATIVE OF AMERICAN HISTORY

I had to leave the United States to begin to understand it. As a soldier in the US Special Forces in Central America in the mid-1980s, I encountered Augusto Sandino everywhere I went. Murals of the Nicaraguan revolutionary's image and his sayings were ubiquitous. Governments that aligned themselves with US interests viewed Sandino's words as seditious. No sooner had the local *policía* scrubbed Sandino's words "Come, you pack of morphine addicts; come to kill us in our own land" off the side of one building, than rebel artists would write, "We will go to the sun of freedom or to death," on a wall across town. My ignorance led me to believe that Augusto César Sandino (1895–1934) was still alive and that he was our greatest enemy.

Over two decades later, then a historian, I stumbled upon Augusto Sandino once again. This time I encountered a living, breathing guerrilla leader whose exploits were lionized in the Black press. The Baltimore *Afro-American*, the *Pittsburgh Courier*, and the *Norfolk Journal and Guide* celebrated Sandino as a hero fighting white supremacy and the United States' invasion of Nicaragua. These two meetings with Augusto Sandino taught me that American exceptionalism, the idea that the United States is the freest nation on earth, the champion of the oppressed, and can do no wrong—or at least never intends to do wrong—is a myth. The African American writers who recorded Sandino's exploits knew that the government that denied their citizenship had not sent the Marines to Nicaragua to promote democracy. Decades later, the people of Central America deployed the words of Sandino against me and my fellow soldiers as a reminder that their battle against *our* imperialism was resilient and longstanding.

Years would pass before I finally understood that the idea that the United States could bring democracy to Central America in the 1980s was only possible because we were ignorant of the bloodshed we had inflicted on that region. But the innocence that Americans claim regarding their actions overseas is viewed by the citizens of the Global South as a kind of national disease emanating out from Washington, DC. Mexico's Carlos Fuentes laments, "So we are left with this final image of the United States: a democracy inside but an empire outside; Dr. Jekyll at home, Mr. Hyde in Latin America."[1] What blinded my generation to the history of US imperialism are the doctrine of American exceptionalism and the myth of isolationism. Both ideas are firmly disproved when we approach US history from African American and Latinx perspectives.

If American exceptionalism is a harmful fable, then what do we replace it with? We can begin by continuing to learn more about ordinary people's capacity to create democracy in action. One of the great benefits of comparative ethnic studies is the opportunity it affords to explore the capacity of workers, immigrants, and marginalized people to organize for social change. Two of the best case studies of social-movement building may be found in the mass strikes launched by African Americans and Latinx people at two perilous moments in the history of the republic. The Black workers' general strike against slavery saved the Union, and this is the core of Frederick Douglass's observation, in 1863: "But we are not to be saved by the captain, at this time, but by the crew. We are not to be saved by Abraham Lincoln, but by that power behind the throne, greater than the throne itself." This egalitarian logic was on display a century and a half later when the Great American Strike restored the ideas of international solidarity and the dignity of labor to American politics. Whether one looks at events such as the making of the Underground Railroad to Mexico in the 1820s or the 1968 Memphis Sanitation Workers Strike, it is an incontestable fact that the United States advances the most when its most oppressed people achieve power and control over their lives.

Though this history in this book has been told from the perspectives of people whose ancestors hail from Africa, Latin America, and the Caribbean, it is in fact a universal tale. It is the story of anyone who has ever tried to live on poverty wages or no wages at all. It is a portrait of a people who believed that freedom should be enjoyed equally by all. It is the chronicle of individuals who lived their entire lives with their backs against the wall, and still had the faith to build a social movement that led Martin Luther King Jr. to say, "We must rapidly begin the shift from a thing-oriented society to a person-oriented society. When machines and computers, profit motives and property rights, are considered more important than people, the giant triplets of racism, extreme materialism, and militarism are incapable of being conquered."[2]

Teaching American history honestly means ending the unforgivable silences surrounding the debts of gratitude we owe to Haiti, Mexico, and Latin America generally in demonstrating through words and deeds the meanings of justice and freedom. Generations of people in the United States drew inspiration and lessons from the Haitian Revolution, the Mexican War of Independence, and the Cuban War of Liberation, among many other struggles. Scholars should continue to research the threads of emancipation that people in the Americas have attempted to weave together. At this writing, we have only scratched the surface. At his inauguration in 2006, Evo Morales, Bolivia's first Indigenous president, framed a national campaign for autonomy from neoliberalism into a hemispheric-wide liberation struggle: "And above all, I want to say to our Indigenous brothers and sisters who have gathered here in Bolivia: the campaign of 500 years of Indigenous—Black—popular resistance has not been in vain."[3]

We must give credit to immigrants of the Global South for sharing practical visions of liberation that have reinvigorated civic culture in the United States. A basic knowledge of the battles fought by the ancestors of today's immigrants—whether they hail from Latin America or elsewhere—is important if we are to understand contemporary US politics. For example, the oft-ignored role of the citizens of Mexico as carriers of traditions of social democracy to the United States needs to be better understood. Mexican migrants to the United States hail from a country that abolished slavery long before the United States, fought off repeated imperial invasions from Europe, and promoted ideals of sharing the nation's wealth on a roughly equal basis.

Inequality in American life today is not the result of abstract market forces, nor is it the consequence of the now-discredited "culture of poverty" thesis. From the outset, inequality was enforced with the whip, the gun, and the United States Constitution. Jim Crow and Juan Crow laws, backed by law enforcement and paramilitary organizations such as the Ku Klux Klan, stood like flaming sentinels against Black and Brown progress. African Americans and Latinx people were forcibly brought or recruited to the United States to toil and to do work that others could not or would not do. Their labor built this nation, but they were not fairly compensated for their work. Instead, they were starved, tortured, traumatized, and murdered for attempting to exercise rights that others took for granted. When Martin Luther King Jr. was assassinated in Memphis, farmworker organizers in California immediately understood that he had been "killed helping workers to organize."

This history leads me to strongly endorse the demand of African American and Latinx workers in North Carolina who in 2001 called for "reparations for African Americans, Black Farmers, and Mexican Braceros."[4] Centuries of state-sponsored expropriation of labor power, land, resources, and human rights demand redress. The mechanisms for creating reparations policies have been soundly presented by William Darity.[5] He and Darrick Hamilton have also proposed the idea of "public provision of a substantial trust fund for newborns from families that are wealth-poor," in order to finally achieve something approaching equality in the United States.[6] We must finally prove that we are a society based on fairness and equality of opportunities, or else abandon this rhetoric altogether.

As I finish the writing of this book, the United States is facing a period of deep crisis. The Supreme Court has placed even more power in the hands of corporations. Firms pay enormous bonuses to Wall Street CEOs who have been bailed out by public funds. At the same time, 63 percent of school teachers in the United States report that "they buy food for hungry students every month," while 21 percent of children in the richest nation on earth live in poverty.[7] This economy is the heir of racial capitalism, a system in which the accumulation of wealth takes priority over the healthy development of the individual, hence betraying the basic human instinct for freedom. African American and Latinx people have challenged and fought this system for centuries, and a careful study of their histories certainly offers clues on how to confront the current social emergencies faced by increasing numbers of Americans.

Many of today's politicians want to build barriers, both literal and figurative, to divide nations; the individuals highlighted in this book struggled to bring the hemisphere's people together. The United States continues to deny citizenship to millions of this nation's hardest workers despite a rich tradition of emancipatory internationalism that envisioned a new kind of citizenship spanning the Americas. There is a great beauty in this history, which confirms Elizabeth Martinez's insight: "We can choose to believe the destiny of the United States is still manifest: global domination. Or we can seek a transformative vision that carries us forward, not backward. We can seek an origin narrative that lays the groundwork for a multicultural identity centered on the goals of social equity and democracy. We do have choices."[8]

ACKNOWLEDGMENTS

Writing a new interpretation of US history is a humbling experience, a collective effort made possible by many teachers, students, and movement elders who taught me to listen carefully and to pay attention to details. At Bremerton High School, Don Bidwell gave me a literary foundation in Richard Wright, Joseph Conrad, and Shakespeare. At Olympic Community College, Philip Schaeffer and David Toren showed me how history and philosophy can change lives. At Evergreen State College, Stephanie Coontz, Beryl Crowe, and Tom Grissom trained me to ask meaningful and rigorous historical questions. At Duke University, William H. Chafe, Charles Payne, Lawrence Goodwyn, Raymond Gavins, Nancy Hewitt, and Julius Scott demonstrated through personal example that being a university professor and a community organizer were not mutually exclusive vocations.

My father, Paul Pedro Ortiz, and my mother, Johnine Powell MacDonald, instilled in me a love of learning from an early age. (Dad also read the entire manuscript and patiently corrected errors.) My *abuelas*, Tulles Martínez and Julia Martínez Reyna, ensured that our family survived the long nightmare of Juan Crow. My uncle Leonard Ortiz shared with me a piece of family history on the long drive between Houston and San Antonio that helped me frame a significant part of this book.

I am grateful to the following institutions for giving me the opportunity to present ideas and to receive critiques on the manuscript-in-progress: the University of Florida Center for Latin American Studies Research Symposium; the John W. Davidson Lecture Series, Fort Valley State University; the Duke University Human Rights Center Symposium; the Rutgers University Center for Historical Analysis; the University of South Florida, Tampa Office of Community Engagement and Partnerships—Poverty, Equity, and Social Justice Program; the Department of History and the Center on Democracy in a Multiracial Society, University of Illinois Urbana-Champaign; Latino Americans: 500 Years of History Series, Santa Fe College; Symposium in Pan African Studies, Clemson University; the Virginia Tech Department of History's "Legacies of Reconstruction" Speakers Series; and the Columbia University Oral History Master of Arts Speakers Series.

I am immensely thankful for the criticism and ideas offered by commentators and audience members at the following panels and conferences held between 2006 and 2016: A New Vision of Black Freedom: The Manning Marable Memorial Conference, Columbia University; Confronting Racial Capitalism: The Black Radical Tradition, Graduate Center, City University of New York; The Long Civil Rights Movement: Histories, Politics, Memories, Methods, Southern Oral History Program, University of North Carolina, Chapel Hill; Monuments and Memory: Race and History, Duke University Center for the Study of Race, Ethnicity, and Gender in the Social Sciences; Chicanas/os and Latinas/os Read James Baldwin: A Roundtable Discussion, East Side Café, El Sereno, East Los Angeles.

While putting the final touches on this manuscript, I benefited incalculably from being able to share ideas with colleagues as a Havens Center for Social Justice visiting scholar at the University of Wisconsin, Madison, in the fall of 2016. I am also grateful to the Department of History and to the College of Liberal Arts and Sciences at the University of Florida for a year's sabbatical during the academic year 2015–16. Without that sabbatical, this book could not have been written.

The Center for Documentary Studies at Duke University graciously provided free lodging on several research trips that allowed me to access collections at the university's David M. Rubenstein Rare Book and Manuscript Library. I am also grateful to librarians at the University of Florida, the Schomburg Center for Research in

Black Culture at the New York Public Library, the Davis Library at the University of North Carolina, Chapel Hill, and the staff at the Library of Congress for their assistance and direction.

This book has benefited from countless discussions, editorial interventions, and late-night rap sessions. So many friends, colleagues, and movement fellow travelers have contributed to my understanding of this history that I hesitate to begin the process of naming lest I exclude anyone. Here goes: Elizabeth "Betita" Martinez, Cedric J. Robinson, Lawrence Guyot, William Darity, David Roediger, Lawrence Goodwyn, Larry Trujillo, Rosie Cabrera, Thulani Davis, Helen Safa, Carlos Muñoz, Karen Fields, Robin D. G. Kelley, Peter Bohmer, Larry Mosqueda, Suzanne Oboler, Anani Dzidzienyo, Vicki Ruiz, Derrick White, Ruth Wilson Gilmore, Jordan Camp, Christina Heatherton, Donna Murch, Max Krochmal, Genesis Lara, Benjamin Marquez, Jane Landers, Robert P. Wolensky, Zaragosa Vargas, Irvin D. S. Winsboro, William Link, Laura Edwards, Peter Wood, Thavolia Glymph, Melinda Wiggins, John Brown Childs, Gay Zieger and Robert H. Zieger, Hernan Vera, Michael Honey, John Due, Gaye Johnson, William Loren Katz, and Alex Lubin.

I have had the privilege of working with a remarkable array of graduate students whose new ideas and scholarship animate and inspire this book, including Kevin Bird, Sean Burns, Erin Conlin, Chris Dixon, Michael Brandon, Justin Dunnavant, Armin Fardis, Randi Gill-Sadler, Jonathan Gomez, Justin Hosbey, Kevin Jenkins, Allen Kent, Raja Rahim, and Matt Simmons.

My students remind me every year that the historical narratives currently dominating our schools and intellectual culture are in need of a vast overhaul. These students are determined to use history to address contemporary social problems and they inspire me to find new ways to teach old topics. I am particularly indebted to students in my courses such as African Diaspora in the Americas and African American and Latina/o Histories. Many of my students have gone on to become labor organizers, lawyers, teachers, entrepreneurs, and workers dedicated to challenging inequality wherever they find it. I hope that this book honors their passion for justice.

Tomás Villanueva and comrades in the United Farm Workers of Washington State taught me the importance of rigorous, social movement history. The Evergreen State College Labor Center reinforced these lessons during its too-brief existence.

My colleagues in the Oral History Association have been a source of constant encouragement. Students, staff, and volunteers at the Samuel Proctor Oral History Program at the University of Florida have helped me learn anew that historically informed civic engagement is a necessary ingredient in creating an egalitarian future.

My editors at Beacon Press—Gayatri Patnaik, Joanna Green, Jill Petty—and managing editor Susan Lumenello deserve awards for their brilliant editorial guidance and faith that I would finish this book after years of research, ruminating, and writing. I am especially indebted to historian and UC-Santa Cruz colleague Dana Frank for introducing me to Gayatri and Beacon Press in 2005.

My wife, Sheila Payne, and stepson, Joshua Redmond-Payne, served as constant reminders for me to "get the book finished." Josh helped me keep my sanity by taking me to the movies on a regular basis and cheering the Seattle Seahawks to victory. Sheila read every single word of this book—more than once—and her editorial eye vastly improved the final product. I relish our work together in the archives, and Sheila's passionate commitment to peace with justice. I am excited to move on to our next project. *¡Adelante!*

A NOTE ON SOURCES

An African American and Latinx History of the United States is based on archival and oral history research conducted between 1993 to the present. I also draw heavily on secondary works in African American, Chicano, and Latinx histories—as well as on literature in Latin American history and labor and ethnic studies. Many of the oral history interviews were conducted when I was a graduate student fellow for the National Endowment for the Humanities–funded *Behind the Veil: Documenting African American Life in the Jim Crow South*, an oral history project based at the Center for Documentary Studies at Duke University. Subsequent interviews were conducted by staff and students of the Samuel Proctor Oral History Program at the University of Florida.

During the years spent researching this book, I transitioned from reading newspapers in the microfilm collections of the Library of Congress, Duke University Libraries, George A. Smathers Libraries at the University of Florida, and other repositories to increasingly using online databases to find newsletters, pamphlets, and other sources. The African American Newspapers collection via Accessible Archives contains invaluable sources, including the *Christian Recorder*, the *North Star*, *Freedom's Journal*, and other nineteenth-century abolitionist journals. The online database *Ethnic NewsWatch* consists of a plethora of documents, including periodicals and newsletters created by Native American, African American, and Chicano movement organizations between 1959 and the present. The ongoing digitization of primary and secondary documents in African American and Latinx historical sources will make future studies in these fields even more productive and accessible to scholars and to community organizations.

NOTES

INTRODUCTION: "KILLED HELPING WORKERS TO ORGANIZE"

1. "The Pan-American Commission," *Chicago Defender*, June 19, 1915.
2. Ibid.
3. Charles Thompson, *Border Odyssey: Travels Along the U.S./Mexico Divide* (Austin: University of Texas Press, 2015), 6.
4. "Speech of Frederick Douglass on the War," *Douglass' Monthly*, February 1862.
5. David B. Chesebrough, *Frederick Douglass: Oratory from Slavery* (London: Greenwood Press, 1998), 24.
6. "Killed Helping Workers to Organize," *El Malcriado: The Voice of the Farm Worker* 2, no. 4 (April 15, 1968).
7. "The Man They Killed," *El Malcriado* (April 15, 1968): 3.
8. Ibid. For an amplification of the importance of organizing in creating social change, see César Chávez, "Huelga! Tales of the Delano Revolution: The Organizer's Tale," *Ramparts* (July 1966): 43–50. See also Dolores Huerta, interviewed by Paul Ortiz, April 16, 2016, Samuel Proctor Oral History Program, George A. Smathers Libraries, University of Florida (henceforth cited as SPOHP); Lawrence Guyot, interviewed by Paul Ortiz, May 5, 2011, SPOHP, George A. Smathers Libraries, University of Florida.
9. "There Will Be No Boundary War," *Colored American*, May 9, 1840.
10. Francisco P. Ramírez, "Editorials," in *Herencia: The Anthology of Hispanic Literature of the United States*, ed. Nicolás Kanellos (New York: Oxford University Press, 2002), 110.
11. Coretta Scott King, foreword to *Where Do We Go from Here: Chaos or Community?*, by Martin Luther King Jr. (1967; Boston: Beacon Press, 2010), xxiii. In developing this concept about connections between forms of oppression as well as liberation, I have been guided by Kimberlé Crenshaw, "Mapping the Margins: Intersectionality, Identity Politics, and Violence Against Women of Color," *Stanford Law Review* 43, no. 6 (July 1991): 1241–99; Vijay Prashad, *The Darker Nations: A People's History of the Third World* (New York: New

Press, 2007); Fred Ho, *Wicked Theory, Naked Practice: A Fred Ho Reader*, ed. Diane C. Fujino (Minneapolis: University of Minnesota Press, 2009).

12. "Cuba," *Christian Recorder*, March 20, 1869.

13. Jeremy Lamont Austin, "Black Liberation in the African Diaspora," paper presented at the University of California, Santa Cruz, April 24, 2006, in author's collection.

14. Elizabeth Martínez, *De Colores Means All of Us: Latina Views for a Multi-Colored Century* (Cambridge, MA: South End Press, 1998), 48.

15. Danny Romero, "A Chicano in Philadelphia," in *Multicultural America: Essays on Cultural Wars and Cultural Peace*, ed. Ishmael Reed (New York: Penguin Books, 1997), 86.

16. I generally use the term "Global South" to refer to the formerly colonized nations in Latin America, the Caribbean, Africa, and Asia, as well as the Middle East.

17. "Telling Histories: A Conversation with Laurent Dubois and Greg Grandin," *Radical History Review* 2013, no. 115 (Winter 2013): 19.

18. Critical texts include John Hope Franklin and Alfred A. Moss Jr., *From Slavery to Freedom*, 8th ed., vol. 1 (1947; New York: McGraw Hill, 1999); Rodolfo F. Acuña, *Occupied America: A History of Chicanos* (1972; New York: Pearson Longman, 2007); Vincent Harding, *There Is a River: The Black Struggle for Freedom in America* (1981; New York: Mariner Books, 1993); Cedric Robinson, *Black Marxism: The Making of the Black Radical Tradition* (1983; Chapel Hill: University of North Carolina Press, 2000); Vicki L. Ruiz, *From Out of the Shadows: Mexican Women in Twentieth Century America* (1998; New York: Oxford University Press, 2008); Ronald Takaki, *A Different Mirror: A History of Multicultural America* (New York: Little, Brown, 1993).

19. King, *Where Do We Go from Here*, 5.

20. Oliver Cromwell Cox, *Capitalism and American Leadership* (New York: Philosophical Library, 1962), 228.

21. Juan González, *Harvest of Empire: A History of Latinos in America*, rev. ed. (New York: Penguin, 2011).

22. For the impact of US military interventions in Central America and the resulting flight of many of the region's residents to the United States, see Gonzalez, *Harvest of Empire*, 129–48.

23. Quoted in *Harvest of Empire: The Untold Story of Latinos in America*, dir. Peter Getzels and Eduardo López, Onyx Films, 2012, a film based on the book *Harvest of Empire* by Juan González.

24. Ruiz, *From Out of the Shadows*, xii. For a brilliant historical study of Chicano identity, see George J. Sanchez, *Becoming Mexican American: Ethnicity, Culture, and Identity in Chicano Los Angeles, 1900–1945* (New York: Oxford University Press, 1993).

25. The pronunciation of this term is "Latin X." "What Does 'Latinx' Mean?," Latinx graduation ceremony brochure, University of Florida, April 19, 2017, in author's collection. Roberto Rodriquez explains the rise of the term "Latinx" in "The X in LatinX," *Diverse Issues in Higher Education* (June 7, 2017), http://diverseeducation.com/article/97500/.

26. Martha Menchaca, *Recovering History, Constructing Race: The*

198   Notes

Indian, Black, and White Roots of Mexican Americans (Austin: University of Texas Press, 2001). See also Laura Gómez, *Manifest Destinies: The Making of the Mexican American Race* (New York: New York University Press, 2007).

27. Marta E. Sánchez, *"Shakin' Up" Race and Gender: Intercultural Connections in Puerto Rican, African American, and Chicano Narratives and Culture (1965–1995)* (Austin: University of Texas Press, 2005).

28. Miriam Jiménez Román and Juan Flores, *The Afro-Latin@ Reader: History and Culture in the United States* (Durham: Duke University Press, 2010); Kathryn J. McKnight and Leo J. Garofalo, *Afro-Latino Voices: Narratives from the Early Modern Ibero-Atlantic World, 1550–1812* (Indianapolis: Hackett, 2009); Jack D. Forbes, *Africans and Native Americans: The Language of Race and the Evolution of Red-Black Peoples* (Urbana: University of Illinois Press, 1993).

29. Bobby Vaughn, "Mexico Negro: From the Shadows of Nationalist Mestizaje to New Possibilities in Afro-Mexican Identity," *Journal of Pan African Studies* 6, no. 1 (July 2013): 227–40. This essay was part of a special issue of *Pan African Studies* titled "Africans in Mexico: History, Race and Place," ed. Alva Moore Stevenson. See also Ann Shetterly, "Black in Mexico: The Complexion of *Mexicanidad* Along the Costa Chica," *Inside Mexico* (April 2007): 14–21.

30. Kimberlé Crenshaw, "Demarginalizing the Intersection of Race and Sex: A Black Feminist Critique of Antidiscrimination Doctrine, Feminist Theory and Antiracist Politics," *University of Chicago Legal Forum* 140, no. 1 (1989): 139–67.

31. Manuel Pastor, Stewart Kwoh, and Angela Glover Blackwell, *Searching for the Uncommon Common Ground: New Dimensions on Race in America* (New York: W. W. Norton, 2002), 81.

32. "Programa para los niños," *El Malcriado*, July 1, 1968.

CHAPTER 1: THE HAITIAN REVOLUTION
AND THE BIRTH OF EMANCIPATORY INTERNATIONALISM

1. In the Spanish Empire, *mestizos* were mixed-race people. *Libertos* were generally defined as free Blacks. On the rebellion, see Elvia Duque Castillo, *Aportes del Pueblo Afrodescendiente: La Historia Oculta de América Latina* (Bloomington, IN: iUniverse, 2013), 249; Charles F. Walker, *The Tupac Amaru Rebellion* (Cambridge, MA: Harvard University Press, 2014); Nicholas A. Robins, *Native Insurgencies and the Genocidal Impulse in the Americas* (Bloomington: Indiana University Press, 2005); Jaime Ramón Olivares, "Tupac Amaru," *Encyclopedia of Slave Resistance and Rebellion*, vol. 2: *O-Z and Primary Documents*, ed. Junius P. Rodriguez (London: Greenwood Press, 2007), 526–28; Matthew R. Lamothe, "While the English Colonies Fought for Independence, Tupac Amaru Wages a People's War in Peru," *Military History* 19, no. 4 (October 2002): 74.

2. Simon Shama, *Rough Crossings: The Slaves, the British, and the American Revolution* (New York: HarperPerennial, 2007); Woody Holton, *Forced Founders: Indians, Debtors, Slaves, and the Making of the American Revolu-*

tion in Virginia (Chapel Hill: University of North Carolina Press, 1999); Gerald Horne, *The Counter Revolution of 1776: Slave Resistance and the Origins of the United States of America* (New York: New York University Press, 2014); Alfred W. Blumrosen, *Slave Nation: How Slavery United the Colonies and Sparked the American Revolution* (New York: Sourcebooks, 2006).

3. Gordon Wood, *The Creation of the American Republic, 1776–1787* (1969; Chapel Hill: University of North Carolina Press, 1998), 3–50.

4. *The Fundamental Constitutions of Carolina*, authored by John Locke in 1669, is one example of this philosophy in action. See Robert Bernasconi and Anika Maaza Mann, "The Contradictions of Racism: Locke, Slavery, and the *Two Treatises*," in *Race and Racism in Modern Philosophy*, ed. Andrew Valls (Ithaca, NY: Cornell University Press, 2005), 89–107. See also Theresa Richardson, "John Locke and the Myth of Race in America: Demythologizing the Parodoxes of the Enlightenment as Visited in the Present," *Philosophical Studies in Education* 42 (January 2011): 101–12; Peter Linebaugh and Marcus Rediker, *The Many-Headed Hydra: Sailors, Slaves, Commoners, and the Hidden History of the Revolutionary Atlantic* (Boston: Beacon Press, 2000), 139. On class conflicts in the Revolutionary era, see Alfred F. Young, ed., *The American Revolution: Explorations in the History of American Radicalism* (DeKalb: Northern Illinois University Press, 1976); Jesse Lemisch, *Jack Tar vs. John Bull: The Role of New York's Seamen in Precipitating the Revolution* (New York: Garland, 1997); Alfred F. Young, Gary Nash, and Ray Raphael, eds., *Revolutionary Founders: Rebels, Radicals, and Reformers in the Making of the Nation* (New York: Alfred A. Knopf, 2011).

5. C. L. R. James, "Black Studies and the Contemporary Student," *The C. L. R. James Reader*, ed. Anna Grimshaw (Oxford, UK: Blackwell, 1992), 396. In a related sense, James argued, in *Black Jacobins*, that "the slave-trade and slavery were the economic basis of the French Revolution." *The Black Jacobins: Toussaint L'Ouverture and the San Domingo Revolution* (1938; London: Vintage Books, 1989), 47. The relationship between slavery and capitalism has been explored more recently in Anne Farrow, Joel Lang, and Jennifer Frank, *Complicity: How the North Promoted, Prolonged, and Profited from Slavery* (2006; New York: Ballantine Books, 2015); Walter Johnson, *River of Dark Dreams: Slavery and Empire in the Cotton Kingdom* (Cambridge, MA: Harvard University Press, 2013); Edward Baptist, *The Half Has Never Been Told: Slavery and the Making of American Capitalism* (New York: Basic Books, 2014); Sven Beckert, *Empire of Cotton: A Global History* (New York: Alfred A. Knopf, 2014); Andrew J. Torget, *Seeds of Empire: Cotton, Slavery, and the Transformation of the Texas Borderlands, 1800–1850* (Chapel Hill: University of North Carolina Press, 2015).

6. Adam Smith, *An Inquiry into the Nature and Causes of the Wealth of Nations*, 1775, ed. with introduction and notes by Kathryn Sutherland (Oxford, UK: Oxford University Press, 1998), 238–39.

7. "Anyone Person," *South Carolina Gazette*, November 25, 1777. See also "Brought to the Workhouse," *South Carolina Gazette*, September 19, 1775; "Runaway," *South Carolina Gazette*, September 26, 1775. Copies of the *South Carolina Gazette* and many of the eighteenth- and nineteenth-century news-

papers cited in the early chapters of this book may be found in the microfilm collections of Duke University Libraries.

8. "Will Be Sold," *South Carolina Gazette*, December 19, 1774.

9. On the practice of breeding humans for profit, see Frederick Bancroft, *Slave Trading in the Old South* (1931; Columbia: University of South Carolina Press, 1996), 67–87; Edward E. Baptist, "'Cuffy,' 'Fancy Maids,' and 'One-Eyed Men': Rape, Commodification, and the Domestic Slave Trade in the United States, *American Historical Review* 106, no. 5 (December 2001): 1619–50; Walter Johnson, *Soul by Soul: Life Inside the Antebellum Slave Market* (Cambridge, MA: Harvard University Press, 1999), 82–88; Ned Sublette and Constance Sublette, *The American Slave Coast: A History of the Slave-Breeding Industry* (Chicago: Lawrence Hill Books, 2016).

10. Advertisements in the *South Carolina Gazette:* "Runaway," October 17, 1774; "Runaway," October 31, 1774: "Absented Himself," December 5, 1774; "Fifty Pounds Reward," March 13, 1775; "Runaway," June 16, 1777; "Ten Pounds Reward," April 3, 1775. For additional examples of "artful" slaves, see Freddie L. Parker, *Running for Freedom: Slave Runaways in North Carolina, 1775–1840* (New York: Garland, 1993); John Hope Franklin and Loren Schweninger, *Runaway Slaves: Rebels on the Plantation* (New York: Oxford University Press, 1999).

11. "Absented Himself," *South Carolina Gazette*, December 5, 1774.

12. Robinson, *Black Marxism*. Robinson's work is a reminder that Black radical intellectuals have long studied the relationship between slavery, racial capitalism, and imperialism. His influence suffuses the pages of this book. For works that connect slavery, capitalism, and modern forms of racial and class oppression, see also T. Thomas Fortune, *Black & White: Land, Labor, and Politics in the South* (1884; New York: Washington Square Press, 2007); W. E. B. Du Bois, *Black Reconstruction: An Essay Toward a History of the Part Which Black Folk Played in the Attempt to Reconstruct Democracy in America, 1860–1880* (1935; New York: Meridian Books, 1964); James, *Black Jacobins*; Eric Williams, *Capitalism and Slavery* (Chapel Hill: University of North Carolina Press, 1944); Oliver Cromwell Cox, *Caste, Class, and Race: A Study in Social Dynamics* (New York: Doubleday, 1948); Manning Marable, *How Capitalism Underdeveloped Black America: Problems in Race, Political Economy and Society* (1983; Boston: South End Press, 2000); Michael O. West, William G. Martin, and Fanon Che Wilkins, eds., *From Toussaint to Tupac: The Black International Since the Age of Revolution* (Chapel Hill: University of North Carolina Press, 2009); Jeffrey B. Perry, *Hubert Harrison: The Voice of Harlem Radicalism, 1883–1918* (New York: Columbia University Press, 2008); Paul Ortiz and Derrick White, "C.L.R. James on Oliver Cox's *Caste, Class, and Race*: An Introduction," *New Politics* 15, no. 4 (Winter 2006): 43–47; and Samuel Proctor Oral History Program, eds., "C.L.R. James: The Class Basis of the Race Question in the United States," *New Politics* 15, no. 5 (Winter 2006): 48–60.

13. Cedric J. Robinson and Elizabeth P. Robinson, preface, *Futures of Black Radicalism*, ed. Gaye Theresa Johnson and Alex Lubin (London: Verso, 2017), 3.

14. Paul Ortiz, "'Washington, Toussaint, and Bolívar, the Glorious Advocates of Liberty': Black Internationalism and Reimagining Emancipation," in *Rethinking American Emancipation: Legacies of Slavery and the Quest for Black Freedom*, ed. William A. Link and James J. Broomall (New York: Cambridge University Press, 2015), 187–215; Paul Ortiz, "Anti-Imperialism as a Way of Life: Emancipatory Internationalism and the Black Radical Tradition in the Americas," in Johnson and Alex Lubin, *Futures of Black Radicalism*.

15. Staughton Lynd and David Waldstreicher, "Free Trade, Sovereignty, and Slavery: Toward an Economic Interpretation of American Independence," *William and Mary Quarterly* 68, no. 4 (October 2011): 597–630; Blumrosen, *Slave Nation*.

16. Gerald Horne, *The Counter-Revolution of 1776: Slave Resistance and the Origins of the United States of America* (New York: New York University Press, 2014). In the fall of 1774, an emergency meeting of Charleston's General Committee was called to hear a report of the colony's delegates to the Continental Congress. The delegates had argued for enhanced representation for "rice and indigo planters" in the Continental Congress. The local committee called for elections and stated "that the only Persons qualified to vote for such Deputies be, every white Freeholder and other free white Men" who possessed a substantial amount of property. See "Charles-Town," *South Carolina Gazette*, November 21, 1774. See also Jerome Nadelhaft, "The Somerset Case and Slavery: Myth, Reality, and Repercussions," *Journal of Negro History* 51 (1966): 193–201; David Brion Davis, *The Problem of Slavery in the Age of Revolution, 1770–1823* (Ithaca: Cornell University Press, 1975), 480–501.

17. "Charles-Town."

18. "Extract of a Letter from London, February 10, 1775," *South Carolina Gazette*, May 29, 1775.

19. Benjamin Quarles, *The Negro in the American Revolution* (1961; Chapel Hill: University of North Carolina Press, 1996), 22.

20. "Third Draft by Jefferson Before June 1776," *Founders Online*, National Archives, http://founders.archives.gov/documents/Jefferson/01-01-02-0161 -0002 (accessed May 9, 2017).

21. *The Writings of Thomas Paine*, ed. Moncure Daniel Conway (New York: G. P. Putnam's Sons, 1894), 7.

22. Ibid.

23. Staughton Lynd, *Class Conflict, Slavery, and the United States Constitution* (1967; New York: Cambridge University Press, 2009), 180.

24. "Taxation No Tyranny: An Answer to the Revolutions and Address of the American Congress, by Samuel Johnson," 1775, http://www.samueljohn son.com/tnt.html (accessed January 26, 2016).

25. Timothy Mather Cooley, *Sketches of the Life and Character of the Rev. Lemuel Haynes, A.M.* (New York: John S. Taylor, 1839), 45–48; Ruth Bogin, "The Battle of Lexington: A Patriotic Ballad by Lemuel Haynes," *William and Mary Quarterly* 42, no. 4 (October 1985): 499–506; Rita Roberts, "Patriotism and Political Criticism: The Evolution of Political Consciousness in the Mind of a Black Revolutionary Soldier," *Eighteenth-Century Studies* 27, no. 4 (Summer 1994): 569–88. For more information on Haynes, see also "The National

Capital," *New York Globe*, February 2, 1884; "Black History," *Greater Milwaukee Star*, October 19, 1968.

26. Ruth Bogin, " 'Liberty Further Extended': A 1776 Antislavery Manuscript by Lemuel Haynes," *William and Mary Quarterly* 40, no. 1 (January 1983): 85–105.

27. Ibid., 94–95.

28. Articles by Arthur A. Schomburg: "Free Negroes in the Formation of the American Republic," *New York Amsterdam News*, February 12, 1930; "Crispus Attucks—Free Patriot," *New York Amsterdam News*, August 24, 1935; "Jupiter Hammon Before the New York African Society," *New York Amsterdam News*, January 22, 1930.

29. Gail Buckley, *American Patriots: The Story of Blacks in the Military from the Revolution to Desert Storm* (New York: Random House, 2002), 4. See also J. A. Rogers, "Ruminations: Crispus Attucks, Revolutionary Martyr," *New York Amsterdam News*, February 28, 1934.

30. "Friends of Haiti to Send Funds to Restore Citadel of Christophe," *Negro Star* (Wichita, KS), August 19, 1932; "Hayti's Aid in 1779: How Eight Hundred of Her Freedmen Fought for America," *New York Tribune*, July 6, 1921.

31. Quarles, *The Negro in the American Revolution*, xxix; Thomas Fleming, in his new introduction to Joseph Plumb Martin, *A Narrative of a Revolutionary Soldier: Some of the Adventures, Dangers, and Sufferings of Joseph Plumb Martin*, 1830 (New York: Signet Classics, 2001), notes, "By 1780, every seventh soldier in the ranks was black" (xx).

32. For an overview of these petitions, see Herbert Aptheker, ed., *Documentary History of the Negro People in the United States*, 2 vols. (New York: International Publishers, 1951), 1: 6–10; Thomas J. Davis, "Emancipation Rhetoric, Natural Rights, and Revolutionary New England: A Note on Four Black Petitions in Massachusetts, 1773–1777," *New England Quarterly* 62, no. 2 (June 1989): 248–63.

33. "Peter Bestes and Other Slaves Petition for Freedom (April 20, 1773)," in Aptheker, *Documentary History of the Negro People in the United States*, 7–8. See also Herbert Gutman, *The Black Family in Slavery and Freedom, 1750–1925* (New York: Vintage, 1977), 350.

34. Franklin and Moss, *From Slavery to Freedom*, 8th ed., vol. 1 (New York: McGraw Hill, 1999), 65–66.

35. Gary Nash, *The Forgotten Fifth: African Americans in the Age of Revolution* (Cambridge, MA: Harvard University Press, 2006); Herbert Aptheker, *The Negro in the American Revolution* (New York: International Publishers, 1940); Quarles, *The Negro in the American Revolution*; "Run Away About a Month Ago," *South Carolina Gazette*, advertisement, November 25, 1777; William Loren Katz, *Black Indians: A Hidden Heritage*, rev. ed. (1986; New York: Simon & Schuster, 2012).

36. Sylvia Frey, *Water from the Rock: Black Resistance in a Revolutionary Age* (Princeton, NJ: Princeton University Press, 1991), 117. Peter Wood, " 'The Dream Deferred': Black Freedom Struggles on the Eve of Independence," in *In Resistance: Studies in African, Caribbean, and Afro-American History*, ed.

Gary Y. Okihiro (Amherst: University of Massachusetts Press, 1986), states that during the Revolution, "In every Southern colony, from Maryland to Georgia, slaves threatened armed revolt" (173).

37. Quarles, *Negro in the American Revolution*, xxvii.

38. "Continental Congress Motion of Protest Against British Practice of Carrying Off American Negroes [26 May 1783]," *Founders Online*, National Archives, http://founders.archives.gov/documents/Hamilton/01-03-02-0239 (accessed May 9, 2017).

39. "The Definitive Treaty of Peace, 1783," available online at the *Avalon Project: Documents in Law, History and Diplomacy*, http://avalon.law.yale .edu/18th_century/paris.asp.

40. Thomas Jefferson, "To the British Minister, May 29th," in *The Works of Thomas Jefferson*, 12 vols., ed. Paul Leicester Ford (New York: G.P. Putnam's Sons, 1904), 7: 41.

41. Beckles Willson, *Friendly Relations: A Narrative of Britain's Ministers and Ambassadors to America, 1791–1930* (Boston: Little, Brown, 1934), 17.

42. Lynd, *Class Conflict, Slavery, and the United States Constitution*, 153–54.

43. Paul Finkelman, "The Proslavery Origins of the Electoral College," *Cardoza Law Review* 23, no. 4 (2002): 1145–57.

44. "Race—The Power of an Illusion," timeline, PBS, http://www.pbs.org /race/000_About/002_03_d-godeeper.htm (accessed November 10, 2015).

45. Evelyn Nakano Glenn argues, "Of all wealthy countries in the world, the United States is the only one to have substantially relied, for its economic development, on the labor of peoples from all three nonwhite areas of the globe: Africa, Latin America, and Asia. Thus, a central feature of the U.S. economy has been its reliance on racialized and gendered systems of control, including coercion. Racialization in the labor market has been buttressed by a system of citizenship designed to reinforce the control of employers and to constrain the mobility of workers." In Glenn, *Unequal Freedom: How Race and Gender Shaped American Citizenship and Labor* (Cambridge, MA: Harvard University Press, 2004), 5.

46. Thomas Law to James Madison, October 18, 1797, *Founders Online*, National Archives, http://founders.archives.gov/documents/Madison/01-17-02-0040 (accessed May 9, 2017). On Thomas Law, see George Alfred Townsend, "Thomas Law, Washington's First Rich Man," *Records of the Columbia Historical Society* (Washington, DC: 1901): 222–45, https:// archive.org/stream/jstor-40066782/40066782#page/n23/mode/2up.

47. Julius Scott, "The Common Wind: Currents of Afro-American Communication in the Era of the Haitian Revolution," PhD diss., Duke University, 1986; James, *Black Jacobins*.

48. Gerald Horne, *Confronting Black Jacobins: The United States, the Haitian Revolution, and the Origins of the Dominican Republic* (New York: Monthly Review Press, 2015); David P. Geggus, ed., *The Impact of the Haitian Revolution in the Atlantic World* (Columbia: University of South Carolina Press, 2002); George Reid Andrews, *Afro-Latin America: Black Lives, 1800–2000* (New York: Oxford University Press, 2004); Laurent Dubois and

Julius Scott, eds., *Origins of the Black Atlantic* (New York: Routledge, 2009); Robin Blackburn, *The American Crucible: Slavery, Emancipation and Human Rights* (London: Verso, 2013); "Telling Histories: A Conversation with Laurent Dubois and Greg Grandin," *Radical History Review* 115 (Winter 2013): 11–25.

49. "Annual Examination," *Frederick Douglass' Paper*, May 6, 1859; "Hayti no. IV," *Freedom's Journal*, June 15, 1827; "The Republic of Haiti," *Christian Recorder*, May 8, 1873; "All Signs Point," *Freeman* (Indianapolis), December 5, 1896; "Sad Bereavement," *Colored American*, July 3, 1903; "Beautiful Haiti and Its Brave Hearted People," *Negro World*, February 21, 1925; Mitch Kachun, "Antebellum African Americans, Public Commemoration, and the Haitian Revolution: A Problem of Historical Mythmaking," in *African Americans and the Haitian Revolution: Selected Essays and Historical Documents*, ed. Maurice Jackson and Jacqueline Bacon (New York: Routledge, 2009), 93–106. African Americans in Durham, North Carolina, named their community "Hayti," and it became known as the "Black Wall Street" in the twentieth century. See Leslie Brown, *Upbuilding Black Durham: Gender, Class, and Black Community Development in the Jim Crow South* (Chapel Hill: University of North Carolina Press, 2008).

50. Douglas R. Egerton, *Gabriel's Rebellion: The Virginia Slave Conspiracies of 1800 and 1802* (Chapel Hill: University of North Carolina Press, 1993), 102.

51. Daniel Rasmussen, *American Uprising: The Untold Story of America's Largest Slave Revolt* (New York: Harper, 2011), 102.

52. Douglas Egerton, *He Shall Go Out Free: The Lives of Denmark Vesey* (1999; Lanham, MD: Rowman & Littlefield, 2004).

53. This account is based on *The Life, Travels, and Opinions of Benjamin Lundy: Including His Journeys* (Philadelphia: William D. Parish, 1847); 206–7; Ralph Clayton, "Baltimore's Own Version of 'Amistad': Slave Revolt," *Baltimore Chronicle*, January 7, 1998, http://www.baltimorechronicle.com/slave_ship2.html (accessed October 27, 2015); Eric Robert Taylor, *If We Must Die: Shipboard Insurrections in the Era of the Atlantic Slave Trade* (Baton Rouge: Louisiana State University Press, 2006), 147–50.

54. Sublette and Sublette, *American Slave Coast*, 426–32; Bancroft, *Slave Trading in the Old South*, 120–22; "A Bitter Inner Harbor Legacy: The Slave Trade," *Baltimore Sun*, July 12, 2000; Johnson, *Soul by Soul*; Michael Tadman, *Speculators and Slaves: Masters, Traders, and Slaves in the Old South* (Madison: University of Wisconsin, 1989).

55. *Niles-Register* story cited in "Domestic Slave Trade," *National Anti-Slavery Standard*, July 17, 1845.

56. "The Secret History of the Slave Trade [in Baltimore]," *Baltimore Sun*, June 20, 1999.

57. Frederick Douglass, *Frederick Douglass: Selected Speeches and Writings*, ed. Philip S. Foner (1950; Chicago: Lawrence Hill Books, 1999), 196. For other reports of the slave trade in Baltimore, see "Summary of News," *Friends Review: A Religious, Literary and Miscellaneous Journal* 1, no. 32

(April 1848): 512; "The Readers of the Review," *Friends Review* 1, no. 34 (May 1848): 538.

58. Sublette and Sublette, *American Slave Coast*, 24.

59. Rashauna Johnson, *Slavery's Metropolis: Unfree Labor in New Orleans During the Age of Revolutions* (New York: Cambridge University Press, 2016).

60. Beckert, *Empire of Cotton*, 403–6.

61. Calvin Schermerhorn, "What Else You Should Know About Baltimore," History News Network, May 4, 2015, http://historynewsnetwork.org /article/159294; Calvin Schermerhorn, *The Business of Slavery and the Rise of American Capitalism, 1815–1860* (New Haven, CT: Yale University Press, 2015).

62. "Blessings of Slavery in Baltimore Maryland!," *Freedom's Journal*, October 31, 1828. The writer is borrowing from Thomas Jefferson's famous dictum on slavery, "I tremble for my country when I reflect that God is just; that his justice cannot sleep forever."

63. "Kidnapping Children," *North Star*, April 10, 1851.

64. "Wrongs of the Colored People," *Colored American*, January 30, 1841.

65. "Baltimore Correspondence," *National Era*, August 26, 1847. See also "Domestic Slave Trade," *Freedom's Journal*, March 7, 1829; "A Little Matter," *Frederick Douglass' Paper*, March 1, 1850.

66. Cuban Anti-Slavery Committee, *Slavery in Cuba: A Report of the Proceedings of the Meeting* (New York: Powers, MacGowan & Slipper, 1873), 17; *A Memorial Discourse by Rev. Henry Highland Garnet* (Philadelphia: Joseph M. Wilson, 1865), 23.

67. James Still, *Early Recollections and Life of Dr. James Still* (Philadelphia: J. B. Lippincott & Co., 1877), 105–10.

68. John Blassingame, *Slave Testimony: Two Centuries of Letters, Speeches, Interviews, and Autobiographies* (Baton Rouge: Louisiana State University Press, 1977), 415.

69. "Underground Railroad Made Stops in Baltimore," *Baltimore Sun*, October 22, 1993.

70. Frank Rosengarten, *Urbane Revolutionary: C. L. R. James and the Struggle for a New Society* (Jackson: University Press of Mississippi, 2008), 39–40; Franklin, *Runaway Slaves*; Larry Eugene Rivers, *Rebels and Runaways: Slave Resistance in Nineteenth-Century Florida* (Urbana: University of Illinois Press, 2012).

71. "200 Dollars Reward," *Baltimore Sun*, advertisement, September 14, 1842, in "Runaway Slave Ads, Baltimore County, Maryland," http://www .afrigeneas.com/library/runaway_ads/balt-1842.html (accessed September 13, 2015).

72. Historian John Hope Franklin used the term "quasi-free Blacks" to highlight the pervasive legal, economic, and social discrimination faced by "free" African Americans in the antebellum era. Franklin and Moss, *From Slavery to Freedom*, 148–70; T. Stephen Whitman, *The Price of Freedom: Slavery and Manumission in Baltimore and Early National Maryland* (Lexington: University Press of Kentucky, 1997).

73. "Slavery in Maryland," *National Anti-Slavery Standard*, August 7, 1845.

74. "Wrongs of the Colored People," *Colored American*, January 30, 1841.

75. Sally E. Hadden, *Slave Patrols: Law and Violence in Virginia and the Carolinas* (Cambridge, MA: Harvard University Press, 2003).

76. "The Runaway Negroes," *National Anti-Slavery Standard*, July 17, 1845.

77. Hadden, *Slave Patrols*. This may be seen as an example of what George Lipsitz refers to as the "possessive investment of whiteness." See Lipsitz, *The Possessive Investment in Whiteness: How White People Profit from Identity Politics*, rev. and expanded ed. (Philadelphia: Temple University Press, 2006), vii–viii.

78. "Baltimore Justice!," *Freedom's Journal*, August 3, 1827. Historian Barbara Fields notes that in Baltimore, "vagrant free blacks (that is to say, those refusing to hire their services to white employers) could be bound or sold for annually renewable terms at the direction of a magistrates' or orphans' court." Fields, *Slavery and Freedom on the Middle Ground: Maryland During the Nineteenth Century* (New Haven, CT: Yale University Press, 1985), 35. Historian Seth Rockman notes, "The liberal promises of the American Revolution stood beyond the reach of these workers, for whom economic failure was far more common than the upward mobility so widely associated with the era of the early republic." Rockman, *Scraping By: Wage Labor, Slavery, and Survival in Early Baltimore* (Baltimore: Johns Hopkins University Press, 2009), 2.

79. "Travelling Scraps," *Freedom's Journal*, August 15, 1828.

80. "The Day We Celebrate," *Christian Recorder*, May 5, 1866.

81. "Benjamin Lundy and His Times," *Baltimore Sun*, January 27, 1872.

82. "Twenty-Ninth Congress," *Baltimore Sun*, March 19, 1846; "Stampede Among the Slaves—The Underground Railroad," *Baltimore Sun*, October 27, 1849; "Opposition to the Underground Railroad," *Baltimore Sun*, October 29, 1849.

83. "Methodism and Slavery," *Freedom's Journal*, November 23, 1827.

84. Martha S. Jones, "The Case of Jean Baptiste, un Creole de Saint-Domingue: Narrating Slavery, Freedom, and the Haitian Revolution in Baltimore City," Public Law and Legal Theory Research Paper Series, vol. 376 (2013).

85. Conor Cruise O'Brien, *The Long Affair: Thomas Jefferson and the French Revolution, 1785–1800* (Chicago: University of Chicago Press, 1996), 290–92.

86. "Haytien Independence," *Genius of Universal Emancipation and Baltimore Courier*, September 12, 1825.

87. Alexander Allen, "U.S. Owes Haitians Gratitude, Not Abuse," *Crisis* 89, no. 8 (October 1982): 47. African Americans interpreted events in the Global South through selective lenses and their ideas of freedom struggles throughout the Americas were influenced by the chronic social crises they faced in the United States. As Frank Guridy notes, "The forging of diasporic linkages necessarily entails, as literary scholar Brent Edwards has shown, the messy process

of translation and, inevitably, misunderstandings. Projections, mistranslations, and disagreements over meaning are embedded in all forms of Afro-diasporic interaction." Frank Andrew Guridy, *Forging Diaspora: Afro-Cubans and African Americans* (Chapel Hill: University of North Carolina Press, 2010), 6–7. It may also be useful to extend Benedict Anderson's idea of "imagined community" to the African American project of creating imagined communities of struggle that transcended national borders. See Benedict Anderson, *Imagined Communities: Reflection on the Origin and Spread of Nationalism* (London: Verso, 1991).

88. Frances Ellen Watkins Harper, "Bury Me in a Free Land," Academy of American Poets, https://www.poets.org/poetsorg/poem/bury-me-free-land (accessed October 28, 2015).

89. "The Revolt in Texas," *Freedom's Journal*, April 20, 1827.

90. "From John Adams to John Taylor, 18 January 1815," *Founders Online,* National Archives, http://founders.archives.gov/documents/Adams/99-02-02 -6397 (accessed May 9, 2017).

91. "Toussaint L'Ouverture," *Freedom's Journal*, May 4, 1827.

92. "Gomez and Blanco," *Afro-American*, June 18, 1898.

93. Historian Laurent Dubois echoes this assessment when he writes, "Haiti, not the US or France, was where the assertion of true universal values reached its defining climax during the Age of Revolution." Dubois, "Atlantic Freedoms," *Aeon*, November 7, 2016, https://aeon.co/essays/why-haiti-should -be-at-the-centre-of-the-age-of-revolution.

94. "Frederick Douglass 1893 Speech in Chicago," Professor Bob Corbett's Home Page, Webster University, http://faculty.webster.edu/corbetre/haiti/his tory/1844–1915/douglass.htm (accessed January 6, 2016).

95. "The Superstition of Fanaticism," *National Anti-Slavery Standard*, April 15, 1865. The *Standard* reprinted this item, which had originally been published in Benjamin Wood's *New York Daily News* the same month.

96. C. L. R. James, *A History of Negro Revolt* (New York: Haskell House, 1938), 29. This insight was recently reaffirmed by Sven Beckert: "When we think of capitalism, we think of wage workers, yet this prior phase of capitalism was based not on free labor but on slavery. We associate industrial capitalism with contracts and markets, but early capitalism was based as often as not on violence and bodily coercion." Beckert, *Empire of Cotton*, xvi.

97. See Staughton Lynd's essay, "Beard, Jefferson, and the Tree of Liberty," in Lynd, *Class Conflict, Slavery, and the United States Constitution*, 247–69. See also Robin Blackburn's chapter, "The Planters Back Colonial Revolt," in Blackburn, *The American Crucible*, 131–44.

98. "William Whipper's Letters, no. II," *Colored American*, February 20, 1841.

99. "Editorial Correspondence," *National Anti-Slavery Standard*, June 17, 1847. The idea that the anti-slavery cause intersected with anti-imperialism may be found in "Verge of a War with the Mexican Republic," *National Enquirer*, November 19, 1836. In 1854, the Western Anti-Slavery Society in Salem, Ohio, critiqued US-based efforts to seize Cuba in order to extend American slavery.

See "Resolutions," *Frederick Douglass' Paper*, September 15, 1854. See also "National Rapacity," *Pennsylvania Freeman*, February 19, 1846. Historians have stressed the connections between slavery and imperialism. See James, *Black Jacobins*; Cox, *Caste, Class, and Race*; Johnson, *River of Dark Dreams*.

CHAPTER 2: THE MEXICAN WAR OF INDEPENDENCE AND US HISTORY

1. *Sentimientos de la Nación de José María Morelos: Antología Documental* (Mexico City: Instituto Nacional de Estudios Históricos de las Revoluciones de México, 1913), 116–24. For broader treatments of the Mexican War of Independence, see Theodore G. Vincent, *The Legacy of Vicente Guerrero, Mexico's First Black Indian President* (Gainesville: University Press of Florida, 2001); Virginia Guedea, "The Process of Mexican Independence," *American Historical Review* 105, no. 1 (February 2000): 116–30; Josefina Zoraida Vázquez, "The Mexican Declaration of Independence" *Journal of American History* 85, no. 4 (March 1999): 1362–69; Andrews, *Afro-Latin America*, 53–115; Christon I. Archer, ed., *The Birth of Modern Mexico, 1780–1824* (Lanham, MD: Rowman & Littlefield, 2007). On the critical role of muleteers in New Spain, see José Adrián Barragán-Alvarez, "The Feet of Commerce: Mule-Trains and Transportation in Eighteenth-Century New Spain," PhD diss., University of Texas, Austin, 2013.

2. On Morelos and his role in the Mexican War of Independence, see Rubén Hermensdorf, *Morelos: Hombre Fundamental de México* (Mexico: Aeromexico-Grijalbo, 1985); H. G. Ward, *Mexico in 1827* (London: Henry Colburn, 1828), 185–226; John Charles Chasteen, *Americanos: Latin America's Struggle for Independence* (New York: Oxford University Press, 2008), 89–121; Wilbert H. Timmons, *Morelos: Priest, Soldier, Statesman of Mexico* (El Paso: Texas Western College Press, 1963); Peter F. Guardino, "The War of Independence in Guerrero, New Spain, 1808–1821," in *The Wars of Independence in Spanish America*, ed. Christon I. Archer (Wilmington, DE: Scholarly Resources, 2000), 93–140. Drawing on the racial categories imposed by imperial New Spain in the colonial era, I define "mestizo" as any combination or admixture of European, Indigenous, and African blood. Scholars have established that race is a social construction—one with real consequences. In imperial New Spain, the *sistema de castas*, the *casta* system of racial categorization, defined one's access to wealth, profession, and even rates of taxation, and this was facilitated by the information priests wrote on infant baptismal records as well as census records. For the *casta* system and racial formation in colonial Latin America, see Menchaca, *Recovering History, Constructing Race*; Ilona Katzew, *Casta Painting: Images of Race in Eighteenth-Century Mexico* (New Haven, CT: Yale University Press, 2004); Herman L. Bennett, *Colonial Blackness: A History of Afro-Mexico* (Bloomington: Indiana University Press, 2009).

3. Alexander von Humboldt, *Political Essay on the Kingdom of New Spain With Physical Sections and Maps*, vol. 1, trans. John Black (London: Longman, Hurst, Rees, 1811), 246. Laura Gómez writes, "Both the Spanish and the American colonial enterprises were grounded in racism—in a system of status inequality built on presumed racial difference." Gomez, "Opposite One-Drop

Rules: Mexican Americans, African Americans, and the Need to Reconceive Turn-of-the-Twentieth-Century Race Relations," in *How the United States Racializes Latinos: White Hegemony and Its Consequences*, ed. José A. Cobas, Jorge Duany, and Joe R. Feagin (New York: Paradigm Publishers, 2009), 89.

4. Vincent, *Legacy of Vicente Guerrero*, 8.

5. Ibid., 84; Andrews, *Afro-Latin America*, 87.

6. Ward, *Mexico in 1827*, 185.

7. "Pastoral letter of November 28, 1812, addressed to parish priests and other clergy of the diocese of Durango by the dean and chapter of the cathedral," in *Caste and Politics in the Struggle for Mexican Independence*, Newberry Library, n.d., http://dcc.newberry.org/collections/caste-and-politics -in-mexican-independence#the-insurgency (accessed September 14, 2015).

8. Guedea, "The Process of Mexican Independence," 119. See also Marixa Lasso, "Race War and Nation in Caribbean Gran Colombia, Cartagena, 1810–1832," *American Historical Review* 111, no. 2 (April 2006): 338.

9. Ward, *Mexico in 1827*, 512.

10. Peter B. Hammond, "Mexico's Negro President," *Negro Digest* (May 1951), 11.

11. Ward, *Mexico in 1827*, 197.

12. José Maria Morelos to James Madison, July 14, 1815 (author's translation), *Founders Online*, National Historical Publications and Records Commission, National Archives, http://founders.archives.gov/documents /Madison/99–01–02–4516 (accessed March 11, 2015).

13. Ibid.

14. John Quincy Adams to George William Erving, November 28, 1818, in *The Writings of John Quincy Adams, Volume VI: 1816–1819*, ed. Worthington Chauncey Ford (New York: Macmillan, 1913), 489; David S. Heidler and Jeane T. Heidler, *Old Hickory's War: Andrew Jackson and the Quest for Empire* (Mechanicsburg, PA: Stackpole Books, 1996).

15. John Quincy Adams, "Speech of John Quincy Adams, in the House of Representatives, on the State of the Nation Delivered May 25, 1836" (1836; Whitefish, MT: Kessinger Publishing, 2010), 13. See also David Waldstreicher and Matthew Mason, *John Quincy Adams and the Politics of Slavery: Selections from the Diary* (New York: Oxford University Press, 2017); Harlow Giles Unger, *John Quincy Adams* (Boston: Da Capo Press, 2012).

16. John Quincy Adams to Thomas Boylston Adams, April 14, 1818, *Founders Online*, National Archives, http://founders.archives.gov/documents /Adams/99-03-02-3489 (accessed November 25, 2014). For Adams on Latin America as well as subsequent developments, see Lars Schoultz, *Beneath the United States: A History of U.S. Policy Toward Latin America* (Cambridge, MA: Harvard University Press, 1998).

17. These included the Third Servile War (73–71 BC), led by Spartacus. Adams used the concept of "servile war" on other occasions. See Thomas Fleming, *A Disease in the Public Mind: A New Understanding of Why We Fought the Civil War* (Boston: Da Capo Press, 2013), 144–45.

18. John Quincy Adams to John Adams, December 21, 1817, in Ford, *The Writings of John Quincy Adams*, 6: 276.

19. John Quincy Adams to George William Erving, November 28, 1818, in *The Writings of John Quincy Adams, Volume VII: 1820–1823*, ed. Worthington Chauncey Ford (New York: Macmillan, 1917), 476. For information on Erving, see J. L. M. Curry, *Diplomatic Services of George William Erving* (Cambridge, MA: John Wilson & Son, 1890).

20. John Quincy Adams to George William Erving in Ford, *The Writings of John Quincy Adams*, 6: 476. Thomas Jefferson also subsequently defended Jackson's conduct in the Seminole War. See Thomas Jefferson to James Madison, March 3, 1819, *Founders Online*, National Archives, https://founders.archives.gov/?q=seminole&s=1111311111&sa=&r=25&sr= (accessed June 15, 2016).

21. For details on the framing of the Adams-Onis Treaty, see Samuel F. Bemis, *John Quincy Adams and the Foundations of American Foreign Policy* (New York: Alfred A. Knopf, 1949).

22. John Quincy Adams to George William Erving, November 28, 1818, in Ford, *The Writings of John Quincy Adams*, 6: 495; "Remembering the Battle of Negro Fort," Fusion.net, July 27, 2016, http://fusion.net/story/330065/battle-of-negro-fort-anniversary/.

23. John Quincy Adams to George William Erving, November 28, 1818, in Ford, *The Writings of John Quincy Adams*, 6: 496–98.

24. Gómez, *Manifest Destinies*, views the notion of manifest destiny "as a cluster of ideas that relied on racism to justify a war of aggression against Mexico" (3).

25. On the racialization of Mexicans, see Menchaca, *Recovering History, Constructing Race*; Gómez, *Manifest Destinies*; Ian Haney-López, *White by Law: The Legal Construction of Race* (New York: New York University Press, 2006).

26. Eric Williams, *From Columbus to Castro: The History of the Caribbean* (1970; New York: Vintage Books, 1984), 410–18; Stephen M. Chambers, *No God but Gain: The Untold Story of Cuban Slavery, the Monroe Doctrine, and the Making of the United States* (London: Verso, 2015).

27. John Quincy Adams to Hugh Nelson, April 28, 1823, in Ford, *The Writings of John Quincy Adams*, 7: 370.

28. Carey McWilliams, *Brothers Under the Skin*, rev. ed. (Boston: Little, Brown, 1951), 196; Horne, *Race to Revolution*, 45–64.

29. "Annexation of Territory," *National Era*, February 4, 1847.

30. Ibid.

31. "Prejudice Against Color," *Colored American*, September 5, 1840.

32. "Slavery," *Freedom's Journal*, November 30, 1827.

33. "First of August Address, at Canandaigua, by Frederick Douglass," *National Anti-Slavery Standard*, August 19, 1847.

34. Ibid.

35. Loring Moody, *A History of the Mexican War, or Facts for the People, Showing the Relation of the United States Government to Slavery* (Boston: Bela Marsh, 1848), 102; "Resolution," *Journal of the House of Representatives of the United States*, 1826–1827, 19th Congress, 2nd Session (Washington:

Gales & Seaton, 1826), 7. Brent presented his resolution on Monday, December 18, 1826, and it was approved by the House of Representatives the following day.

36. Moody, *History of the Mexican War*, 102. For further details on the Mexican congress's refusal to accede to US demands to return "fugitive slaves," see Jose Maria Herrera, "The Blueprint for Hemispheric Hegemony: Joel Roberts Poinsett and the First United States Diplomatic Mission to Mexico," PhD diss., Purdue University, 2008, 307–8.

37. William Loren Katz interview with Paul Ortiz, SPOHP, George A. Smathers Libraries, University of Florida, June 22, 2012. See also William Loren Katz's keynote address at the 2012 Underground Railroad Conference, ed. Deborah Hendrix, prod. Samuel Proctor Oral History Program, http://williamlkatz.com/media/videos/.

38. "Mississippi—The Connection of Things," *National Anti-Slavery Standard*, September 3, 1840.

39. "From East Tennessee," *National Anti-Slavery Standard*, December 31, 1840.

40. "Slavery Question in Oregon," *Sacramento Daily Union*, September 30, 1857.

41. "Annexation of Territory," *National Era*, February 4, 1847.

42. Benjamin Lundy, *The War in Texas: A Review of Facts and Circumstances Showing that this Contest Is a Crusade Against Mexico Set on Foot and Supported by Slaveholders, Land-Speculators, &c. in Order to Re-Establish, Extend, and Perpetuate the System of Slavery and the Slave Trade*, 2nd ed. (Philadelphia: Merrihew & Gunn, 1837), 5.

43. "Interesting Letter," *Liberator*, May 26, 1832.

44. Irvin D. S. Winsboro and Joe Knetsch, "Florida Slaves, the 'Saltwater Railroad' to the Bahamas, and Anglo-American Diplomacy," *Journal of Southern History* 74, no. 1 (February 2013): 51–78; Margo Harakas, "Underground Railroad Made Tracks to Bahamas," *Sun-Sentinel* (FL), April 14, 2005.

45. John K. Mahon, *History of the Second Seminole War, 1835–1842* (1976; Gainesville: University Press of Florida, 2010); "Documentary Proposal by John Mahon: Osceola and the Seminole Wars," grant proposal, National Endowment for the Humanities, November 1992, http://ufdc.ufl.edu /AA00007635/00001/4j (accessed March 12, 2016). The Samuel Proctor Oral History Program at the University of Florida, in partnership with the National Park Service and the Organization of American Historians, has recently conducted oral history interviews with descendants of Florida's Black Seminoles who relocated to Oklahoma, Texas, Mexico, and the Bahamas in the wake of the Second Seminole War (1835–42). These interviews are currently being processed for scholarly use.

46. Charles Bingham Reynolds, *Old Saint Augustine: A Story of Three Centuries* (St. Augustine, FL: E. H. Reynolds, 1888), 113; Kenneth Porter Wiggins, *The Black Seminoles: History of a Freedom-Seeking People*, rev. and ed. by Alcione M. Amos and Thomas P. Senter (Gainesville: University Press of Florida, 1996).

47. Rivers, *Rebels and Runaways*, 131–46; Martin Van Buren, "First Annual Message to Congress," December 5, 1837, Miller Center, University of Virginia, https://millercenter.org/the-presidency/presidential-speeches /december-5-1837-first-annual-message-congress (accessed May 9, 2017); Cantor Brown, "Race Relations in Territorial Florida, 1821–1845," *Florida Historical Quarterly* 73 (January): 287–307.

48. "Speech of John Quincy Adams, in the House of Representatives . . . May 25, 1836." See also William Lee Miller, *Arguing About Slavery: John Quincy Adams and the Great Battle in the United States* (New York: Vintage Books, 1995).

49. "Speech of John Quincy Adams in the House of Representatives . . . May 25, 1836," 9.

50. Joseph Wheelan, *Mr. Adams's Last Crusade: John Quincy Adams's Extraordinary Post-Presidential Life in Congress* (New York: Perseus Books, 2008).

51. "Speech of John Quincy Adams in the House of Representatives . . . May 25, 1836," 10.

52. Ibid., 9.

53. Lundy, *The War in Texas*, 53; Congreso General de Mexico, *Manifiesto del Congreso en el Presente Año, 1836* (Mexico City: Imprenta de J.M.F. de Lara, 1836). Adams became renowned for his eloquent defense of the *Amistad* rebels in 1841. See Marcus Rediker, *The Amistad Rebellion: An Atlantic Odyssey of Slavery and Freedom* (New York: Penguin Books, 2012), 188–90.

54. "Cuba," *Frederick Douglass' Paper*, October 29, 1852. See also "Southern Patriotism & Florida War," *National Enquirer*, January 28, 1837; "Cuba and the United States," *Frederick Douglass' Paper*, September 4, 1851; "Cuba—The Reason," *Provincial Freeman*, June 3, 1854.

55. "Treachery, Vile and Unblushing," *Colored American*, February 3, 1838.

56. "Mexico and Texas," *Colored American*, January 30, 1841.

57. "The Present Position of Mexico," *Colored American*, February 2, 1839. See also Christopher Klein, "The Pastry War, 175 Years Ago," "History in the Headlines," *News Network*, November 27, 2013, http://www.history .com/news/the-pastry-war-175-years-ago (accessed May 9, 2017).

58. James McCune Smith, "Introduction," in *A Memorial Discourse by Rev. Henry Highland Garnet* (Philadelphia: Joseph M. Wilson, 1865), 25. See also Harding, *There Is a River*, 120–24; David Fiske, Clifford W. Brown Jr., and Rachel Seligman, *Solomon Northup: The Complete Story of the Author of "Twelve Years a Slave"* (Santa Barbara, CA: Praeger, 2013); Marjorie Waters, "Before Solomon Northup: Fighting Slave Catchers in New York," *History News Network*, October 18, 2013, http://historynewsnet work.org/article/153653 (accessed May 7, 2107).

59. Smith, *A Memorial Discourse*, 30; "The Brief but Courageous Life of Noyes Academy," *Dartmouth Life*, December, 2005, http://www.dartmouth .edu/~dartlife/archives/15-5/noyes.html (accessed March 5, 2015).

60. *Minutes of the National Convention of Colored Citizens Held at Buffalo* (New York: Piercy & Reed, 1843), 15–18.

61. Frederick Douglass, "Texas, Slavery, and American Prosperity: An

Address Delivered in Belfast, Ireland, on January 2, 1846," at John Blassingame et al, eds., *The Frederick Douglass Papers: Series One—Speeches, Debates, and Interviews*, Gilder Lehrman Center for the Study of Slavery, Resistance, and Abolition, http://glc.yale.edu/texas-slavery-and-american-prosperity (accessed May 9, 2017).

62. "On Mexico," *Liberator*, June 8, 1849. See also editorial in the *North Star*, January 21, 1848.

63. "M. R. Delany," *Frederick Douglass' Paper*, May 19, 1848. See also "The Conduct of the War," *National Era*, March 18, 1847; "An Appeal to the Friends of Justice, Humanity, Peace, and Liberty in the United States," *National Anti-Slavery Standard*, May 21, 1846.

64. "Letter from Frederick Douglass," *National Anti-Slavery Standard*, September 9, 1847.

65. "Anti-Slavery Petitions," *Frederick Douglass' Paper*, February 4, 1848.

66. "The Feeling of Mexico," *National Era*, August 31, 1848.

67. David E. Hayes-Bautista, *El Cinco de Mayo: An American Tradition* (Berkeley: University of California Press, 2012), 83–84.

68. "Revolution in Northern Mexico," *National Era*, October 16, 1851. See also "Negro Conspiracy," *Frederick Douglass' Paper*, July 24, 1851; Wendell G. Addington, "Slave Insurrections in Texas," *Journal of Negro History* 35 (October 1950): 408–34; William W. White, "The Texas Slave Insurrection of 1860," *Southwestern Historical Quarterly* 52 (January 1949): 259–61.

69. "A New Plot of the Slave-Drivers," *National Anti-Slavery Standard*, August 4, 1855; Addington, "Slave Insurrections in Texas," 412.

70. "Negro in Latin America, Mexico and 1856 Slave Rebellion," editorial, *Philadelphia Tribune*, January 15, 1944; Bill Stein, "Capital Punishment in Colorado County History," *Nesbitt Memorial Library Journal: A Journal of Colorado County History* 1, no. 5 (June 1990): 131–32.

71. "Letter from B. F. Remington," *Frederick Douglass' Paper*, February 19, 1852. Remington's thesis is supported by Matthew Karp, *This Vast Southern Empire: Slaveholders at the Helm of American Foreign Policy* (Cambridge, MA: Harvard University Press, 2016).

72. William Walker, *The War in Nicaragua* (New York: S. H. Goetzel, 1860), 261. See also Karl Bermann, *Under the Big Stick: Nicaragua and the United States Since 1848* (Boston: South End Press, 1986); Johnson, *The River of Dark Dreams*, 366–94.

73. "Annexation of Cuba," *Richmond Enquirer*, June 3, 1854.

74. For anti-imperial and antislavery critiques of the filibusters, see "The Workings of the Compromise—More Slave Territory," *Frederick Douglass' Paper*, July 24, 1851; "Let the People Be Roused," *Frederick Douglass' Paper*, March 30, 1855; "Nicaragua as It Is," *Provincial Freeman*, May 17, 1856; "Later for Nicaragua—The Plot Consummated," *National Era*, October 23, 1856.

75. "Cuba and the United States," *Frederick Douglass' Paper*, September 4, 1851.

76. Hayes-Bautista, *El Cinco de Mayo*, 83.

77. "Political Aspect of the Colored People," *Provincial Freeman*, October 13, 1855.

78. Richard Newman, Patrick Rael, and Philip Lapansky, eds., *Pamphlets of Protest: An Anthology of Early African-American Protest Literature, 1790–1860* (New York: Routledge, 2001), 98.

79. Dorothy Sterling, ed., *The Trouble They Seen: The Story of Reconstruction in the Words of African Americans* (1976; reprint, New York: Da Capo Press, 1994), 29.

80. "Interesting Letter."

81. "An Address to the People of the United States," *Proceedings of the Colored National Convention Held in Franklin Hall, Philadelphia, October 16th, 17th and 18th, 1855* (Salem, NJ: National Standard, 1856), 32.

82. "What Is to Be Done?," *Frederick Douglass' Paper*, May 6, 1852.

83. On the American Party, popularly known as the Know-Nothing Party, see Tyler Anbinder, *Nativism & Slavery: The Northern Know Nothings & the Politics of the 1850s* (New York: Oxford University Press, 1992).

84. "Diplomatic Revelations," *New Orleans Tribune*, June 9, 1865.

85. Henry Highland Garnet, "The Past and Present Condition, and Destiny of the Colored Race: A Discourse Delivered at the Fifteenth Anniversary of the Female Benevolent Society of Troy, N.Y., Feb. 14, 1848," *Electronic Texts in American Studies*, Paper 13, http://digitalcommons.unl.edu/etas/13, 21 (accessed July 8, 2016).

86. José Martí, "The Washington Pan-American Congress," in José Martí, *Inside the Monster: Writings on the United States and American Imperialism*, ed. Phillip S. Foner, trans. Elinor Randall et al. (New York: Monthly Review Press, 1975), 347.

87. Jack O'Dell, "Foundations of Racism in American Life," *Freedomways* 4, no. 4 (Fall 1964): 98–99. For an overview of O'Dell's writings, see Nikhil Pal Singh, ed., *Climbin' Jacob's Ladder: The Freedom Movement Writings of Jack O'Dell* (Berkeley: University of California Press, 2010).

88. William Appleman Williams, *Empire as a Way of Life: An Essay on the Causes and Character of America's Present Predicament Along with a Few Thoughts About an Alternative* (New York: Oxford University Press, 1980); see also William Appleman Williams, "Empire as a Way of Life," *Nation* 231 (August 2–9, 1980): 104–19. Williams's thesis is supported by Steven Hahn in *A Nation Without Borders: The United States and Its World in an Age of Civil Wars* (New York: Viking, 2016).

CHAPTER 3: "TO BREAK THE FETTERS OF SLAVES ALL OVER THE WORLD"

1. Ernesto Galarza, *Spiders in the House and Workers in the Field* (Notre Dame, IN: University of Notre Dame Press, 1970); Natalia Molina, *How Race Is Made in America: Immigration, Citizenship, and the Historical Power of Racial Scripts* (Berkeley: University of California Press, 2014), 91–111; Linda Heidenreich, *"This Land Was Mexican Once": Histories of Resistance from Northern California* (Austin: University of Texas Press, 2007); Carol Anderson, *White Rage: The Unspoken Truth of Our Racial Divide* (New York: Bloomsbury, 2016).

2. Richard Griswold del Castillo, *The Treaty of Guadalupe Hidalgo: A*

Legacy of Conflict (Norman: University of Oklahoma Press, 1990); Acuña, *Occupied America*, 48–50; Zaragosa Vargas, *Crucible of Struggle: A History of Mexican Americans* (New York: Oxford University Press, 2011), 100–3.

3. Leon Litwack, *North of Slavery: The Negro in the Free States* (Chicago: University of Chicago Press, 1961), 70. Litwack notes, "Most of the new states, particularly those carved out of the Northwest Territory, either explicitly barred Negroes or permitted them to enter only after they had produced certified proof of their freedom and had posted a bond, ranging from $500 to $1,000, guaranteeing their good behavior." On repressive legislation against African Americans in Oregon and California, see "The State Constitutional Convention," *Daily Alta California*, September 13, 1857; "Free Persons of Color," *Sacramento Daily Union*, May 4, 1858; "Illustration of a Disgraceful Law," *Marysville Daily Appeal*, March 22, 1862.

4. "The Workings of the Compromise," *Frederick Douglass' Paper*, July 24, 1851.

5. John Steinbeck, *The Grapes of Wrath* (1939; New York: Penguin Books, 2002), 231. For the politics of expropriation, see also Alexander Saxton, *The Rise and Fall of the White Republic: Class Politics and Mass Culture in Nineteenth Century America* (1991; New York: Verso, 2003).

6. Franklin and Moss, *From Slavery to Freedom*, 184–91; Litwack, *North of Slavery*, 100–102.

7. "Speech of John S. Rock, Esq.," *Christian Recorder*, February 22, 1862. All speech excerpts that follow are from this source.

8. Ramírez quoted in Jesse Alemán, "The Invention of Mexican America," in *The Oxford Handbook of Nineteenth-Century American Literature*, ed. Russ Castronovo (New York: Oxford University Press, 2012), 92. See also Paul Bryan Gray, *A Clamor for Equality: Emergence and Exile of Californio Activist Francisco P. Ramirez* (Lubbock: Texas Tech University Press, 2012), 25–26. See also Félix Gutiérrez, "Francisco P. Ramírez: Californio Editor and Yanqui Conquest," in *Profiles in Journalistic Courage*, ed. Robert Giles, Robert W. Snyder, and Lisa DeLisle (New Brunswick, NJ: Transaction, 2001), 19–28; José Luis Benavides, "Californios! Whom Do You Support? El Clamor Público's Contradictory Role in the Racial Formation Process in Early California," *California History* 84, no. 2 (Winter 2006–7): 54–66; Arturo Romero Nunez, "*Freedom's Journal* and *El Clamor Público*: African American and Mexican American Cultural Fronts in Nineteenth-Century Newsprint," PhD diss., University of California, Berkeley, 2010.

9. Hayes-Bautista, *El Cinco de Mayo*, 49–50.

10. "Getting Up to Date on a 19th Century L.A. Activist," editorial, *Los Angeles Times*, January 8, 2013.

11. Gutiérrez, "Francisco P. Ramírez," 24.

12. Gómez, *Manifest Destinies*, 1; Guadalupe T. Luna, "On the Complexities of Race: The Treaty of Guadalupe Hidalgo and Dred Scott v. Sandford," *University of Miami Law Review* 53 (1999), 691–716; William S. Kiser, *Turmoil on the Rio Grande: The Territorial History of the Mesilla Valley, 1846–1865* (College Station: Texas A&M University Press), 33–45.

13. Menchaca, *Recovering History, Constructing Race*, 215–76; Takaki,

A Different Mirror, 166–90; Molina, *How Race Is Made in America,* 25–26, 87–88.

14. See, for example, Raúl A. Ramos, *Beyond the Alamo: Forging Mexican Ethnicity in San Antonio, 1821–1861* (Chapel Hill: University of North Carolina Press, 2008).

15. Galarza, *Farm Workers and Agribusiness in California,* 88.

16. On the decline of the economic and political rights of Latinx people in the West, see Acuña, *Occupied America,* 109–24; Albert Camarillo, *Chicanos in a Changing Society: From Mexican Pueblos to American Barrios in Santa Barbara and Southern California, 1848–1930* (1979; Dallas: Southern Methodist University Press, 2005), 33–53; Gómez, *Manifest Destinies,* 47–80; McWilliams, *Brothers Under the Skin,* 113–39.

17. Alemán, "Invention of Mexican America," 92.

18. Vargas, *Crucible of Struggle,* 116.

19. Jean Pfaelzer, *Driven Out: The Forgotten War Against Chinese Americans* (Berkeley: University of California Press, 2007), 38–39.

20. William D. Carrigan and Clive Webb, *Forgotten Dead: Mob Violence Against Mexicans in the United States, 1848–1928* (New York: Oxford University Press, 2013); Menchaca, *Recovering History, Constructing Race,* 228–71; Heidenreich, *"This Land Was Mexican Once."*

21. Carrigan and Webb, *Forgotten Dead;* Menchaca, *Recovering History, Constructing Race,* 228–71; Heidenreich, *"This Land Was Mexican Once";* Benjamin Heber Johnson, *Revolution in Texas: How a Forgotten Rebellion Turned Mexicans into Americans* (New Haven, CT: Yale University Press, 2003).

22. Benjamin Madley, *An American Genocide: The United States and the California Indian Catastrophe* (New Haven, CT: Yale University Press, 2016).

23. Richard Street, *Beasts of the Field: A Narrative History of California Farmworkers, 1769–1913* (Palo Alto, CA: Stanford University Press, 2004); Stacey L. Smith, *Freedom's Frontier: California and the Struggle over Unfree Labor, Emancipation, and Reconstruction* (Chapel Hill: University of North Carolina Press, 2013).

24. Ernesto Galarza, *Farm Workers and Agri-Business in California, 1947–1960* (Notre Dame, IN: University of Notre Dame Press, 1977), 88.

25. Camarillo, *Chicanos in a Changing Society,* 4. Zaragosa Vargas finds that employers paid Mexican miners in Arizona "about a third less than Anglo miners for the same work." Vargas, *Crucible of Struggle,* 153.

26. Ibid., 333.

27. Litwack, *North of Slavery,* 69–74.

28. David Roediger, *The Wages of Whiteness: Race and the Making of the American Working Class* (1991; New York: Verso, 2007); David Roediger, *Working Toward Whiteness: How America's Immigrants Became White: The Strange Journey from Ellis Island to the Suburbs* (New York: Basic Books, 2005); Matthew Frye Jacobson, *Whiteness of a Different Color: European Immigrants and the Alchemy of Race* (Cambridge, MA: Harvard University Press, 1998).

29. Gregory R. Nokes, *Breaking Chains: Slavery on Trial in the Oregon Territory* (Corvallis: Oregon State University Press, 2013).

30. *Transactions of the Twenty-Fifth Annual Reunion of the Oregon Pioneer Association for 1897* (Portland: Geo H. Himes and Company, 1898), 42.

31. Nokes, *Breaking Chains*; Charles H. Carey, *The Oregon Constitution and Proceedings and Debates of the Constitutional Convention of 1857* (Salem, OR: State Printing Dept., 1926).

32. Cheryl A. Brooks, "Race, Politics, and Denial: Why Oregon Forgot to Ratify the Fourteenth Amendment," *Oregon Law Review* 83 (2004): 731–62.

33. Stephen Jay Gould, *The Mismeasure of Man*, rev. ed. (1981; New York: W.W. Norton, 1996), 88.

34. For an overview of scientific racism, see Gould, *Mismeasure of Man*; Samuel J. Redman, *Bone Rooms: From Scientific Racism to Human Prehistory in Museums* (Cambridge, MA: Harvard University Press, 2016); Tony Platt, "Engaging the Past: Charles M. Goethe, American Eugenics, and Sacramento State University," *Social Justice* 32, no. 2 (2005): 17–33; Ibram X. Kendi, *Stamped from the Beginning: The Definitive History of Racist Ideas in America* (New York: Nation Books, 2016); William H. Tucker, *The Funding of Scientific Racism: Wickliffe Draper and the Pioneer Fund* (Urbana: University of Illinois Press, 2002).

35. "American Slavery—Its Effects Upon the Rights and Interests," *North Star*, May 12, 1848.

36. "South Carolina Declaration of Independence," *Sacramento Daily Union*, December 4, 1860.

37. "Slavery Question in Oregon," *Sacramento Daily Union*, September 30, 1857.

38. Caitlin Rosenthal, "Plantations Practiced Modern Management," *Harvard Business Review* (September 2013), https://myhbp.org/leadingedge/d/cla?&c=28097&i=28099&cs=9780836848f84f739c7616ab61d4ecao.

39. Phil Fixico, interviewed by Ryan Morini, June 6, 2012, Black Seminole/Underground Railroad South Collection, SPOHP; Katz, *Black Indians*.

40. "Stampede," *Rome Courier*, December 26, 1850; "Texas Rangers—Wild Cat—The Fugitive Law," *National Era*, October 30, 1851; "The Mexican Border Troubles," *Frederick Douglass' Paper*, November 16, 1855. For an oral account of these border struggles for freedom by a descendent of the Black Seminoles, see William "Dub" Warrior, interviewed by Paul Ortiz, SPOHP, June 21, 2012.

41. Genevieve Payne Benson, interviewed by Ryan Morini, SPOHP, June 21, 2012. See also Rafaela Brown, interviewed by Marna Weston, SPOHP, June 22, 2012.

42. Vargas, *Crucible of Struggle*, 123.

43. "Slave Stampede and Resistance," *Placer Times*, January 5, 1850.

44. "The Civil War in Ohio," *Sacramento Daily Union*, July 2, 1857.

45. "The Boston Fugitive Slave Riot," *Daily Alta California*, July 2, 1854.

46. C. L. R. James, *A History of Pan-African Revolt* (1939; Chicago: Charles H. Kerr, 1995), 57.

47. William Watson Davis, *Civil War and Reconstruction in Florida* (New York: Columbia University, 1913), 38–42. See also Paul Goodman, "David Donald's Charles Sumner Reconsidered," *New England Quarterly* 37, no. 3 (September 1964): 373–87; and Samuel Proctor, ed., "The Call to Arms: Secession from a Feminine Point of View," *Florida Historical Quarterly* 35, no. 3 (January 1957): 269. Davis's thesis on slavery as the causative factor of the Civil War has encouraged newer generations of Florida historiography. See, for example, Daniel Schafer, *Thunder on the River: The Civil War in Northeast Florida* (Gainesville: University Press of Florida, 2010), x–xi; Paul Ortiz, "The Not So Strange Career of William Watson Davis's Civil War and Reconstruction in Florida," in *The Dunning School: Historians, Race, and the Meaning of Reconstruction*, ed. John David Smith and J. Vincent Lowery (Lexington: University Press of Kentucky, 2013).

48. *Constitution or Form of Government for the People of Florida: Ordinance of Secession* (Tallahassee: Dyke & Carlisle, 1861), 7, https://babel.hathitrust.org/cgi/pt?id=dul1.ark:/13960/t8w960178;view=1up;seq=2⸗

49. "Letter from Niagara," *National Anti-Slavery Standard*, July 22, 1847.

50. "The Pulpit and Press on the War," *Christian Recorder*, August 24, 1861.

51. Adam Goodheart, "The South Rises Again—and Again, and Again," *New York Times*, January 27, 2011; Pleasant A. Stovall, *Robert Toombs: Statesman, Speaker, Soldier, Sage* (New York: Cassell Publishing Co., 1892); William C. Davis, *The Union That Shaped the Confederacy: Robert Toombs & Alexander H. Stephens* (Lawrence: University Press of Kansas, 2001).

52. Edward A. Miller Jr., "Garland H. White, Black Army Chaplain," *Civil War History* 43, no. 2 (1997): 201–18.

53. "Letter from the 25th U.S.C.T.," *Christian Recorder*, November 4, 1864.

54. "Letter from Richmond," *Christian Recorder*, April 22, 1865.

55. Hayes-Bautista, *El Cinco De Mayo*, 81–84. Whether this was true or not is the subject of debate. Karl Marx argued in 1867 that Maximilian had planned to bring slavery back in Mexico under the guise of peonage. However, what ultimately matters in this instance is the belief among many African Americans in the United States that a European army was in Mexico in order to reestablish empire and slavery. See Jon Elster, ed., *Karl Marx: A Reader* (Cambridge, UK: Cambridge University Press, 1986), 138.

56. "Brilliant Achievements," *Hartford Daily Courant*, January 30, 1863; "The News from Mexico," *Christian Recorder*, July 26, 1862.

57. "Army of the Potomac," *Christian Recorder*, May 23, 1863. See also "From Havana and Mexico," *Christian Recorder*, December 27, 1862; "The French in Mexico," *Christian Recorder*, April 25, 1863.

58. "The French in Mexico," *Christian Recorder*, January 31, 1863.

59. "Mexico," *Christian Recorder*, November 14, 1863.

60. Hayes-Bautista, *El Cinco de Mayo*, 81.

61. "Vera Cruz," *Christian Recorder*, May 23, 1863; "Republican Form of Government by Rev. H. M. Turner," *Christian Recorder*, October 3, 1863.

62. Jerry Thompson, *Cortina: Defending the Mexican Name in Texas* (Col-

lege Station: Texas A&M University Press, 2007), 153–54; John Hope Franklin, *George Washington Williams: A Biography* (Chicago: University of Chicago Press, 1985), 5–6; "A Mexican War, After Our Rebellion, Shall Maximilian Be Driven Out?" *Black Republican* (New Orleans), April 15, 1865.

63. "Opinion," *New Orleans Tribune*, July 12, 1867.

64. "Slavery in Cuba," and "Maximilian and Slavery," *South Carolina Leader* (Charleston), November 25, 1865.

65. The South sought to emulate the success of the Union Army—much too late—by passing a measure to recruit African American soldiers into their depleted columns. See "Gen. Lee's Testimony," *Anti-Slavery Advocate*, April 1, 1865.

66. "The Army and the Negroes," *Anti-Slavery Standard*, February 18, 1865.

67. P. K. Rose, "Black Dispatches: Black American Contributions to Union Intelligence During the Civil War," Central Intelligence Agency, March 16, 2007, https://www.cia.gov/library/center-for-the-study-of-intelligence/csi-pub lications/books-and-monographs/black-dispatches/.

68. "Letter from 3rd U.S.C.T.," *Christian Recorder*, August 12, 1865.

69. "'God Bless the Negroes!'" *Anti-Slavery Advocate*, April 1, 1865.

70. Sarah H. Bradford, *Harriet: The Moses of Her People* (New York: Geo. R. Lockwood & Son, 1886); Catherine Clinton, *Harriet Tubman: The Road to Freedom* (New York: Little, Brown, 2005); Liane Hansen, "Harriet (Tubman) The Spy," National Public Radio, *Weekend Edition*, August 30, 2009, http://www.npr.org/templates/story/story.php?storyId=112384583 (accessed May 9, 2017).

71. "From Camp WM Penn.," *Christian Recorder*, April 15, 1865.

72. Kate Clifford Larson, *Bound for the Promised Land: Harriet Tubman, Portrait of an American Hero* (New York: Ballantine Books, 2004), 366.

73. "Senator Sherman on Suffrage," *National Anti-Slavery Standard*, July 1, 1865.

74. Ibid.

75. Abraham Lincoln, "Interview with John T. Mills, August 15, 1864," *American Presidency Project*, http://www.presidency.ucsb.edu/ws/?pid=591 (accessed May 9, 2017).

76. John Stauffer, *Giants: The Parallel Lives of Frederick Douglass and Abraham Lincoln* (New York: Twelve, 2008), 288; C. L. R. James, "Black Studies and the Contemporary Student," in *At the Rendezvous of Victory: Selected Writings* (London: Allison and Busby, 1984), 404.

77. Du Bois, *Black Reconstruction in America* (1935; New York: Meridian Books, 1964), 33–127; C. L. R. James, "The Black Jacobins and Black Reconstruction: A Comparative Analysis," *Small Axe* 8 (September 2000): 86; C. L. R. James, *American Civilization*, ed. Anna Grimshaw and Keith Hart (Cambridge, MA: Blackwell, 1993), 92.

78. Du Bois, *Black Reconstruction in America*, 67.

79. James, "The Black Jacobins and Black Reconstruction."

80. Frederick Douglass, "Emancipation, Racism, and the Work Before Us,"

in *"The Real War Will Never Get in the Books"*: *Selections from Writers During the Civil War*, ed. Louis P. Masur (New York: Oxford University Press, 1993), 118.

81. "Black Suffrage," *National Anti-Slavery Standard*, April 8, 1865.

82. "Appeal to the American People," *National Anti-Slavery Standard*, June 24, 1865.

83. Ibid.

84. "From Boston," *New Orleans Tribune*, March 2, 1865.

CHAPTER 4: GLOBAL VISIONS OF RECONSTRUCTION

1. Howard Thurman, *Jesus and the Disinherited* (1949; Boston: Beacon Press, 1996). On the development of African American Christianity, see Albert J. Raboteau, *Slave Religion: The "Invisible Institution" in the Antebellum South* (1978; New York: Oxford University Press, 2004); C. Eric Lincoln and Lawrence H. Mamiya, *The Black Church in the African American Experience* (1990; Durham: Duke University Press, 2003).

2. Thurman, *Jesus and the Disinherited*, 13.

3. "Slavery in the West Indies," *Christian Recorder*, February 20, 1873.

4. "The Boston Meetings," *National Anti-Slavery Standard*, February 3, 1866.

5. "Wm. Lloyd Garrison, Esq." *Christian Recorder*, February 24, 1866.

6. "Thirty-Sixth Anniversary of the American Anti-Slavery Society," *National Anti-Slavery Standard*, May 29, 1869.

7. "Oration," *Elevator* (San Francisco), January 24, 1868.

8. "Liberty in Cuba," *Christian Recorder*, March 21, 1878; "The Present Extent of the Slave Trade," *Christian Recorder*, March 8, 1877.

9. "Fifteenth Amendment Address," *Elevator*, April 15, 1870. African American Fifteenth Amendment observances in California frequently incorporated messages of solidarity with the Cuban struggle. For a description of one such event held in San Francisco, see "Oration," *Elevator*, April 5, 1873. For the fourth-anniversary celebration of the Fifteenth Amendment in Chico, California, where support was expressed for the Cuban patriots, see "Oration," *Elevator*, March 1, 1873, and "Oration," *Elevator*, April 25, 1874.

10. "Ratification Celebration of the Colored Citizens of Virginia City, Nevada," *Territorial Enterprise*, April 8, 1870.

11. "The Slavery Question," *Black Republican*, May 20, 1865. Reports of slave traders seizing African Americans in Alabama and other states in order to sell them to Cuba also alarmed African Americans. See "Slave Trading," *National Anti-Slavery Standard*, March 3, 1866.

12. Cuban Anti-Slavery Committee, *Slavery in Cuba: A Report of the Proceedings of the Meeting Held at Cooper Institute* (New York: Powers, Macgowan & Slipper, 1872), 8, https://archive.org/details/slaveryincubarep00cuba. African Americans commonly underplayed the very real tensions within the nationalist movement in Cuba. These included racism and differences over strategies. See Ada Ferrer, *Insurgent Cuba: Race, Nation, and Revolution, 1868–1898* (Chapel Hill: University of North Carolina Press, 1999), 9–10.

13. For example, see "President's Annual Message," December 2, 1872, in *The Congressional Globe: The Debates and Proceedings of the Third Session, Forty-Second Congress* (Washington, DC: Office of the Congressional Globe, 1873), 5, https://digital.library.unt.edu/ark:/67531/metadc30903/.

14. "Petitions, Resolutions, &c." *Journal of the House of Representatives of the State of South Carolina Being the Regular Session of 1869–70* (Columbia, SC: John W. Denny, Printer to the State, 1870), 55–56.

15. "Forty-First Congress," *New York Times*, February 5, 1870; "Journal of the Senate of the United States of America, 1789–1873" (December 9, 1869), Library of Congress, *American Memory*, https://memory.loc.gov/ (accessed October 12, 2015).

16. Members of the Cuban Junta in New York held different political tendencies and attitudes toward US involvement in Cuba's Ten Years' War. See Vanessa Michelle Ziegler, "The Revolt of 'The Ever-Faithful Isle': The Ten Years' War in Cuba, 1868–1878," PhD diss., University of California, Santa Barbara, 2007, 185–206.

17. For information on Governor Pinchback, see Agnes Smith Grosz, "The Political Career of Pinckney Benton Stewart Pinchback," *Louisiana Historical Quarterly* 27 (April 1944): 527–612.

18. "Speeches and Resolutions of the Colored National Convention," *Pacific Appeal* (San Francisco), May 4, 1872.

19. "Correspondence Salt Lake, U.T.," *Elevator*, July 4, 1873.

20. See *Facts About Cuba* (New York: Sun Job Prtg. Off., 1870). For an outstanding account of the movement, see Nancy Raquel Mirabal, *Suspect Freedoms: The Racial and Sexual Politics of Cubanidad in New York, 1823–1957* (New York: New York University Press, 2017).

21. Carla Peterson, "Black Elites and the Draft Riots," *New York Times*, July 13, 2013.

22. The following account is taken primarily from the booklet on the proceedings, published by the Cuban Anti-Slavery Committee, titled *Slavery in Cuba*.

23. José Martí, "Henry Garnet, Famous Negro Orator," in Foner, *Inside the Monster*, 69.

24. Cuban Anti-Slavery Committee, *Slavery in Cuba*, 16.

25. Ibid., 16.

26. Ibid., 5.

27. "The Colored Citizens of New York," *Christian Recorder*, December 21, 1872.

28. "Public Meetings," *Elevator*, December 28, 1872; "Cuban Independence," *Elevator*, February 15, 1873.

29. "Cuban Anti-Slavery Meeting—Addresses and Resolutions," *Sun* (Baltimore), February 14, 1873. Several meeting summaries of the Cuban Anti-Slavery Committee note the participation of women. Given the leadership roles that Black women played in African American communities, they undoubtedly played a major role in the national petition campaign. See "Enthusiastic Meeting in Cooper Institute," *New York Times*, October 25, 1877.

30. Ibid.

31. "Slavery in Cuba," *New York Herald*, February 1, 1873.

32. "Cuban Independence," *Elevator*, February 15, 1873.

33. For reports of meetings, see "Sympathy with Cuba," *New York Times*, February 8, 1873; "Colored Men on Spanish Slavery Meeting in Washington," *New York Times*, March 8, 1873; "The Colored Men and Cuba," *New York Times*, March 11, 1873. On movement culture, see Lawrence Goodwyn, *The Populist Moment: A Short History of the Agrarian Revolt in America* (New York: Oxford University Press, 1978), xix.

34. "The Colored People of the District of Columbia," *New York Times*, November 19, 1873.

35. "Duty of the Colored Population," *Elevator*, December 6, 1873; "The Civil Rights Convention," *New York Times*, December 15, 1873.

36. "Oration," *Elevator*, April 25, 1874.

37. "Emancipation of Cuban Slaves," *Christian Recorder*, September 10, 1870; "Slavery in Cuba," *New York Times*, July 13, 1877; "Samuel R. Scottron," *Cleveland Gazette*, June 4, 1887.

38. "The Corresponding Secretary to the Bishop and Conference," *Christian Recorder*, July 23, 1870. Lawrence S. Little, *Disciples of Liberty: The African Methodist Episcopal Church in the Age of Imperialism, 1884–1916* (Knoxville: University of Tennessee Press, 2000).

39. "Cuba et Puerto Rico," *Christian Recorder*, November 7, 1868.

40. *Official Journal of the Proceedings of the Senate of the State of Louisiana* (New Orleans: Office of The Republican, 1872), 113; "Hon. J. Henri Burch," *Weekly Louisianan*, January 25, 1873.

41. Charles Vincent, *Black Legislators in Louisiana During Reconstruction* (Baton Rouge: Louisiana State University Press, 1976), 165–66.

42. "The Louisiana Colored Men," *New York Times*, November 28, 1873.

43. "Louisiana State Republican Resolutions and Platform," *Weekly Louisianan*, September 26, 1874.

44. "Colored Men on Spanish Slavery Meeting in Washington," *New York Times*, March 8, 1873; "The Colored Men and Cuba," *New York Times*, March 11, 1873.

45. "Civil Rights Demonstration," *Weekly Louisianan*, June 27, 1874.

46. *A Journal of the Proceedings of the Assembly of the State of Florida at the Sixth Session Held in the Capitol in The City of Tallahassee on Tuesday, January 7, 1873* (Tallahassee, FL: S. B. McLin, 1873), 192–93.

47. "Speech of Hon. Josiah Walls, of Florida, In the House of Representatives, January 24, 1874, On the Joint Resolution Declaring the Right of the Cuban Republic to Recognition as Belligerent," *Appendix to the Congressional Record, Congressional Record: Forty-Third Congress, First Session*, vol. 2 (Washington: Government Printing Office, 1874), 27–29.

48. "Samuel R. Scottron: An Interesting Biographical Sketch of a Successful Member of the Race," *Cleveland Gazette*, June 4, 1887; "Petition to Accord Belligerent Rights to Cuba," *New York Times*, February 20, 1873; "Correspondence," *Elevator*, April 12, 1873.

49. "Meeting of Congress, President's Message," *Weekly Louisianan*, December 7, 1872; "Petition to Accord Belligerent Rights to Cuba," *New York*

Times, February 20, 1873; "The Spanish Republic," *New York Times*, February 24, 1873; "Correspondence," *Elevator*, March 25, 1873.

50. Allan Nevins, *Hamilton Fish: The Inner History of the Grant Administration*, rev. ed., vol. 1 (New York: Frederick Ungar, 1957), 180–81.

51. Richard H. Bradford, *The Virginius Affair* (Boulder: Colorado University Press, 1980), 14–15. See also Ziegler, "Revolt of 'The Ever-Faithful Isle,'" 175–89.

52. "Cuba," *Christian Recorder*, March 6, 1873.

53. "Cuba," *Savannah Tribune* (Georgia), November 11, 1876.

54. "Protest Against Cuban Slavery," *Christian Recorder*, November 8, 1877; "The Freedom of Cuba," *New York Times*, October 25, 1877.

55. J. Morgan Kousser, *The Shaping of Southern Politics: Suffrage Restriction and the Establishment of the One-Party South, 1880–1910* (New Haven, CT: Yale University Press, 1974).

56. Martí, "Henry Garnet, Famous Negro Orator," 68–69.

57. "Emancipation Celebration in Florida," *National Anti-Slavery Standard*, February 11, 1865.

58. Menard wrote a poem in homage to the struggle against slavery in Cuba and Brazil in 1879. See "Hail Free Cuba!" *People's Advocate* (Washington, DC), September 27, 1879. For information on Menard, see "Elected to Congress, Menard Lost Seat in Bitter Contest," *Chicago Defender*, November 21, 1925; "Florida Citizens Meet with President Hayes," *Sunland Tribune*, March 31, 1877; John Willis Menard, *Lays in Summer Lands*, ed. Larry Eugene Rivers, Richard Mathews, and Canter Brown Jr. (Tampa, FL: University of Tampa Press, 2002). Menard also served as principal of the Douglas School on the island. See "The National Capital," *New York Globe*, December 1, 1883.

59. "Grant in Cuba," *Daily Inter Ocean*, January 31, 1880. Gerald E. Poyo, "Cuban Revolutionaries and Monroe County Reconstruction Politics, 1868–1876," *Florida Historical Quarterly* 55 (April 1977): 407–22.

60. José Martí, "To Cuba!," in *José Martí: Selected Writings*, ed. and trans. Esther Allen (New York: Penguin Books, 2002), 321.

61. Paul Ortiz, *Emancipation Betrayed: The Hidden History of Black Organizing and White Violence in Florida from Reconstruction to the Bloody Election of 1920* (Los Angeles: University of California Press, 2005), 34–43.

62. Ron Hayduk, "Florida History: Resident Noncitizen Voting in Florida," 2016, http://ronhayduk.com/immigrant-voting/around-the-us/state-histories/florida-history/ (accessed November 16, 2016); Virginia Harper-Ho, "Noncitizen Voting Rights: The History, the Law and Current Prospects for Change," *Law and Inequality Journal* 18 (Summer 2000): 273–83. Alexander Keyssar discusses the rise and fall of declarant alien voting nationally in *The Right to Vote: The Contested History of Democracy in the United States* (New York: Basic Books, 2000), 136–71.

63. "Constitution of the State of Florida, 1868," Florida Constitution Revision Commission, http://archive.law.fsu.edu/crc/conhist/1868con.html (accessed January 3, 2016).

64. Knights of Labor, *Proceedings of the General Assembly of the Knights of Labor of America* (General Assembly, 1887), 1385, 1717; John Rogers Com-

mons et al., *History of Labour in the United States: Nationalisation*, vol. 1 (New York: Macmillan Company, 1918), 463; Melton McLaurin, *The Knights of Labor in the South* (Westport, CT: Greenwood Press, 1984), 81–82; Canter Brown Jr., "Prelude to the Poll Tax: Black Republicans and the Knights of Labor in 1880s Florida," in *Florida's Heritage of Diversity: Essays in Honor of Samuel Proctor*, ed. Mark I. Greenberg, William Warren Rogers, and Canter Brown, Jr. (Tallahassee: Sentry Press, 1997), 69–81. See also Leon Fink, *Workingman's Democracy: The Knights of Labor and American Politics* (Urbana: University of Illinois Press, 1983), 28; Laura Edwards, *Gendered Strife and Confusion: The Politics of Reconstruction* (Urbana: University of Illinois Press, 1997), 218–54; Philip S. Foner and Ronald L. Lewis, *Black Workers: A Documentary History from Colonial Times to the Present* (Philadelphia: Temple University Press, 1989), 209–35; Ileen A. DeVault, *United Apart: Gender and the Rise of Craft Unionism* (Ithaca: Cornell University Press, 2004), 147–51.

65. *Report of the Royal Commission on Strikes* (Sydney: George Stephen Chapman Government Printers, 1891), 209; Eleanor Marx and Edward Aveling, *The Working-Class Movement in America* (London: Swan Sonnenschein & Co., 1891), 5.

66. Winston James, *Holding Aloft the Banner of Ethiopia: Caribbean Radicalism in Early Twentieth-Century America* (London: Verso, 1998), 232–57; Gerald E. Poyo, "Cuban Patriots in Key West, 1878–1886: Guardians at the Separatist Ideal," *Florida Historical Quarterly* 61 (January 1979): 20–36; Horne, *Race to Revolution*, 141–42.

67. On the expansion of these markets, see C. B. Rogers to W. J. Lutterloh, January 5, 1870, File #5, Washington J. Lutterloh Papers, Southern Historical Collection, University of North Carolina, Chapel Hill.

68. "Peculiarities of Key West," *New York Age*, November 3, 1888; "Florida Market Gardens," *New York Times*, November 24, 1889.

69. "Peculiarities of Key West."

70. J. W. Menard to Joseph E. Lee, January 24, 1880, Joseph Lee Papers, Private Manuscript Collection of Ike Williams III, Jacksonville, Florida (henceforth cited as Joseph Lee Papers). The Cigar Makers International Union of America counted at least 300 union members in Key West as late as 1903. See "Organization," *Cigar Makers Official Journal* 28 (April 15, 1904): 9.

71. William Artrell to Joseph E. Lee, April 27, 1880, Joseph Lee Papers.

72. "Peculiarities of Key West."

73. Sheriff Dupont's obituary in 1938 noted, "A political division which led to a coalition between Negroes and Spanish-Americans brought about his election with a considerable majority." "Florida's Only Negro Sheriff," quoted in *Tampa Sunday Tribune*, October 2, 1938, box 1, folder "1938," Florida Negro Papers, Florida Works Progress Administration, University of South Florida, Tampa; Horne, *Race to Revolution*, 141. For a brief profile of Dean, see "A Beautiful City," *Freeman* (Indianapolis), November 29, 1890.

74. Prior to the election of 1888, a white candidate for the county judgeship stepped aside in favor of James Dean. For Dean's plan to use slavery reparations to fund Florida's public schools, see *The Proceedings of the State Conference of the Colored Men of Florida Held at Gainesville, February, 5, 1884* (Wash-

ington, DC: 1884), reel 10, frame 27, Frederick Douglass Papers, Manuscript Division, Library of Congress.

75. "Freest Town in the South: No Bulldozing Attempted at Key West," *New York Age*, November 24, 1888. Livingston would go on to become US consul in Haiti.

76. Ibid.

77. On the stresses in the Republican coalition in Key West, see William Artrell to Joseph E. Lee, October 4, 1881, Joseph Lee Papers.

78. "Freest Town in the South."

79. Ortiz, *Emancipation Betrayed*, 33–55.

80. *Christian Recorder*, editorial, July 6, 1882.

81. Quoted in Du Bois, *Black Reconstruction*, 621.

82. "Everyone Favors the Bill," *Florida Times-Union*, April 9, 1889; Samuel Proctor, *Napoleon Bonaparte Broward: Florida's Fighting Democrat* (Gainesville: University Press of Florida, 1950).

83. *Florida Times-Union*, editorial, April 13, 1889. See also "The Negro Can't Be Assimilated," *Pensacola Commercial*, October 5, 1888.

84. I am using the term "Jim Crow/Juan Crow segregation" to describe the overarching systems of segregation in the Sunbelt that were used by political elites to disenfranchise African American and Latinx workers. I use the term "Sunbelt" to refer to the South, the Southwest, and the agriculturally important areas of California.

85. J. Clay Smith Jr., *Emancipation: The Making of the Black Lawyer, 1844–1944* (Philadelphia: University of Pennsylvania Press, 1999), 276.

86. On the development of white business supremacy in the South, see Ortiz, *Emancipation Betrayed*, 11–59.

87. "Pensacola Free," *Pensacola Commercial*, March 15, 1885.

88. Equal Justice Initiative, *Lynching in America: Confronting the Legacy of Racial Terror* (Montgomery, AL: 2015).

89. "Florida Topics," *New York Freeman*, June 25, 1887.

90. William W. Rogers, "The Negro Alliance in Alabama," *Journal of Negro History* 45, no. 1 (January 1960): 39.

91. Fortune, *Black and White*, xxxi–xxxii; William H. Skaggs, *The Southern Oligarchy: An Appeal on Behalf of the Silent Masses of Our Country Against the Despotic Rule of the Few* (New York: Devin-Adair Company, 1924).

92. Keyssar, *The Right to Vote*, 99; Alexander Saxton, *The Indispensable Enemy: Labor and the Anti-Chinese Movement in California* (1971; Berkeley: University of California Press, 1995), 89–90; Vargas, *Crucible of Struggle*, 151–52.

93. Keyssar, *The Right to Vote*, 98.

94. "Democratic Doctrine," *New York Globe*, September 20, 1884.

95. Steel boss Andrew Carnegie on the importance of voter suppression in the South: "In the South, the ignorant are the immense majority. To give suffrage without restriction to the blacks would mean that the intelligent whites were powerless, overwhelmed. Government would be in the hands of men steeped in ignorance of political responsibilities to a degree impossible for Northern

people to imagine. Only residence among them can give a true impression." "Mr. Carnegie on the Negro," *Florida Times-Union*, March 2, 1904.

96. "Governor Fowler [*sic*] Interviewed," *State Chronicle* (NC), May 10, 1889.

97. Robert Winston, "An Unconsidered Aspect of the Negro Question," *South Atlantic Quarterly* 1, no. 1 (January 1902): 265. See also Dwight Farnham, "Negroes a Source of Industrial Labor," *Industrial Management* 56, no. 2 (August 1918): 75.

98. "Relations of Whites and Blacks" *News and Observer* (Raleigh, NC), April 14, 1901.

99. Du Bois, *Black Reconstruction*, 727.

100. Ibid., 706.

101. William Appleman Williams, *The Tragedy of American Diplomacy* (1959; New York: W. W. Norton, 1972).

CHAPTER 5: WAGING WAR ON THE GOVERNMENT
OF AMERICAN BANKS IN THE GLOBAL SOUTH

1. On the life and work of Ida B. Wells-Barnett, see Paula J. Giddings, *Ida: A Sword Among Lions* (New York: HarperCollins, 2008); Sarah L. Silkey, *Black Woman Reformer: Ida B. Wells, Lynching, and Transatlantic Activism* (Athens: University of Georgia Press, 2015); Patricia Schechter, *Ida B. Wells-Barnett and American Reform, 1880–1930* (Chapel Hill: University of North Carolina Press, 2001).

2. "The Act of an Arkansas Mob," *New York Times*, February 21, 1892.

3. José Martí, "A Town Sets A Black Man on Fire," in *Selected Writings*, 313; Oscar Montero discusses Martí's complex approach to US race relations in "Jose Marti Against Race," in *The Cuban Republic and Jose Marti: Reception and Use of a National Symbol*, ed. Mauricio A. Font and Alfonso W. Quiroz (New York: Lexington Books, 2006). See also Manfred Berg and Simon Wendt, eds., *Globalizing Lynching History: Vigilantism and Extralegal Punishment from an International Perspective* (New York: Palgrave Macmillan, 2011), 53–68.

4. Juan González and Joseph Torres, *News for All the People: The Epic Story of Race and the American Media* (London: Verso, 2011), 170.

5. Martí, "The Truth About the United States," in *Selected Writings*, 330–31.

6. Jacqueline Jones Royster, ed., *Southern Horrors and Other Writings: The Anti-Lynching Campaign of Ida B. Wells, 1892–1900* (New York: Bedford/St. Martins, 1997), 70.

7. José Martí, "Antonio Maceo," in *Our America by José Martí: Writings on Latin America and the Struggle for Cuban Independence*, ed. Philip S. Foner, trans. Elinor Randall (New York: Monthly Review Press, 1977), 374. On Maceó, see Philip S. Foner, *Antonio Maceo: The 'Bronze Titan' of Cuba's Struggle for Independence* (New York: Monthly Review Press, 1977); Robert C. Nathan, "Imagining Antonio Maceo: Memory, Mythology and Nation in Cuba, 1896–1959," master's thesis, University of North Carolina, Chapel Hill,

2007; José Martí, "The Washington Pan-American Congress," in Foner, *Inside the Monster*, 340–41.

8. "Resolutions Adopted," *Freeman* (Indianapolis), January 2, 1897.

9. Ibid; "Chicago Sympathizes with Cuba," *Enterprise* (Omaha), January 1, 1897.

10. "Gen. Antonio Maceo, A Brilliant Figure Around Whom the Aspiring Negro May Twine His Brightest Hopes for the Future," *Freeman*, October 30, 1897.

11. "Maceo's Death Arouses Them," *Cleveland Gazette*, December 19, 1896.

12. "Emancipation Address Delivered by Rev. C. Dillard," *Cleveland Gazette*, May 1, 1897.

13. Edward A. Johnson, *History of the Colored Soldiers in the Spanish American War* (1899), http://www.gutenberg.org/files/11102/11102-h/11102-h.htm (accessed February 9, 2015).

14. In recent years, scholars have been transcending binary thinking on race. See, for example, Manuel Pastor, Stewart Kwoh, and Angela Glover Blackwell, *Searching for the Uncommon Common Ground: New Dimensions on Race in America* (New York: W. W. Norton, 2002).

15. "Sketches; Gen. Antonio Maceo," *Cleveland Gazette*, November 14, 1896. See also "A Grand Record in the History of Cuba," *Cleveland Gazette*, March 4, 1899; "The Colored Man in Cuba Knows No Color Lines," *Fair Play* (Fort Scott, KS), March 10, 1899; Sarah Watts, *Rough Rider in the White House: Theodore Roosevelt and the Politics of Desire* (Chicago: University of Chicago Press, 2003), 84–85.

16. "The Colored Man in Cuba Knows No Color Lines."

17. "Cuba's Mulatto Hero," *Freeman*, April 30, 1898. See also "All Signs Point," *Freeman*, December 6, 1896. In contrast, Florida's superintendent of public instruction, W. M. Sheats, lectured: "Those of us who love the Anglo-Saxon race and this great American republic are willing to do almost anything to preserve race purity and to save the South from the spectacle witnessed in Hayti, Jamaica, Mexico, and wherever there are no race distinctions." "The Florida Disgrace," *Southwestern Christian Advocate*, September 12, 1895.

18. See "Another Cuban Hero Fell," *Cleveland Gazette*, April 9, 1898; "Social Equality Discussed," *Freeman*, July 31, 1897; "All Over the World Brave, Banderas," *Iowa State Bystander*, September 3, 1897; "The Cuban Patriots," *Cleveland Gazette*, November 28, 1896.

19. See Louis A. Pérez Jr., *The War of 1898: The United States & Cuba in History & Historiography* (Chapel Hill: University of North Carolina Press, 1998), 81–133.

20. "'The White Man's Burden': Kipling's Hymn to U.S. Imperialism," *History Matters: The U.S. Survey Course on the Web*, http://historymatters.gmu.edu/d/5478/ (accessed January 10, 2016); Hans Schmidt, *The United States Occupation of Haiti: 1915–1934* (1971; New Brunswick, NJ: Rutgers University Press, 1995), 44.

21. "Cuban Women: Some of Their Daring Acts of Bravery," *Fair Play*,

March 24, 1899. Edward A. Johnson also noted the participation of Cuban women as combatants in the War of Independence. See *A School History of the Negro Race in America, from 1619 to 1890: Combined with a History of the Negro Soldiers in the Spanish-American War*, rev. ed. (New York: Isaac Goldmann Co., 1911).

22. Ibid.

23. Ibid. "It is easy to be heroes with women such as these," José Martí remarked. See Lynn K. Stoner, *From the House to the Streets: The Cuban Woman's Movement for Legal Reform, 1898–1940* (Durham: Duke University Press, 1991), 20. See also Linda L. Reif, "Women in Latin American Guerilla Movements: A Comparative Perspective," *Comparative Politics* 18, no. 2 (January 1986): 147–69; Karen Kampwirth, *Women and Guerilla Movements: Nicaragua, El Salvador, Chiapas, Cuba* (University Park: Pennsylvania State University Press, 2002).

24. José Martí, "Letter to Manuel Mercado," in *Selected Writings*, 347. On the intersections of race and empire in the United States, see Paul A. Kramer, *The Blood of Government: Race, Empire, the United States and the Philippines* (Chapel Hill: University of North Carolina Press, 2006); Paul A. Kramer, "Power and Connection: Imperial Histories of the United States in the World," *American Historical Review* 116, no. 5 (December 2011): 1348–91.

25. "Race News," *Plain Dealer* (Cleveland), November 24, 1899; "Race Echoes," *Iowa State Bystander*, December 1, 1899.

26. "J.H. Wheaton Objects to American Interference in Cuban Affairs," *Enterprise* (Omaha), February 6, 1897.

27. African Americans often understated racism in the former nations of the Spanish Empire in their efforts to contrast race relations in Latin America with social relations in the United States. On racism in the Cuban nationalist movement, see Ferrer, *Insurgent Cuba*. More generally, see Matt D. Childs, *The 1812 Aponte Rebellion in Cuba and the Struggle Against Atlantic Slavery* (Chapel Hill: University of North Carolina Press, 2006); Eduardo Galeano, *Upside Down: A Primer for the Looking-Glass World* (New York: Picador, 2001); Peter Wade, *Race and Ethnicity in Latin America* (1997; New York: Pluto Press, 2010).

28. James A. Le Roy, "Race Prejudice in the Philippines," *Atlantic Monthly*, July–December, 1902, 103. See Alfred W. McCoy, *Policing America's Empire: The United States, the Philippines, and the Rise of the Surveillance State* (Madison: University of Wisconsin Press, 2009); Willard B. Gatewood, *"Smoked Yankees" and the Struggle for Empire: Letters from Negro Soldiers, 1898–1902* (Fayetteville: University of Arkansas Press, 1987).

29. "Unfairness of the United States," *Afro-American*, November 13, 1909.

30. For an example of labor struggles in the sugar industry, see Santiago Iglesias, "Strike of Porto Rican Agricultural Workers," *American Federationist* 22, no. 1 (April 1915): 264–67; "Strike in Porto Rico Becoming More General," *Facts About Sugar* 4, no. 8 (February 24, 1917): 86; "Letter from Porto Rico, Labor Troubles Are Quite Acute," *Louisiana Planter and Sugar Manufacturer* 54, no. 1 (February 27, 1915): 139.

31. "Porto Rico Misery Laid to Americans," *Negro World*, March 7, 1925.

32. "U.S. Hurts, Doesn't Help, Puerto Rico in Solving Island Ills of Hunger," *Chicago Defender*, May 22, 1943.

33. Gonzalez, *Harvest of Empire*, 280–82; Carlos Alamo-Pastrana, *Seams of Empire: Race and Radicalism in Puerto Rico and the United States* (Gainesville: University Press of Florida, 2016).

34. Serafín Méndez-Méndez with Ronald Fernández, *Puerto Rico Past and Present: An Encyclopedia*, 2nd ed. (Denver: Greenwood Press, 2015), 220–21; Ronald Schmidt Sr. et al., *Newcomers, Outsiders, and Insiders: Immigrants and American Racial Politics in the Early Twenty-First Century* (Ann Arbor: University of Michigan Press, 2010), 86.

35. "Statement From the Annual Meeting of the Niagara Movement at Sea Island, NJ," *Afro-American*, September 18, 1909; "Right to Work Is Question," *Afro-American*, September 18, 1909.

36. "Independent Political League Adopts Strong Address against US Intervention in Cuba," *Afro-American Ledger*, July 20, 1912. Historian Arthur S. Link discusses the work of the National Independent Political League in *Wilson: The Road to the White House* (Princeton, NJ: Princeton University Press, 1947), 503–6. See also National Independent Political League, *Fifty Years of Physical Freedom and Political Bondage, 1862–1912* (Washington, DC: National Independent Political League, 1912).

37. W. E. B. Du Bois, "The African Roots of War," *Atlantic Monthly* 115 (May 1915): 707–14.

38. "The Haitian Affliction," *Washington Bee*, October 23, 1920. On the role of the National City Bank of New York in American imperialism and politics, see Peter James Hudson, "The National City Bank of New York and Haiti, 1909–1922," *Radical History Review* 115 (Winter 2013): 91–114; Louis Brandeis, *Other People's Money and How the Bankers Use It* (New York: Frederick A. Stokes Company, 1914), 28. On the Wilmington Massacre, see H. Leon Prather, *We Have Taken a City: The Wilmington Racial Massacre and Coup of 1898* (Wilmington, NC: Dram Tree Books, 2006).

39. "Neval H. Thomas Speaks Out for Equal Rights and Justice for All American Citizens," *Negro Star* (Wichita, KS), September 17, 1920.

40. "Political Power 'Distorted' Says Dr. Du Bois," *Plain Dealer* (Topeka, KS), June 29, 1928.

41. "N.A.A.C.P. Publishes Text of Address." *Amsterdam News*, July 18, 1928.

42. "Imperialism? Turn to Haiti," *Pittsburgh Courier*, February 11, 1928.

43. "Pan American Conference," *Western Outlook* (Oakland, CA), February 4, 1928.

44. The continuation of Black internationalist ideas throughout the twentieth century can be traced in Singh, *Climbin' Jacob's Ladder*; Conrad J. Lynn, *There Is a Fountain: The Autobiography of Conrad Lynn* (1979; New York: Lawrence Hill Books, 1993); Vijay Prashad, *Everybody Was Kung Fu Fighting: Afro-Asian Connections and the Myth of Cultural Purity* (Boston: Beacon Press, 2002); Penny M. Von Eschen, *Race Against Empire: Black Americans*

and Anticolonialism, 1937–1957 (Ithaca, NY: Cornell University Press, 1997); Susan Greenbaum, *More Than Black: Afro-Cubans in Tampa* (Gainesville: University Press of Florida, 2002).

45. For critical analyses of these organizations and Black internationalist tendencies in general, see James, *A History of Pan-African Revolt*; Frantz Fanon, *The Wretched of the Earth* (1961; New York: Grove Press, 2005); Ula Yvette Taylor, *The Veiled Garvey: The Life and Times of Amy Jacques Garvey* (Chapel Hill: University of North Carolina Press, 2001); Michelle Mitchell, *Righteous Propagation: African Americans and the Politics of Racial Destiny After Reconstruction* (Chapel Hill: University of North Carolina Press, 2004); Minkah Makalini, *In the Cause of Freedom: Radical Black Internationalism from Harlem to London* (Chapel Hill: University of North Carolina Press, 2011); Christopher J. Lee, *Making a World After Empire: The Bandung Moment and Its Political Afterlives* (Columbus: Ohio University Press, 2010); Fred Ho and Bill V. Mullen, *Afro Asia: Revolutionary Political and Cultural Connections Between African Americans and Asian Americans* (Durham, NC: Duke University Press, 2008); Tony Martin, *Race First: The Ideological and Organizational Struggles of Marcus Garvey and the Universal Negro Improvement Association* (Dover, MA: Majority Press, 1986).

46. I have drawn heavily on the works of Cedric Robinson and Edward W. Said in making these points about the relationship between social theory and resistance. See Edward W. Said, "Traveling Theory Reconsidered," in *Critical Reconstructions: The Relationship of Fiction and Life*, ed. Robert M. Polhemus and Roger Henkle (Stanford, CA: Stanford University Press, 1994), 251–65; Cedric Robinson, *The Terms of Order: Political Science and the Myth of Leadership* (1980; Chapel Hill: University of North Carolina Press, 2016).

47. "Kaiser Sam Critique of US Foreign Policy," *Pittsburgh Courier*, January 22, 1927.

48. "Brutal Official Rule in Spanish Honduras," *Negro World*, October 11, 1924; "A Disgraceful Chapter," *Philadelphia Tribune*, November 6, 1920. See also Jason M. Colby, *The Business of Empire: United Fruit, Race, and U.S. Expansion in Central America* (Ithaca, NY: Cornell University Press, 2011).

49. "Haitian Laws Disregarded by US Tyrants," *Philadelphia Tribune*, March 13, 1926 (this investigation had been jointly conducted by the Patriotic Union of Haiti and the NAACP). For an analysis of the role of US banks in promoting US imperialism, see Hudson, "National City Bank of New York and Haiti."

50. "Haitian Laws Disregarded."

51. "US Get Out of Haiti," *New York World*, April 10, 1927. Chester M. Wright served as English Language Secretary of the Pan-American Federation of Labor and was a major figure in the American Federation of Labor.

52. Building on the work of Lawrence Goodwyn and other democratic theorists, Harry C. Boyte promoted the idea that "political knowledge is importantly social and experiential." See Harry C. Boyte, "Populism and John Dewey: Convergences and Contradictions," University of Michigan Dewey Lecture, March 29, 2007, 2 (transcript in author's collection), https://archive

.org/stream/populism_devey/populism_devey_djvu.txt. See also Goodwyn, *Populist Moment*.

53. Blair L. M. Kelley, *Right to Ride: Streetcar Boycott and African American Citizenship in the Era of Plessy v. Ferguson* (Chapel Hill: University of North Carolina Press, 2010).

54. "Day by Day," *Afro-American*, June 20, 1925.

55. Ibid.

56. Ibid. On the issue of American citizens' land holdings in Mexico, see McLynn, *Zapata and Villa*, 16–18.

57. On the upsurge in Pan-African activity in this era, see James, *A History of Pan-African Revolt*.

58. "Beautiful Haiti and Its Brave Hearted People," *Negro World*, February 7, 1925. On Holly, see "The New and Brilliant French Editor of the Negro World," *Negro World*, February 7, 1925. See also Brenda Gayle Plummer, "The Afro-American Response to the Occupation of Haiti, 1915–1934," in *Race and U.S. Foreign Policy from the Colonial Period to the Present*, ed. Michael L. Krenn (New York: Garland, 1998), 70.

59. Between 1825 and 1947, the French government extorted approximately 90 million gold francs from the Haitians. See "M. Sarkozy, rendez à Haïti son argent extorqué," *Libération*, August 15, 2010, http://www.liberation.fr/planete/2010/08/16/m-sarkozy-rendez-a-haiti-son-argent-extorque_672275 (accessed January 3, 2017); Isabel Macdonald, "France's Debt of Dishonour to Haiti," *Guardian*, August 16, 2010.

60. "Heroic Women of Haiti," *Negro World*, February 21, 1925.

61. "Bolivar and San Martin," *Negro World*, December 20, 1924.

62. Ibid. See also "Sad Bereavement," *Colored American*, July 11, 1903; "Song of Toussaint L'Ouverture," *Negro World*, September 15, 1923; "Mexico's Black Lincoln [Vicente Guerrero]," *Plain Dealer* (Kansas City), February 16, 1945.

63. Martin, *Race First*, 92–100.

64. Taylor, *The Veiled Garvey*, 52–54.

65. "UNIA Continues to Sweep Cuba," *Negro World*, October 6, 1923.

66. For example, see "Propaganda en Contra de la Aspiracíon Filipina," *Negro World*, November 3, 1923; "Discontented Porto Rico Clamors for Justice," *Negro World*, November 10, 1923; "Disturbances in China Are Laid to the British," *Negro World*, June 27, 1925; "Can Britain Hold India in the Empire?," *Negro World*, April 4, 1925; "Nicaragua y Estados Unidos," *Negro World*, November 29, 1924.

67. "US Get out of Haiti and Colonial Traitors," *New York World*, April 10, 1927

68. "Race and Class Struggle Fierce in South Africa," *Negro World*, August 1, 1925.

69. "The Degradation of Labor in South Africa," *Negro World*, November 15, 1924.

70. "'Be Free Men and Women in Africa,'" *Negro World*, April 25, 1925. For background on the ICU, see Helen Bradford, *A Taste of Freedom: The ICU*

in Rural Africa, 1924–1930 (New Haven, CT: Yale University Press, 1988); C. Kadalie, *My Life and the ICU: The Autobiography of a Black Trade Unionist in South Africa* (New York: Humanities Press, 1970).

71. "Our Labor Troubles Are World-Embracing and Perplexing," *Negro World*, April 25, 1925.

72. "The Cotton Revolution and Trouble in the African Sudan," *Negro World*, December 6, 1924.

73. "Procedimientos Inhumanos," *Negro World*, November 29, 1924.

74. "Cubans Appreciate U.S. Support of U.N.I.A.," *Negro World*, August 8, 1925.

75. "Should Protest Butler as Military Governor of Cuba," *Christian Recorder*, August 11, 1898; "The Black Man in Cuba," *Plain Dealer*, February 3, 1899; "The 'Color Devil' in Cuba," *Christian Recorder*, March 2, 1899; "A Lesson to Learn," *Afro-American*, December 10, 1910; "Uprising in Cuba," *Philadelphia Tribune*, May 25, 1912; "Color Line in Cuba," *Philadelphia Tribune*, June 8, 1912.

76. "A Lesson to Learn," *Afro-American*, December 10, 1910; Julie Greene, *The Canal Builders: Making America's Empire at the Panama Canal* (New York: Penguin Books, 2010).

77. "More Outrages in Haiti," *Negro World*, November 24, 1923.

78. "Urges Race to Fight Facisti Movement," *Pittsburgh Courier*, April 28, 1928.

79. "The Lynching of Haitians," *Cleveland Gazette*, January 22, 1921. In a similar manner, the *Negro World* simultaneously critiqued Jim Crow and imperialism, showing how the two worked together in one provocative headline: "How American Occupation of Haiti Is Demoralizing Oppressor and Oppressed. Ignorant and Licentious Young Men Drawn Chiefly from the Negro-Hating South Sowing Seeds of Strife. Tax on Island's Chief Product Benefits Only National City Bank of New York—U.S. Advised to Get Out." *Negro World*, April 23, 1927.

80. James Weldon Johnson, "Self-Determining Haiti: The American Occupation," *Nation* 111 (August 28, 1920), http://windowsonhaiti.com/windowsonhaiti/haiti_oc_series_03.shtml (accessed December 15, 2014). See also "White Hell in Black Haiti: U.S. Military Law Rules," *Washington Bee*, September 11, 1920.

81. "Annexing Another Colony," *Pittsburgh Courier*, November 19, 1927. On March 18, 1911, the *Savannah Tribune* published a story on how William Taft's administration attempted to meddle in the Mexican Revolution: "Chain Guard Along Border; Taft Admits the Real Purpose of the Mobilization."

82. Ibid.

83. See "Haitian Laws Disregarded by US Tyrants"; "Haiti Conditions As Described by a Native," *Washington Bee*, June 18, 1921; "Haiti Speaks!" *Cleveland Gazette*, June 11, 1921; "Nicaraguan War as Forum Topic," *New York Amsterdam News*, January 25, 1928.

84. "New York Virgin Islanders Hold Big Mass Meeting to Protest Bad Economic Rule," *Pittsburgh Courier*, February 23, 1924.

85. "Virgin Islands Ask U.S. For Citizenship," *Baltimore Afro-American*, March 7, 1924.

86. "Uncle Sam's Hot Potato," *Pittsburgh Courier*, January 14, 1928. "Nicaraguan War as Forum Topic"; Neill Macaulay, *The Sandino Affair* (1985; Micanopy, FL: Wacahoota Press, 1998); Thomas W. Walker, *Nicaragua: Living in the Shadow of the Eagle* (Boulder, CO: Westview Press, 2003); Max Boot, *The Savage Wars of Peace: Small Wars and the Rise of American Power* (New York: Basic Books, 2003), 231–52.

87. "Says Sandino Served," *New York Times*, January 6, 1928; "Republic or Empire?" *New York Amsterdam News*, February 22, 1928.

88. "Our Nicaraguan War," *Norfolk Journal and Guide*, July 23, 1927.

89. "Rah! For the Dominicans!" *Cleveland Gazette*, June 25, 1921.

90. "Views and Reviews," *Pittsburgh Courier*, May 12, 1928.

91. "Aggressors Pay for the Robberies," *Pittsburgh Courier*, October 16, 1943.

92. Ibid. See also Schuyler's essay, "The Caucasian Problem," which appeared in Rayford Logan, ed., *What the Negro Wants* (Chapel Hill: University of North Carolina Press, 1944). Schuyler traveled to Liberia in 1931 and developed a more positive opinion of the Firestone plantations. See Oscar Renal Williams, *George S. Schuyler: Portrait of a Black Conservative* (Knoxville: University of Tennessee Press, 2007), 55–56.

93. Smedley Butler, *War Is a Racket* (1935; New York: Skyhorse Publishing, 2013), 4–5.

94. "Mr. Hoover Says," *Afro-American*, April 7, 1928.

95. Ibid. For Howard University president Mordecai Johnson's on-air critiques of US imperialism, see "More Howard University Air Programs," *Afro-American*, November 30, 1929

96. "Haiti Speaks," *Washington Bee*, June 4, 1921.

97. "Democracy in Dixieland," *Negro World*, January 1, 1927.

98. Bernardo Ruiz Suarez, *The Color Question in the Two Americas*, trans. John Crosby Gordon (New York: Hunt Publishing, 1922), 19.

99. Ibid., 95.

CHAPTER 6: FORGOTTEN WORKERS OF AMERICA

1. Marcus Rediker, *The Slave Ship: A Human History* (New York: Viking, 2007).

2. For an overview, see Nell Irvin Painter, *Standing at Armageddon: The United States, 1877–1919* (1987; New York: W.W. Norton, 2008); Louis Adamic, *Dynamite: The Story of Class Violence in America* (1931; New York: AK Press, 2008); David Montgomery, *Beyond Equality: Labor and the Radical Republicans, 1862–1872* (1967; Urbana: University of Illinois Press, 1981); Paul Krause, *The Battle for Homestead, 1880–1892: Politics, Culture and Steel* (Pittsburgh: University of Pittsburgh Press, 1992); Graham Adams, *The Age of Industrial Violence, 1910–1915* (New York: Columbia University Press, 1966); David Montgomery, *The Fall of the House of Labor: The Workplace, the State,*

and American Labor Activism, 1865–1925 (Cambridge, UK: Cambridge University Press, 1987); Jeremy Brecher, *Strike!*, rev. ed. (1972; Cambridge, MA: South End Press, 1997); Robert Michael Smith, *From Blackjacks to Briefcases: A History of Commercialized Strikebreaking and Unionbusting in the United States* (Athens: Ohio University Press, 2003); Robin Archer, *Why Is There No Labor Party in the United States?* (Princeton, NJ: Princeton University Press, 2007); Josiah Lambert, *If Workers Took a Notion: The Right to Strike and American Political Development* (Ithaca, NY: Cornell University Press, 2005).

3. On the pro-employer bent of labor law in the United States, see Christopher L. Tomlins, *The State and the Unions: Labor Relations, Law, and the Organized Labor Movement in America, 1880–1960* (Cambridge, UK: Cambridge University Press, 1985); Christopher L. Tomlins, *Law, Labor, and Ideology in the Early American Republic* (New York: Cambridge University Press, 1993).

4. Karen Orren, *Belated Feudalism: Labor, the Law, and Liberal Development in the United States* (New York: Cambridge University Press, 1991).

5. Vargas, *Crucible of Struggle*, 237.

6. William H. Skaggs, *The Southern Oligarchy: An Appeal in Behalf of the Silent Masses of Our County Against the Despotic Rule of the Few* (New York: Devin-Adair Co., 1924), 299.

7. Vargas, *Crucible of Struggle*, 181–82.

8. Carolyn Ashbaugh, *Lucy Parsons: An American Revolutionary* (1976; Chicago: Haymarket Books, 2012), 55.

9. Howard Kester, *Revolt Among the Sharecroppers* (New York: Arno Press, 1969), 46.

10. Gould, *Mismeasure of Man*, 142.

11. "Peace for Capital and Labor" *Florida Times-Union*, May 25, 1901. On the corporate consolidation of power in the Progressive Era, see Gabriel Kolko, *The Triumph of Conservatism: A Reinterpretation of American History, 1900–1916* (1963; New York: Free Press, 1977); Goodwyn, *The Populist Moment*; Nancy Cohen, *The Reconstruction of American Liberalism, 1865–1914* (Chapel Hill: University of North Carolina Press, 2002); James Livingston, *Origins of the Federal Reserve System: Money, Class and Corporate Capitalism, 1890–1913* (Ithaca, NY: Cornell University Press, 1989).

12. "The Color Line That Belts the Earth," *Florida Times-Union*, March 20, 1904. For the relationship between lynching and voter suppression, see Cox, *Caste, Class, and Race*, 555.

13. American Social History Project, Nelson Lichtenstein, Susan Strasser, and Roy Rosenzweig, *Who Built America? Working People and the Nation's Economy, Politics, Culture, and Society, 1877 to the Present* (New York: Worth Publishers, 2000), 2: 167.

14. W. E. B. Du Bois, "The Economics of Negro Emancipation in the United States," *Sociological Review* 4, no. 3 (October 1911): 310.

15. Keyssar, *The Right to Vote*, 136–71.

16. James Green, "Democracy Comes to 'Little Siberia': Aliquippa, Pennsylvania, 1933–1937," *Labor's Heritage* 5 (August 1993): 4–27.

17. Gabriela F. Arredondo, *Mexican Chicago: Race, Identity, and Nation, 1916–39* (Urbana: University of Illinois Press, 2008), 93.

18. For an analysis of the emergence of the Sunbelt in terms of politics, race, and labor, see Joseph Crespino, *Strom Thurmond's America* (New York: Hill and Wang, 2012).

19. For workers' strike actions in California agriculture between the 1880s and 1910s, see Richard Steven Street, *Beasts of the Field: A Narrative History of California Farmworkers, 1769–1913* (Stanford, CA: Stanford University Press, 2004), 81, 92, 319–20, 332–33, 433–34, 454–69; Frank P. Barajas, *Curious Unions: Mexican American Workers and Resistance in Oxnard, California, 1898–1961* (Lincoln: University of Nebraska Press, 2010). The process of corporate consolidation of farming in the West is dramatized in Frank Norris's 1901 novel *The Octopus: A Story of California.*

20. Carey McWilliams, *Factories in the Field: The Story of Migratory Farm Labor in California* (1935; Santa Barbara, CA: Peregrine Publishers, 1971), 139–40.

21. Saxton, *Indispensable Enemy.*

22. "Growers and Shippers to Gather Wage Data," *Florida Grower*, December 25, 1920; "Cause Spread," *Florida Grower*, December 4, 1920.

23. Robert Perkinson, *Texas Tough: The Rise of America's Prison Empire* (New York: Henry Holt, 2010), 55.)

24. Vargas, *Crucible of Struggle*, 170.

25. For a discussion of the implementation of the Dawes Act, see Roxanne Dunbar-Ortiz, *An Indigenous Peoples' History of the United States* (Boston: Beacon Press, 2014), 157–61.

26. Cox, *Capitalism and American Leadership*, 249.

27. Johnson, *Revolution in Texas*; Vargas, *Crucible of Struggle*, 183–87; Gerald Horne, *Black and Brown: African Americans and the Mexican Revolution, 1910–1920* (New York: New York University Press, 2005), 156–80; Charles H. Harris III and Louis R. Sadler, *The Plan de San Diego: Tejano Rebellion, Mexican Intrigue* (Lincoln: University of Nebraska Press, 2013).

28. Carrigan and Webb, *Forgotten Dead.*

29. Kelly Lytle Hernández, *Migra! A History of the U.S. Border Patrol* (Berkeley: University of California Press, 2010), 54–57.

30. The Nazis studied the use of Zyklon B at the US–Mexico border and later used it as a weapon to exterminate Jewish people and others in death camps during the Holocaust. See David Dorado Romo, *Ringside Seat to a Revolution: An Underground Cultural History of El Paso and Juárez* (El Paso: Cinco Puntos Press, 2005), 240–44.

31. Scott Simon, "The Bath Riots: Indignity Along the Mexican Border," interview with J. Burnett, National Public Radio, January 28, 2006, http://www.npr.org/templates/story/story.php?storyId=5176177.

32. Clements quoted in Cletus E. Daniel, *Bitter Harvest: A History of California Farmworkers, 1870–1941* (Berkeley: University of California Press, 1981), 105–6.

33. McWilliams, *Factories in the Field*, 125–26.

34. For deportation campaigns over time, see Ernesto Galarza, *Merchants of Labor: The Mexican Bracero Story* (Santa Barbara, CA: McNally & Loftin, 1964), 39–40; Julie M. Weise, *Corazón de Dixie: Mexicanos in the U.S. South Since 1910* (Chapel Hill: University of North Carolina, 2015), 45–46; Nestor P. Rodriguez and Cecilia Menjívar, "Central American Immigrants and Racialization in a Post–Civil Rights Era," in *How the United States Racializes Latinos: White Hegemony and Its Consequences*, ed. José A. Coba, Jorge Duany, and Joe R. Feagin (Boulder, CO: Paradigm: 2009), 193–94.

35. Dora Anderson, interviewed by Paul Ortiz, August 3, 1994, Tallahassee, Florida, for *Behind the Veil: Documenting African American Life in the Jim Crow South*, Center for Documentary Studies, Duke University (henceforth cited as *Behind the Veil*). See also Robert J. Norrell, *Up from History: The Life of Booker T. Washington* (Cambridge, MA: Harvard University Press, 2009), 113–14. Leon Litwack has written extensively on Jim Crow–era white violence against "successful blacks" in *Trouble in Mind: Black Southerners in the Age of Jim Crow* (New York: Alfred A. Knopf, 1998), 150–63.

36. Du Bois, in "Economics of Negro Emancipation," states, "Of the proportion of farm ownership the Census says that between 1890 and 1900, while the number of Negro farmers probably increased by about 36 or 38 per cent, the number of Negro owners increased over 57 per cent, and the percentage of ownership by 3.5 per cent. So that 187,799 Negro farms, or 25.2 per cent of all Negro farms were owned. The rapid increase of this group between 1890 and 1900 alarmed the merchants" (311).

37. Roland B. Eustler, "Agricultural Credit and the Negro Farmer," *Journal of Social Forces* 8 (1929–30): 420.

38. "Our Good White Folks Way Down in Dixie," *Negro World*, March 28, 1925.

39. For the creation of state systems of forced labor after the formal abolition of slavery, see J. C. Powell, *The American Siberia or Fourteen Years' Experience in a Southern Convict Camp* (1891; Montclair, NJ: Patterson Smith, 1970); Stetson Kennedy, *Southern Exposure* (1946; Boca Raton: Florida Atlantic University Press, 1991); Pete Daniel, *The Shadow of Slavery: Peonage in the South, 1910–1969* (1972; Urbana: University of Illinois Press, 1990); Alex Lichtenstein, *Twice the Work of Free Labor: The Political Economy of Convict Labor in the New South* (London: Verso, 1996); Matthew J. Mancini, *One Dies, Get Another: Convict Leasing in the American South, 1866–1928* (Columbia: University of South Carolina Press, 1996); David M. Oshinsky, *"Worse Than Slavery": Parchman Farm and the Ordeal of Jim Crow Justice* (New York: Free Press, 1996); Talitha L. LeFlouria, *Chained in Silence: Black Women and Convict Labor in the New South* (Chapel Hill: University of North Carolina Press, 2015); Mary Ellen Curtin, *Black Prisoners and Their World: Alabama, 1865–1900* (Charlottesville: University of Virginia Press, 2000); Douglas A. Blackmon, *Slavery by Another Name: The Re-Enslavement of Black Americans from the Civil War to World War II* (New York: Doubleday, 2008).

40. "During the Cotton Picking Season, U.S. Attorney's Claim," *Pittsburgh Courier*, February 19, 1927.

41. "A New Form of Labor Peonage in the Cotton Belt," *Norfolk Journal and Guide*, November 13, 1926.

42. "Imported Porto Rican Laborers Suffering at the Hands of Arizona Cotton Growers," *Pittsburgh Courier*, October 9, 1926.

43. See Angelo Falcon, "A History of Puerto Rican Politics in New York City: 1860s to 1945," in *Puerto Rican Politics in Urban America*, ed. James Jennings and Monte Rivera (Westport, CT: Greenwood Press, 1984), 27–28.

44. Morris Milgram, "Involuntary Servitude in Florida," *Twice A Year: A Book of The Arts, and Civil Liberties*, vol. 14 (Fall–Winter 1946–1947), 410, 413.

45. James, *A History of Pan-African Revolt*, 89.

46. "Why Scarce," *Florida Metropolis*, January 11, 1906.

47. "Punishing Criminals," *Florida Metropolis*, January 9, 1906.

48. "Let It Be Done Here Too," *Florida Metropolis*, January 27, 1907

49. Mario Barrera, *Race and Class in the Southwest: A Theory of Racial Inequality* (Notre Dame: University of Notre Dame Press, 1979), 78–89

50. Michael Honey, *Southern Labor and Black Civil Rights: Organizing Memphis Workers* (Urbana: University of Illinois Press, 1993), 30–37; Sterling D. Spero and Abram L. Harris, *The Black Worker: The Negro and the Labor Movement* (1931; New York: Atheneum, 1974), 173.

51. On union racism, see Spero and Harris, *The Black Worker*, 53–115. Human resources professionals saw the racial wage differential as a key tool in management's arsenal. See D. N. Crosthwait, "Making Up the Labor Shortage," *Industrial Management*, vol. T (May 1918): 412–13. See also Barrera, *Race and Class in the Southwest*, 51–52; McWilliams, *Brothers Under the Skin*, 312–46; George Lipsitz, *Possessive Investment in Whiteness: How White People Profit from Identity Politics*, rev. ed. (Philadelphia: Temple University Press, 2006).

52. Elaine Bernard and John Trumpbour, "Unions and Latinos: Mutual Transformation," in *Latinos: Remaking America*, ed. Marcelo Suárez-Orozco and Mariela Páez (Berkeley: University of California Press, 2002), 126–45.

53. Barrera, *Race and Class in the Southwest*, 89–92; John H. M. Laslett, *Sunshine Was Never Enough: Los Angeles Workers, 1880–2010* (Berkeley: University of California Press, 2014), 203.

54. On the struggle against color bars, see Herbert Hill, *Black Labor and the American Legal System: Race, Work, and the Law* (Madison: University of Wisconsin Press, 1985); Robert H. Zieger, *For Jobs and Freedom: Race and Labor in America Since 1865* (Lexington: University Press of Kentucky, 2007).

55. T. J. Woofter, "The Negro and Industrial Peace," *Survey* 45 (December 18, 1920): 420–21.

56. Kester, *Revolt Among the Sharecroppers*, 21.

57. "Adjust Wages and Working Opportunities," *Afro-American*, May 30, 1925.

58. Carol Shammas, Marylynn Salmon, and Michel Dahlin, *Inheritance in America: From Colonial Times to the Present* (New Brunswick, NJ: Rutgers University Press, 1987), 3; Andrew F. Brimmer, "Preamble: The Economic Cost of Discrimination Against Black Americans," in *A Different Vision: Race and*

Public Policy, vol. 2, ed. Thomas D. Boston (London: Routledge, 1997); Melvin L. Oliver and Thomas M. Shapiro, *Black Wealth/White Wealth: A New Perspective on Racial Inequality* (New York: Routledge, 1997); Maya Wesby, "Why Rich Kids Become Rich Adults and Poor Kids Become Poor Adults," *Wilson Quarterly* (August 13, 2015), https://wilsonquarterly.com/stories/why-rich-kids-become-rich-adults-and-poor-kids-become-poor-adults/.

59. James, *A History of Pan-African Revolt*, 67–101.

60. David Brody, *Steelworkers in America: The Nonunion Era* (1960; Urbana: University of Illinois Press, 1998).

61. "White Men Bomb Home in Effort to Force Family to Vacate Neighborhood," *Pittsburgh Courier*, July 19, 1924; "Kansas City Pastor Escapes Bomb," *Afro-American*, September 26, 1924; "Wrecked by Dynamite," *Afro-American*, September 3, 1912; "Will Blow Up Whole Block, Say Whites," *Pittsburgh Courier*, June 21, 1924; "Police Give No Aid When Mob Menaces Man's Home," *Chicago Defender*, November 22, 1924; "Residential Restriction Working in Chicago," *Negro World*, January 31, 1925. Paul Ortiz, "U.S. Race Riots, 1917–1923," in *The Encyclopedia of Race and Racism*, ed. Nicole Watkins (New York: Macmillan Reference USA, 2007), 438; Douglas S. Massey and Nancy A. Denton, *American Apartheid: Segregation and the Making of the Underclass* (Cambridge, MA: Harvard University Press, 1993), 30–31.

62. Michael R. Belknap, "The Mechanics of Repression: J. Edgar Hoover, the Bureau of Investigation and the Radicals, 1917–1925," *Crime and Social Justice* 7 (Spring–Summer 1977): 49–58.

63. Elliot M. Rudwick, *Race Riot at East St. Louis, July 2, 1917* (Edwardsville: Southern Illinois University Press, 1964), 13–14.

64. James Gregory, *The Southern Diaspora: How the Great Migrations of Black and White Southerners Transformed America* (Chapel Hill: University of North Carolina Press, 2005), 47.

65. James Weldon Johnson, *Along This Way: The Autobiography of James Weldon Johnson* (New York: Viking, 1933), 315.

66. Ortiz, *Emancipation Betrayed*, 206.

67. John Hope Franklin and John Whittington Franklin, eds., *My Life and an Era: The Autobiography of Buck Colbert Franklin* (Baton Rouge: Louisiana State University Press, 1997); Scott Ellsworth, *Death in a Promised Land: The Tulsa Race Riot of 1921* (Baton Rouge: Louisiana State University Press, 1982); Ortiz, "U.S. Race Riots, 1917–1923," 435–43.

68. James Hirsch, *Riot and Remembrance: The Tulsa Race War and Its Legacy* (Boston: Houghton Mifflin, 2002), 8.

69. James Loewen, *Sundown Towns: A Hidden Dimension of American Racism* (New York: Touchstone, 2005).

70. Nan Elizabeth Woodruff, *American Congo: The African American Freedom Struggle in the Delta* (Chapel Hill: University of North Carolina Press, 2012).

71. "Daily Newspapers," *Pittsburgh Courier*, January 23, 1926.

72. "Tampa Mob Burns Race Land Office," *Pittsburgh Courier*, February 6, 1926.

73. "Mob Burns Florida Realty Office," *Chicago Defender*, February 6, 1926.

74. Vargas, *Crucible of Struggle*, 217–20; Sarah Deutsch, *No Separate Refuge: Culture, Class, and Gender on an Anglo-Hispanic Frontier in the American Southwest, 1880–1940* (New York: Oxford University Press, 1987), 164–67; Francisco Balderrama and Raymond Rodríguez, *Decade of Betrayal: Mexican Repatriation in the 1930s* (Albuquerque: University of New Mexico Press, 1995); Acuña, *Occupied America*, 167–68.

75. Vargas, *Crucible of Struggle*, 218.

76. Zaragosa Vargas, *Labor Rights Are Civil Rights: Mexican American Workers in Twentieth-Century America* (Princeton, NJ: Princeton University Press, 2005), 55–58.

77. Vargas, *Crucible of Struggle*, 218.

78. Cox, *Caste, Class, and Race*, 393.

79. McWilliams, *Factories in the Field*, 236–37.

80. Galarza, *Spiders in the House*, 4; Nelson A. Pichardo Almanzar and Brian W. Kulik, *American Fascism and the New Deal: The Associated Farmers of California and the Proto-Industrial Movement* (Lanham, MD: Lexington Books, 2013); McWilliams, *Factories in the Field*, 230.

81. Carey McWilliams, "California Pastoral," *Antioch Review* 2, no. 1 (March 1942): 103–21.

82. Galarza, *Farm Workers and Agri-Business in California*, 363; Galarza, *Merchants of Labor*, 38–40. On agricultural subsidies in Mississippi, see James Cobb, *The Most Southern Place on Earth: The Mississippi Delta and the Roots of Regional Identity* (New York: Oxford University Press, 1994), 193–97; Pete Daniel, *Breaking the Land: The Transformation of Cotton, Tobacco, and Rice Cultures Since 1880* (Urbana: University of Illinois Press, 1986).

83. Carey McWilliams, *Ill Fares the Land: Migrants and Migratory Labor in the United States* (New York: Little, Brown, 1942), 27.

84. Ibid., 260.

85. "Unemployment Means Government Needs to Do Something," *Afro-American*, March 15, 1930.

86. "Hoover, the Bankers, Change System Time," *Afro-American*, October 17, 1931.

87. "Strike," *Gaffney (SC) Ledger*, August 29, 1933.

88. "Bagging Mill Shut as Women Strike," *Charleston (SC) News and Courier*, August 27, 1933. The *Daily Worker* placed the strikers in the wrong state, but it provided sympathetic coverage of the strike. See "800 Negro Workers Strike for More Pay in Charleston, N.C [sic]," *Daily Worker*, September 5, 1933.

89. "Spirit of Jungle Animates Negroes," *Asheville (NC) Advocate*, September 8, 1933, in *The Tuskegee Institute News Clippings File*, ed. John W. Kitchens, on microfilm (Tuskegee, AL: Tuskegee Institute, 1978), reel 44, frame 634.

90. "Mill Head Goes to Code Meeting," *Charleston News and Courier*, August 28, 1933.

91. Barton Bernstein, *Towards a New Past: Dissenting Essays in American History* (New York: Pantheon, 1968), 268.

92. "Bagging Factory to Open Tuesday," *Charleston News and Courier,* September 4, 1933.

93. On the rise of the CIO, see Lizabeth Cohen, *Making a New Deal: Industrial Workers in Chicago, 1919–1939* (New York: Cambridge University Press, 1990); Bruce Nelson, *Workers on the Waterfront: Seamen, Longshoremen, and Unionism in the 1930s* (Urbana: University of Illinois Press, 1990); Staughton Lynd, *We Are All Leaders: The Alternative Unionism of the Early 1930s* (Urbana: University of Illinois Press, 1996); Janet Irons, *Testing the New Deal: The General Textile Strike of 1934 in the American South* (Urbana: University of Illinois Press, 2000).

94. "Negroes on Edisto Look for Big Money," *Charleston News and Courier,* August 28, 1933. For an introduction to domestic work in this era, see Phyllis Palmer, *Domesticity and Dirt: Housewives and Domestic Servants in the United States, 1920–1945* (Philadelphia: Temple University Press, 1990).

95. "Seek 'New Deal' Wages," *Charleston News and Courier,* September 3, 1933.

96. Myrna Fichtenbaum, *The Funsten Nut Strike* (New York: International Publishers, 1991). On Philadelphia, see "Strike," *Baltimore Afro-American,* August 19, 1933. On Birmingham, see Paul Ortiz, "The Last Shall Be First: Black Workers, Civil Rights, and the Birmingham Spring of 1934," *Works in Progress,* March 1995; "In Birmingham," *Afro-American,* March 10, 1934.

97. "Domestic Strikes in Alabama," *Twin City Herald* (Minneapolis), March 10, 1934.

98. "Farm Worker Strike in NJ Tear Gassed," *Afro-American,* July 14, 1934; "Day by Day," *Afro-American,* July 21, 1934.

99. Gerda Lerner, ed., *Black Women in White America: A Documentary History* (New York: Pantheon Books, 1972), 269–70. For the history of FTA Local 22, see Robert Korstad, *Civil Rights Unionism: Tobacco Workers and the Struggle for Democracy in the Mid-Twentieth-Century South* (Chapel Hill: University of North Carolina Press, 2003).

100. "J. C. Long Speaks for Higher Taxes," *Charleston News and Courier,* August 31, 1933.

101. "Higher Prices Mean an Increase in My Salary," *Charleston News and Courier,* August 26, 1933.

102. "Negroes on Edisto Look for Big Money."

103. "N.R.A. Wage Scale Will Nullify Government Aim for Jobs in the South," *Charleston News and Courier,* September 10, 1933.

104. On the exclusion of African American workers from New Deal provisions, Ira Katznelson, *When Affirmative Action Was White: An Untold History of Racial Inequality in Twentieth-Century America* (New York: W. W. Norton, 2006), 53–79. For the marginalization of Southern white workers, see Irons, *Testing the New Deal.*

105. Paul Ortiz, "Segregation and Black Labor Before the CIO," *Against the Current* 138 (January–February 2009), https://www.solidarity-us.org /node/2035 (accessed July 10, 2015).

106. "Police Disperse Bag Mill Crowd," *Charleston News and Courier,*

August 29, 1933; "600 Resume Bag Mill Jobs Today," *Charleston News and Courier*, September 5, 1933.

107. "City Drops Work to Mark Hot but Quiet Labor Day," *Charleston News and Courier*, September 5, 1933.

108. "Colorful Labor Day Parade of Local Negroes Cancelled," *Charleston News and Courier*, September 3, 1933; Mamie Garvin Fields with Karen Fields, *Lemon Swamp and Other Places: A Carolina Memoir* (New York: Free Press, 1985), 29–30.

109. "City Drops Work."

110. "Parade 20 Miles Long," *Charleston News and Courier*, August 31, 1933.

111. Vicki L. Ruiz, *Cannery Women, Cannery Lives: Mexican Women, Unionization, and the California Food Processing Industry, 1930–1950* (Albuquerque: University of New Mexico, 1987).

112. See Nancy A. Hewitt, *Southern Discomfort: Women's Activism in Tampa, Florida, 1880s–1920s* (Urbana: University of Illinois Press, 2003); Vicki L. Ruiz, "Luisa Moreno and Latina Labor Activism," in *Latina Legacies: Identity, Biography, and Community*, ed. Vicki L. Ruiz and Virginia Sánchez Korrol (New York: Oxford University Press, 2005), 175–92.

113. "Luisa Moreno's 1949 Address to California CIO," *Kenneth Burt's Latino History Blog*, http://kennethburt.com/blog/?p=754 (accessed July 3, 2016); "Conference Discusses Negro Workers' Future," *California Eagle*, April 26, 1945.

114. Leon Alexander, interviewed by Paul Ortiz, June 21, 1994, *Behind the Veil*.

115. Francisco Arturo Rosales and Daniel T. Simon, "Mexican Immigrant Experience in the Urban Midwest: East Chicago, Indiana, 1919–1945," *Indiana Magazine of History* 77, no. 4 (1981), http://josotl.indiana.edu/index.php/imh/article/view/10337/14385 (accessed May 10, 2017).

116. Vargas, *Labor Rights Are Civil Rights*, 3–4; Francisco Arturo Rosales, *Chicano! The History of the Mexican American Civil Rights Movement* (Houston: Arte Público Press, 1996), 122.

117. Francisco Arturo Rosales, *Testimonio: A Documentary History of the Mexican-American Struggle for Civil Rights* (Houston: Arte Público Press, 2000), 252

118. Barrera, *Race and Class in the Southwest*, 141–43.

119. Leroy Boyd, interviewed by Paul Ortiz, June 19, 1995, *Behind the Veil*.

120. Earl B. Brown, interviewed by Paul Ortiz, June 28, 1994, *Behind the Veil*.

121. Ralph Thompson, interviewed by Paul Ortiz, July 7, 1995, *Behind the Veil*. On the persistence of racism in unions, see Herbert Hill, *The AFL-CIO and the Black Worker: Twenty-Five Years After the Merger* (Louisville, KY: National Association of Human Rights Workers, 1982); Herbert Hill, *Black Labor and the American Legal System: Race, Work, and the Law* (Madison: University of Wisconsin Press, 1985); Bruce Nelson, *Divided We Stand: American Workers and the Struggle for Black Equality* (Princeton, NJ: Princeton University Press, 2001).

122. William P. Jones, *The March on Washington: Jobs, Freedom, and the Forgotten History of Civil Rights* (New York: W. W. Norton, 2013), 1–40.

123. Brecher, *Strike!*, 237–47; George Lipsitz, *Rainbow at Midnight: Labor and Culture in the 1940s* (Urbana: University of Illinois Press, 1994).

124. Nelson Lichtenstein, *Labor's War at Home: The CIO in World War* II (Cambridge, UK: Cambridge University Press, 1982); James A. Gross, *Broken Promise: The Subversion of U.S. Labor Relations Policy, 1947–1994* (Philadelphia: Temple University Press, 1995); James A. Gross, *The Reshaping of the National Labor Relations Board: National Labor Policy in Transition, 1937–1947* (Albany: State University of New York Press, 1981); Tomlins, *The State and the Unions.*

125. Acuña, *Occupied America*, 261. See also Ernesto Galarza, *Merchants of Labor: The Mexican Bracero Story* (Santa Barbara, CA: McNally-Loftin, 1972), and Deborah Cohen, *Braceros: Migrant Citizens and Transnational Subjects in the Postwar United States and Mexico* (Chapel Hill: University of North Carolina Press, 2013). The historian Erin Conlin notes that Florida's employers could rely on the state to provide them with a large pool of Puerto Rican and Bahamian workers. See Conlin, "Invisible Hands in the Winter Garden: Power, Politics, and Florida's Bahamian Farmworkers in the Twentieth Century," PhD diss., University of Florida, 2014.

126. Michael Honey, *Black Workers Remember: An Oral History of Segregation, Unionism, and the Freedom Struggle* (Berkeley: University of California Press, 2002), 181.

127. Jefferson Cowie, *Capital Moves: RCA's Seventy-Year Quest for Cheap Labor* (1999; New York: New Press, 2001).

128. Ira Katznelson, *Fear Itself: The New Deal and the Origins of Our Time* (New York: Liveright, 2013), 156–94; Austin P. Morris, "Agricultural Labor and National Labor Legislation," *California Law Review* 54, no. 5 (December 1966): 1939–89; Phyllis Palmer, "Outside the Law: Agricultural and Domestic Workers Under the Fair Labor Standards Act," *Journal of Policy History* 7 (1995): 416–40; Katznelson, *When Affirmative Action Was White.* See Crespino, *Strom Thurmond's America*, for the rise of Sunbelt conservatism after World War II.

CHAPTER 7: EMANCIPATORY INTERNATIONALISM
VS. THE AMERICAN CENTURY

1. *Final Act of the Inter-American Conference on Problems in War and Peace: Mexico City, February–March, 1945* (Washington, DC: Pan American Union, 1945), 16. For coverage of the conference, see "Dispute Is Put Off as Inter-American Conference Opened in Mexico City," *New York Times*, February 22, 1945; "Americas Form Peace Alliance," *St. Petersburg Times*, March 4, 1945; "Chapultepec Act Heralds Democracy in the Americas," *Norfolk Journal and Guide*, March 24, 1945. On efforts to enhance inter-American cooperation during the war years, see Darlene J. Sadlier, *Americans All: Good Neighbor Cultural Diplomacy in World War II* (Austin: University of Texas Press, 2012), and Thomas A. Guglielmo, "Fighting for Caucasian Rights: Mexicans, Mexi-

can Americans, and the Transnational Struggle for Civil Rights in World War II Texas," *Journal of American History* 92, no. 4 (March 2006): 1212–37.

2. *Final Act of the Inter-American Conference*, 16.

3. "Conspicuous Daily Visitor," *New York Times*, February 25, 1945.

4. "The Crux of the Disagreement," *New York Times*, March 10, 1945.

5. "Americas Form Peace Alliance, Sanction Force," *St. Petersburg Times*, March 4, 1945. The *New York Times* was also hopeful that the conference would lead to a "new Monroe Act." See "Contradiction Seen in Hemisphere Pact," *New York Times*, March 7, 1945; "Delegates in Dilemma at Mexico Conference: Failure to Provide Means for Guarding Hemisphere Security Debated," *New York Times*, March 4, 1945.

6. "Haiti Demands Smashing of Color Barriers: For Inter-American Unity," *Pittsburgh Courier*, March 10, 1945.

7. "Foes Label Him 'A Negro': Mexico's Padilla Warns U.S. That Race Hatred Must End," *Cleveland Call and Post*, March 31, 1945; "Bias Ban Approved at Mexico Parley," *New York Times*, March 7, 1945; "Inter-American Conference Hailed but Argentina Recuses Equality of Nations Assured Under Latin-American Pact," *Baltimore Afro-American*, March 24, 1945.

8. "Inter-American Conference in Mexico City Hailed," *Amsterdam News*, March 17, 1945.

9. "Inter American Conference Should Serve as a Model for US," *Norfolk Journal and Guide*, March 31, 1945; *Final Act of the Inter-American Conference*, 80.

10. Ibid.

11. Ibid. See also "Praises Inter-American Conference," *Norfolk Journal and Guide*, April 14, 1945.

12. Josef L. Kunz, "The Inter-American Conference on Problems of War and Peace at Mexico City and the Problem of the Reorganization of the Inter-American System," *American Journal of International Law* 39, no. 3 (July 1945): 527–33.

13. "No Jim Crow Among Nations," *Cleveland Call and Post*, March 31, 1945.

14. Ibid.

15. Philippa Strum, *Mendez v. Westminster: School Desegregation and Mexican-American Rights* (Lawrence: University Press of Kansas, 2010); Gilbert G. González, *Chicano Education in the Era of Segregation* (Philadelphia: Balch Institute Press, 1990); Richard R. Valencia, *Chicano Students and the Courts: The Mexican American Legal Struggle for Educational Equity* (New York: New York University Press, 2008).

16. "Separate School Law Violates Constitution," *Baltimore Afro-American*, December 14, 1946.

17. "Racial Problem Is Social, Says Reid," *Atlanta Daily World*, March 29, 1945.

18. "Chapultepec Declaration Impact on US Racism, FEPC Aid to US Latin Relations Says Senator," *Baltimore Afro-American*, March 17, 1945; "Schwellenback, Stassen Rap FEPC Filibusterers," *Baltimore Afro-American*, February 2, 1946; "Chavez to Ask Permanent FEPC at Demo Parley," *Plain Dealer* (Kansas City), July 7, 1944.

19. "National Council Calls on Local Help [in] Fight for Permanent FEPC," *Arkansas State Press*, January 25, 1946; "Chavez Challenges Bilbo Stadium Plan, Reminds of FEPC," *Chicago Defender*, November 10, 1945.

20. "Ghetto Housing Keeps Race Problem Boiling," *Amsterdam News*, July 27, 1946. See also Jeffrey D. Gonda, *Unjust Deeds: The Restrictive Covenant Cases and the Making of the Civil Rights Movement* (Chapel Hill: University of North Carolina Press, 2015).

21. "'Racism Must Go,' High Court Told by Houston," *Baltimore Afro-American*, January 24, 1948.

22. "Cloture Flunks; FEPC Pushed Aside," *Los Angeles Tribune*, February 16, 1946.

23. Harold Preece, "The Klan Declares War," *New Masses*, October 16, 1945, http://www.unz.org/Pub/NewMasses-1945oct16-00003.

24. Michael Anderson, "Lorraine Hansberry's Freedom Family," *American Communist History* 7, no. 2 (2008): 268–69.

25. Greg Grandin, *The Last Colonial Massacre: Latin America in the Cold War*, rev. ed. (Chicago: University of Chicago Press, 2011); Rigoberta Menchu, *I, Rigoberta Menchu: An Indian Woman in Guatemala*, ed. Elisabeth Burgos-Debray, trans. by Ann Wright (1984; London: Verso, 2009); Ariel Dorfman, *Feeding on Dreams: Confessions of an Unrepentant Exile* (New York: Mariner Books, 2011); Colby, *The Business of Empire*.

26. Walter LaFeber, *Inevitable Revolutions: The United States in Central America* (New York: W. W. Norton, 1993), 15.

27. "The World," *New York Times*, June 13, 1954.

28. "U.S. Aid to Grow," *New York Times*, June 3, 1954.

29. Greg Grandin, *Empire's Workshop: Latin America, the United States, and the Rise of the New Imperialism* (2006; New York: Holt Paperbacks, 2010), 42–43.

30. Ibid. See also La Feber, *Inevitable Revolutions*, 113–27; Juan Gonzalez, *Harvest of Empire: A History of Latinos in America*, rev. ed. (New York: Penguin, 2011), 135–43.

31. Scholars have demonstrated that mainstream African American organizations acquiesced to Cold War policies in the 1950s in the hope that compliance might encourage the federal government to take a pro–civil rights stance. It is unlikely, however, that the NAACP's or Urban League's decision to support US foreign policy in the Global South would have enough weight to uproot a centuries-long tradition of Black internationalism at the grassroots. See Carol Anderson, *Eyes Off the Prize: The United Nations and the African American Struggle for Human Rights, 1944–1955* (New York: Cambridge University Press, 2003); Penny M. Von Eschen, *Race Against Empire: Black Americans and Anticolonialism, 1937–1957* (Ithaca, NY: Cornell University Press, 1997).

32. "The Aggrandizing US," *Pittsburgh Courier*, letter to the editor, March 26, 1955.

33. Ralph Matthews, "Yes, We Have No Bananas," *Cleveland Call and Post*, July 3, 1954.

34. Ibid.

35. Cited in Randi Gill-Sadler, "Diasporic Dissonance: Black Women's Lit-

erature, U.S. Imperialism and the Black Diaspora," PhD diss., University of Florida, 2017, 10.

36. Martin Luther King Jr., *Where Do We Go From Here: Chaos or Community?* (Boston: Beacon Press, 1967), 4–5.

37. Ibid., 186.

38. Ernesto Galarza, Herman Gallegos, and Julian Samora, *Mexican Americans in the Southwest* (Santa Barbara, CA: McNally & Loftin, 1970), 61.

39. On the federal government's role in supplying Florida with workers, see Conlin, "Invisible Hands in the Winter Garden"; Cindy Hahamovitch, *No Man's Land: Jamaican Guestworkers in America and the Global History of Deportable Labor* (Princeton, NJ: Princeton University Press, 2012); Cohen, *Braceros.* Julie Weise notes that Mexican farmworkers could sometimes turn to the Mexican consulate for assistance in battling racism and labor exploitation but that over time, even this support dwindled. Weise, *Corazón de Dixie: Mexicanos in the U.S. South Since 1910.*

40. Galarza, Gallegos, and Samora, *Mexican-Americans in the Southwest,* 59.

41. Ibid.

42. Fred Ross, *Conquering Goliath: Cesar Chavez and the Beginning* (Keene, CA: El Taller Grafico Press, 1989), 24.

43. Ibid., 24; Chavez, "Huelga!"

44. Susan Ferriss and Ricardo Sandoval, *The Fight in the Fields: Cesar Chavez and the Farmworkers Movement,* ed. Diana Hembree (New York: Harcourt Brace, 1997), 11–12.

45. Somini Sengupta, "A Duty to Fight," *Los Angeles Times,* August 4, 1992.

46. David Bacon, "The Death of Pete Velasco," *San Francisco Examiner,* December 9, 1995.

47. On the history of the United Farm Workers, see Jacque E. Levy, *Cesar Chavez: Autobiography of La Causa* (1975; Minneapolis: University of Minnesota Press, 2007). Critical works include Randy Shaw, *Beyond the Field: Cesar Chavez, the UFW, and the Struggle for Justice in the 21st Century* (Berkeley: University of California Press, 2008); Matthew Garcia, *From the Jaws of Victory: The Triumph and Tragedy of Cesar Chavez and the Farm Worker Movement* (Berkeley: University of California Press, 2012); Frank Bardacke, *Trampling Out the Vintage: Cesar Chavez and the Two Souls of the United Farm Workers* (London: Verso, 2012).

48. "Huelga Wins One," *Basta Ya!* (San Francisco), August 1970.

49. "Four Negro Groups Support Grape Strike," *Pittsburgh Courier,* January 1, 1966.

50. "Demonstration on November 26, 1968, by United Farm Workers Organizing Committee, Pittsburgh, Pennsylvania," in *FBI Files on Cesar Chavez and the United Farm Workers,* microfilm publication (Wilmington, DE: Scholarly Sources, n.d.), file 100–444762, frames 757–58.

51. *Afro-American,* letter to the editor, November 30, 1968.

52. "Slavery Is Grape War Cry," *Pittsburgh Courier,* December 14, 1968.

53. Sam Kushner, *Long Road to Delano* (New York: International Publishers, 1975), 164.

54. Martin Luther King Jr., *Why We Can't Wait* (1963; New York: Mentor Books, 1964), 24.

55. Jim Harrington, "Filosofia del Boicoteo," *El Campesino*, November 5, 1973.

56. Robert Gordon, "Poisons in the Fields: The United Farm Workers, Pesticides, and Environmental Politics," *Pacific Historical Review* 68 (February 1999): 51.

57. Martin Luther King, Jr., *Stride Toward Freedom: The Montgomery Story* (1958; Boston: Beacon Press, 2010), 73.

58. This analysis is based on Jones, *The March on Washington*. See also William P. Jones, "The Forgotten Radical History of the March on Washington," *Dissent* (Spring 2013), https://www.dissentmagazine.org/article/the-forgotten-radical-history-of-the-march-on-washington.

59. For the full text of A. Philip Randolph's address, see "Claiming and Teaching the 1963 March on Washington," by Bill Fletcher Jr. at *Teaching a People's History: Zinn Education Project*, August 20, 2013, https://zinnedproject.org/2013/08/the-1963-march-on-washington/.

60. Paul Ortiz interview with Lawrence Guyot, May 5, 2011; comments by Lawrence Guyot at "Chaos or Community: Where Do We Go from Here?," Third Annual Civil Rights History Panel, SPOHP, Delta State University, September 21, 2011; Paul Ortiz interview with Hollis Watkins, May 6, 2008, SPOHP, University of Florida.

61. Paul Ortiz interview with Margaret Block, September 18, 2008, SPOHP, University of Florida; Akinyele Omowale Umoja, *We Will Shoot Back: Armed Resistance in the Mississippi Freedom Movement* (New York: New York University Press, 2013); Charles E. Cobb, *This Nonviolent Stuff'll Get You Killed: How Guns Made the Civil Rights Movement Possible* (New York: Basic Books, 2014).

62. On the rise of SNCC and the MFDP, see Charles M. Payne, *I've Got the Light of Freedom: The Organizing Tradition and the Mississippi Freedom Struggle* (Berkeley: University of California Press, 2007); Clayborne Carson, *In Struggle: SNCC and the Black Awakening of the 1960s* (Cambridge, MA: Harvard University Press, 1981); Wesley C. Hogan, *Many Minds, One Heart: SNCC's Dream for a New America* (Chapel Hill: University of North Carolina Press, 2007).

63. Gerald Horne, *Fire This Time: The Watts Uprising and the 1960s* (Charlottesville: University Press of Virginia, 1995), 57. See also Edward J. Escobar, *Race, Police, and the Making of a Political Identity: Mexican Americans and the Los Angeles Police Department, 1900–1945* (Berkeley: University of California Press, 1999).

64. Horne, *Fire This Time*, 149.

65. Ibid., 82.

66. Ibid., 59.

67. Governor's Commission on the Los Angeles Riots, *Violence in the City—An End or a Beginning? A Report* (Los Angeles: State of California, December 2, 1965), 41.

68. Dr. Martin Luther King Jr., "Beyond Vietnam," address delivered at

Riverside Church, April 4, 1967, http://kingencyclopedia.stanford.edu/kingweb/publications/speeches/Beyond_Vietnam.pdf (accessed June 24, 2015).

69. The following analysis of the Poor People's Campaign and Memphis Sanitation Workers' Strike is based on Gordon Mantler, *Power to the Poor: Black-Brown Coalition and the Fight for Economic Justice, 1960–1974* (Chapel Hill: University of North Carolina Press, 2013); Michael K. Honey, *Going Down Jericho Road: The Memphis Strike, Martin Luther King's Last Campaign* (New York: W. W. Norton, 2007); Taylor Branch, *At Canaan's Edge: America in the King Years* (New York: Simon & Schuster, 2006).

70. "Remembering the Forgotten King," *Bowdoin*, January 14, 2011, http://www.bowdoin.edu/news/archives/1academicnews/008141.shtml.

71. The literature on social movements of the era includes Sonia Song-Ha Lee, *Building a Latino Civil Rights Movement: Puerto Ricans, African Americans, and the Pursuit of Racial Justice in New York City* (Chapel Hill: University of North Carolina Press, 2014); Max Krochmal, *Blue Texas: The Making of a Multiracial Democratic Coalition in the Civil Rights Era* (Chapel Hill: University of North Carolina Press, 2016); Donna Jean Murch: *Living for the City: Migration, Education, and the Rise of the Black Panther Party in Oakland, California* (Chapel Hill: University of North Carolina Press, 2010); Armando Navarro, *The Cristal Experiment: A Chicano Struggle for Community Control* (Madison: University of Wisconsin Press, 1998); Frederick Douglass Opie, *Upsetting the Apple Cart: Black-Latino Coalitions in New York City: From Protest to Public Office* (New York: Columbia University Press, 2015); Matthew J. Countryman, *Up South: Civil Rights and Black Power in Philadelphia* (Philadelphia: University of Pennsylvania Press, 2006); Barbara Ransby, *Ella Baker and the Black Freedom Movement: A Radical Democratic Vision* (Chapel Hill: University of North Carolina Press, 2003); Laura Pulido, *Black, Brown, Yellow, and Left: Radical Activism in Los Angeles* (Berkeley: University of California Press, 2006); Gaye Theresa Johnson, *Spaces of Conflict, Sounds of Solidarity: Music, Race, and Spatial Entitlement in Los Angeles* (Berkeley: University of California Press, 2013); Maurice Jourdane, *The Struggle for the Health and Legal Protection of Farm Workers: El Cortito* (Houston: Arte Público Press, 2004); Allen Kent, "The Missing Link: Black Police and Black Power in Chicago, 1965–1987," PhD diss., University of Florida, 2015.

72. Jakobi E. Williams, *From the Bullet to the Ballot: The Illinois Chapter of the Black Panther Party and Racial Coalition Politics in Chicago* (Chapel Hill: University of North Carolina Press, 2013), 125–66.

73. Joshua Bloom and Waldo E. Martin Jr., *Black Against Empire: The History and Politics of the Black Panther Party* (Berkeley: University of California Press, 2013), 292.

74. Jakobi E. Williams, "The Original Rainbow Coalition: An Example of Universal Identity Politics," *Tikkun*, http://www.tikkun.org/nextgen/the-original-rainbow-coalition-an-example-of-universal-identity-politics (accessed December 10, 2016).

75. "United Construction Workers Association," Seattle Civil Rights and Labor History Project, http://depts.washington.edu/civilr/ucwa.htm (accessed December 6, 2015).

76. "Who We Are," *No Separate Peace* 1, no. 1 (May 15, 1975): 2.
77. Ibid.
78. Piri Thomas, *Down These Mean Streets* (1967; New York: Vintage Books, 1997).
79. Piri Thomas, "Voices of Fighters Against Oppression," *New York Amsterdam News*, November 16, 1985.
80. "Brickmaking Machine," *Swaan Call: The Newsletter of Washington's State-Wide Anti-Apartheid Network*, no. 3 (October–November 1986): 5.
81. "Latinos Want South Africa Free," *New York Amsterdam News,* November 16, 1985.
82. Ibid.
83. "Latinos to Join Soweto March," *New York Amsterdam News,* June 14, 1986; "March for Motherland," *New York Amsterdam News,* June 21, 1986.
84. Ronald Smothers, "Jackson Hears Mexican View of Cuba," *New York Times,* May 29, 1984; "Jackson Pleased with Mexican Trip," *Baltimore Afro-American,* May 1, 1984; Bradford Martin, *The Other Eighties: A Secret History of America in the Age of Reagan* (New York: Hill & Wang, 2011), 33, 131–37; Crystal Nix, "Many in U.S. Protest on South Africa," *New York Times,* October 12, 1985.
85. Jesse Jackson, "1984 Democratic National Convention Address," July 18, 1984, San Francisco, *American Rhetoric: Top 100 Speeches,* http://www.americanrhetoric.com/speeches/jessejackson1984dnc.htm (accessed May 10, 2017).
86. Paul Ortiz, "From Slavery to Cesar Chavez and Beyond: Farmworker Organizing in the United States," in *The Human Cost of Food: Farmworkers' Lives, Labor, and Advocacy,* ed. Charles Dillard Thompson and Melinda Wiggins (Austin: University of Texas Press, 2002), 249–76.
87. JoAnn Wypijewski, "Rainbow's Gravity," *Nation,* July 26, 2004, http://www.alternet.org/story/19332/rainbow's_gravity/?page=entire. For a critique of the National Rainbow Coalition, see Adolph Reed, *The Jesse Jackson Phenomenon: The Crisis of Purpose in Afro-American Politics* (New Haven, CT: Yale University Press, 1986).
88. Manning Marable, *Race, Reform and Rebellion: The Second Reconstruction in Black America, 1945-1982* (1984; Jackson: University Press of Mississippi, 1988), 125; Nelson Blackstock, *Cointelpro: The FBI's Secret War on Political Freedom* (New York: Pathfinder Press, 1988); Seth Rosenfeld, *Subversives: The FBI's War on Student Radicals, and Reagan's Rise to Power* (New York: Farrar, Straus & Giroux, 2012).

CHAPTER 8: *EL GRAN PARO ESTADOUNIDENSE*

1. Anita Hamilton, "A Day Without Immigrants: Making a Statement," *Time,* May 1, 2006, http://content.time.com/time/nation/article/0,8599,1189899,00.html; Antonio Valencia, "El gran paro: boicot Latino contra Estados Unidos," *La Nación* (Chile), piensaChile.com, May 1, 2006, http://piensachile.com/2006/05/el-gran-paro-boicot-latino-contra-estados-unidos/; William I. Robinson, "La lucha por los derechos de inmigrantes," piensaChile.com, April

29, 2006, http://piensachile.com/2006/04/eeuu-la-lucha-por-los-derechos-de
-inmigrantes/.

2. On the mass strikes of the Vietnam War era, see Brecher, *Strike!*, 221–
42. For an overview of neoliberalism, see Miguel A. Centeno and Joseph N.
Cohen, "The Arc of Neoliberalism," *Annual Review of Sociology* 38 (August
2012): 317–40; Jason Hackworth, *The Neoliberal City: Governance, Ideology, and the Development of American Urbanism* (Ithaca, NY: Cornell University Press, 2007); Stephen Graham, *Cities Under Siege: The New Military
Urbanism* (London: Verso, 2011); Jasmin Hristov, "Freedom and Democracy
or Hunger and Terror: Neoliberalism and Militarization in Latin America,"
Social Justice 32, no. 2 (2005): 89-114. For analyses that frame neoliberalism
as a counterattack against democratic insurgencies, including the Chicano, civil
rights, and Black liberation movements, see Jordan T. Camp, *Incarcerating the
Crisis: Freedom Struggles and the Rise of the Neoliberal State* (Oakland: University of California Press, 2017); Jordan T. Camp and Christina Heatherton,
eds., *Policing the Planet: Why the Policing Crisis Led to Black Lives Matter*
(New York: Verso, 2016); Ruth Wilson Gilmore, *Golden Gulag: Prisons, Surplus, Crisis, and Opposition in Globalizing California* (Berkeley: University
of California Press, 2007); Cedric Johnson, ed., *The Neoliberal Deluge: Hurricane Katrina, Late Capitalism, and the Remaking of New Orleans* (Minneapolis: University of Minnesota Press, 2011); Heather Thompson, *Blood in
the Water: The Attica Prison Uprising of 1971 and Its Legacy* (New York:
Pantheon, 2016); William Greider, *Who Will Tell the People: The Betrayal of
American Democracy* (New York: Simon & Schuster, 1992); Jane Mayer, *Dark
Money: The Hidden History of the Billionaires Behind the Rise of the Radical Right* (New York: Doubleday, 2016); Kathryn Edin and H. Luke Shaefer,
"20 Years Since Welfare 'Reform,'" *Atlantic*, August 22, 2016, http://www.the
atlantic.com/business/archive/2016/08/20-years-welfare-reform/496730/.

3. "Volcker Asserts US Must Trim Living Standard," *New York Times,*
October 18, 1979. For a broader analysis of the ways that the Federal Reserve
intervened to revolutionize labor relations, see William H. Greider, *Secrets of
the Temple: How the Federal Reserve Runs the Country* (New York: Simon &
Schuster, 1989).

4. Thomas Friedman, "A Manifesto for the Fast World," *New York Times
Magazine*, March 28, 1999, https://www.nytimes.com/books/99/04/25/reviews
/friedman-mag.html.

5. Grover Norquist: "I don't want to abolish government. I simply want to
reduce it to the size where I can drag it into the bathroom and drown it in the
bathtub." "Conservative Advocate," *Morning Edition*, National Public Radio,
May 25, 2001, http://www.npr.org/templates/story/story.php?storyId=1123439.

6. For an overview of the DLC movement, see Al From, "Recruiting Bill
Clinton," *Atlantic*, December 3, 2013, http://www.theatlantic.com/politics/
archive/2013/12/recruiting-bill-clinton/281946/; William Greider, *One World,
Ready or Not: The Manic Logic of Global Capitalism* (New York: Simon
& Schuster, 1997); Charles Peters, "A Neoliberal's Manifesto," *Washington
Monthly*, May 1983, 9-19; Thomas Ferguson and Joel Rogers, *Right Turn: The
Decline of the Democrats and the Future of American Politics* (New York: Hill

& Wang, 1986). Neoliberalism in the United States was part of an international trend. See Curtis Atkins, "The Third Way International," *Jacobin* 20 (Winter 2016) https://www.jacobinmag.com/2016/02/atkins-dlc-third-way-clinton-blair-schroeder-social-democracy/ (accessed August 5, 2016).

7. Patrick J. McDonnell, "Seeds of Discontent Grow in Watsonville," *Los Angeles Times*, May 26, 1996.

8. "Trading Up," *Texas Observer*, June 2017, 6.

9. United Farm Workers of Washington, "Public Action Organizers," state memo, October 13, 1994 (in author's collection).

10. The US Commission on Civil Rights, *Voting Irregularities in Florida During the 2000 Presidential Election* (Washington, DC: 2001), http://www.usccr.gov/pubs/vote2000/report/exesum.htm (accessed June 12, 2014).

11. Thomas Sugrue, *The Origins of the Urban Crisis: Race and Inequality in Postwar Detroit* (1996; Princeton, NJ: Princeton University Press, 2014); Massey and Denton, *American Apartheid*; Merrit Kennedy, "Lead-Laced Water in Flint: A Step-By-Step Look at the Makings of a Crisis," *The Two-Way: Breaking News from NPR*, NPR.org, April 20, 2016, http://www.npr.org/sections/thetwo-way/2016/04/20/465545378/lead-laced-water-in-flint-a-step-by-step-look-at-the-makings-of-a-crisis (accessed May 15, 2016).

12. Julian Borger, "US Conservatives Round on Bush over Katrina Aid Pledges," *Guardian*, September 17, 2005; Julian Borger, "Hurricane Aid Used to 'Test Out Rightwing Social Policies,'" *Guardian*, September 22, 2005; John Brown Childs, ed., *Hurricane Katrina: Response and Responsibilities*, 2nd ed. (2005; Santa Cruz, CA: New Pacific Press, 2008).

13. "Reports of Anarchy at Superdome Overstated," *Seattle Times*, September 26, 2005, http://community.seattletimes.nwsource.com/archive/?date=20050926&slug=katmyth26.

14. Justin Hosbey, "Consumption and Conviviality: Charter Schools and the Delectability of Black Death in Post-Katrina New Orleans," PhD diss., University of Florida, 2016; "Latino Workers Helped Rebuild New Orleans, but Many Weren't Paid," *NBC News*, August 28, 2015, http://www.nbcnews.com/storyline/hurricane-katrina-anniversary/families-scattered-hurricane-katrina-still-making-their-way-home-n417661; "Guest Workers Sue New Orleans Hotel Chain," *Washington Post*, August 17, 2006; Southern Poverty Law Center, "SPLC Exposes Exploitation of Immigrant Workers," news release, August 15, 2006, https://www.splcenter.org/news/2006/08/16/splc-exposes-exploitation-immigrant-workers.

15. Mary Bauer, *Close to Slavery: Guestworker Programs in the United States* (Montgomery, AL: Southern Poverty Law Center, 2013), https://www.splcenter.org/20130218/close-slavery-guestworker-programs-united-states.

16. Mark Brenner, "Katrina's Aftermath Transforms Work in the Gulf Region," *Labor Notes* (March 2006), http://labornotes.org/node/201 (accessed May 10, 2017).

17. Thomas D. Boston, *A Different Vision: Race and Public Policy*, vol. 2 (New York: Routledge, 1996).

18. Jonathan Kozol, *The Shame of the Nation: The Restoration of Apart-

heid Schooling in America (New York: Three Rivers Press, 2005); Michelle Alexander, *The New Jim Crow: Mass Incarceration in the Age of Colorblindness* (2010; New York: New Press, 2012); Gerald Markowitz and David Rosner, *Lead Wars: The Politics of Science and the Fate of America's Children* (2013; Berkeley: University of California Press, 2014); Manuel Pastor et al., *In the Wake of the Storm: Environment, Disaster and Race After Katrina* (New York: Russell Sage Foundation, 2006); M. Shahid Alam, *Challenging the New Orientalism: Dissenting Essays on the "War Against Islam* (North Haledon, NJ: Islamic Publications International, 2007); David Roediger, *How Race Survived US History: From the American Revolution to the Present* (London: Verso, 2008); Lipsitz, *Possessive Investment in Whiteness.*

19. Deborah Wallace and Rodrick Wallace, *A Plague on Your Houses: How New York Was Burned Down and National Public Health Crumbled* (London: Verso, 1998); Joe Flood, *The Fires: How a Computer Formula, Big Ideas, and the Best of Intentions Burned Down New York City—and Determined the Future of Cities* (New York: Riverhead Books, 2010); Lydia R. Otero, *La Calle: Spatial Conflict and Urban Renewal in a Southwest City* (Tucson: University of Arizona Press, 2010); Joe Flood, "Why the Bronx Burned," *New York Post*, May 16, 2010, http://nypost.com/2010/05/16/why-the-bronx-burned.

20. Kim Probasco, "For the Greater Good or Greed? Redistributing Private Space Through Eminent Domain Power: Relocating The Dallas Cowboys Stadium to Arlington, Texas," master's thesis, University of Texas, Arlington, 2007. For broader discussions of the intersection of race, eminent domain, and public policy, see N. D. B. Connolly, *A World More Concrete: Real Estate and the Remaking of Jim Crow South Florida* (Chicago: University of Chicago Press, 2016); Xavier Perez, "Gentrification and Crime: A Study of Changing Lives in a Puerto Rican Community," PhD thesis, University of Illinois, Chicago, 2010; Mindy Thompson Fullilove, *Eminent Domain & African Americans: What Is the Price of the Commons?*, vol. 1, *Perspectives on Eminent Domain Abuse* (Institute for Justice, February 2007), http://ij.org/report/eminent-domain-african-americans (accessed March 10, 2016).

21. Carol Anderson, *White Rage: The Unspoken Truth of Our Racial Divide* (New York: Bloomsbury, 2016), 2; John A. Eterno, ed., *The New York City Police Department: The Impact of Its Policies and Practices* (New York: Taylor & Francis, 2015).

22. Camp, *Incarcerating the Crisis.*

23. Ibid.

24. Jonathan Kozol, *Savage Inequalities: Children in America's Schools* (1991; New York: Broadway Books, 2012), 119–20.

25. Ibid.

26. Gary Orfield, Susan E. Eaton, and the Harvard Project on School Desegregation, *Dismantling Desegregation: The Quiet Reversal of Brown v. Board of Education* (New York: W. W. Norton, 1996), xiii.

27. Eduardo Porter, "In Public Education, Edge Still Goes to the Rich," *New York Times*, November 5, 2013, http://www.nytimes.com/2013/11/06/business/a-rich-childs-edge-in-public-education.html.

28. Bonnie Kristian, "Why The Pentagon Budget Is Out of Control," *Fiscal Times*, March 28, 2016, http://www.thefiscaltimes.com/2016/03/28/Why -Pentagon-Needs-Audit-Now.

29. "The Sorry State of Corporate Taxes: What Fortune 500 Firms Pay (or Don't Pay)," Citizens for Tax Justice, http://www.ctj.org/corporatetaxdodgers /sorrystateofcorptaxes.php (accessed January 12, 2017).

30. David Zucchino, *Myth of the Welfare Queen: A Pulitzer Prize-Winning Journalist's Portrait of Women on the Line* (New York: Simon & Schuster, 1999). For a historical analysis of blame-the-poor policies and political narratives, see Michael B. Katz, *The Undeserving Poor: America's Enduring Confrontation with Poverty*, 2nd ed. (New York: Oxford University Press, 2013); Michael B. Katz, *In the Shadow of the Poorhouse: A Social History of Welfare in America* (1986; New York: Perseus Books, 1996).

31. Columbia University, National Center for Children in Poverty, "By Race, White Children Make Up the Biggest Percentage of America's Poor," news release, November 20, 2007, http://www.nccp.org/media/releases/release _34.html.

32. Franklin D. Gilliam Jr., The 'Welfare Queen' Experiment: How Viewers React to Images of African-American Mothers on Welfare," *Nieman Reports*, June 15, 1999, http://niemanreports.org/articles/the-welfare-queen-experi ment/ (accessed July 12, 2017).

33. Lipsitz, *Possessive Investment in Whiteness*, 19.

34. King, *Where Do We Go From Here*.

35. Richard Reeves and Joanna Venator, "Saving Horatio Alger: The Data Behind the Words," *Social Mobility Memos* (blog), Brookings Institution, August 21, 2014, https://www.brookings.edu/blog/social -mobility-memos/2014/08/21/saving-horatio-alger-the-data-behind-the-words -and-the-lego-bricks/ (accessed May 24, 2015); William Julius Wilson, ed., *The Ghetto Underclass: Social Science Perspectives* (1989; Newbury Park, CA: Sage Publications, 1993); Lawrence M. Mead, *Beyond Entitlement: The Social Obligations of Citizenship* (New York: Free Press, 1986); Charles Murray and Richard Herrnstein, *The Bell Curve: Intelligence and Class Structure in American Life* (New York: Free Press, 1994).

36. Jim Naureckas, "Joe Klein: Media Spokesperson for White People," FAIR (Fairness & Accuracy in Reporting), July 1, 1992, http://fair.org/extra /joe-klein-media-spokesperson-for-white-people/ (accessed May 11, 2017); Ta-Nehisi Coates, "The New Republic: An Appreciation," *Atlantic*, December 9, 2014, http://www.theatlantic.com/politics/archive/2014/12/the-new-repub lic-an-appreciation/383561/.

37. Amy Davidson, "Donald Trump and the Central Park Five," *New Yorker*, June 23, 2014; Sarah Burns, *The Central Park Five: The Untold Story Behind One of New York City's Most Infamous Crimes* (New York: Vintage, 2012).

38. Elizabeth Martinez, "Beyond Black/White: The Racisms of Our Time," in *The Latino/a Condition: A Critical Reader*, ed. Richard Delgado and Jean Stefancic (New York: New York University Press, 1998), 469.

39. Gonzalez, *Harvest of Empire*, 167–275; Rubén Martínez, *The Other*

Side: Notes from the New L.A., Mexico City, and Beyond (New York: Vintage, 1993); Leo R. Chavez, *The Latino Threat: Constructing Immigrants, Citizens, and the Nation* (Stanford, CA: Stanford University Press, 2008).

40. T. Watanabe, "Civil Activists Join Latino Wage Suit," *Los Angeles Times*, May 16, 2007.

41. Nano Riley, *Florida's Farmworkers in the Twenty-First Century* (Gainesville: University Press of Florida, 2002), 55; Greg Asbed, "For Pickers, Slavery Tastes Like Tomatoes," *Palm Beach Post*, March 30, 2003, Coalition of Immokalee Workers, http://www.ciw-online.org/gapbpoped.html; "Report: Modern-Day Slavery Alive and Well in Florida," Associated Press, February 25, 2004, in http://www.washingtonpost.com/wp-dyn/articles/A4555-2004Feb25 .html?sections=http://www.washingtonpost.com/wp-dyn/nation; D. Moffett, "Slavery? In Florida? In 2003? Yes," *Palm Beach Post*, November 23, 2003.

42. "Anti-Slavery International Chooses CIW to Receive Its 2007 Anti-Slavery Award," Coalition of Immokalee Workers, November 12, 2007, http:// www.ciw-online.org/blog/2007/11/anti-slavery-international-chooses-ciw-to -receive-its-2007-anti-slavery-award/.

43. David Bacon, "Common Ground on the Kill Floor: Organizing Smithfield," *Labor Notes* (April 20, 2012).

44. Human Rights Watch, *Blood, Sweat and Fear: Workers' Rights in U.S. Meat and Poultry Plants* (New York: Human Rights Watch, 2005); Christopher D. Cook, "Fowl Trouble," *Harper's*, August 1999, 78–79.

45. Human Rights Watch, *Blood, Sweat and Fear*.

46. See Nick Wood, "Mt. Olive: Blood on the Cucumbers," *Against the Current* 102 (January–February 2003), https://www.solidarity-us.org /node/681. I discuss aspects of coalition building in the Farm Labor Organizing Committee's campaign in Ortiz, "From Slavery to Cesar Chavez and Beyond," 249–76.

47. Farm Labor Organizing Committee and Black Workers for Justice, "Juneteenth" news release, United Electrical Workers Local 150, June 16, 2001 (in author's collection).

48. Ibid. The boycott ended with a union victory in 2005.

49. "Case Farms Workers Walked Off the Job," *News Herald* (Morganton, NC), June 10, 2005; "Glove Charge Sparks Strike at Case Farms," *News Herald*, October 28, 2006.

50. Leon Fink, *The Maya of Morganton: Work and Community in the Nuevo New South* (Chapel Hill: University of North Carolina Press, 2003).

51. "Worker Unrest at Case Farms: Employees at Poultry Plant Meet to Discuss Forming Union," *Charlotte Observer*, November 12, 2006.

52. C. Sanchez, "Protesters Hope to Create a Political Movement," *Sarasota Herald-Tribune*, May 3, 2006; Jon Wiener, "L.A.'s Two May Day Marches," *Nation*, May 2, 2006, available at *AlterNet*, http://www.alternet. org/story/35722/l.a.%27s_two_may_day_marches.

53. Paul Ortiz, "We Are the Ghosts Who Clean: Building the Movement in Santa Cruz, California, 2004–2008," roundtable presentation, American Studies Association Annual Meeting, "The May Day Protests, Grassroots Mobilization, and the Politics of Citizenship," Washington, DC, November 6, 2009.

54. C. Siemaszko, "N.Y. Immigrants Rally for Rights," *New York Daily News*, May 2, 2006.

55. Sonja Maria Diaz, "Written Reflection on May Day," November 9, 2009, unpublished essay (in author's collection).

56. Ortiz, "We Are the Ghosts Who Clean."

57. "Immigrants' Boycott Move Strikes Home," *Herald-Sun* (Durham, NC), May 2, 2006; "Day Without Immigrants Draws Millions to Streets; Many Local Residents Take Day Off to Show Support," *Star News* (Wilmington, NC), May 2, 2006; "Thousands Demonstrate at Springdale Park Rally," *Arkansas Democrat-Gazette*, May 2, 2006.

58. Randal Archibold, "Immigrants Take to U.S. Streets in Show of Strength," *New York Times*, May 2, 2006; Dan Whitcomb, "U.S. Latinos Expect a Momentous May Day," *Star-Ledger* (Newark, NJ), April 28, 2006.

59. Juan Gonzalez, "On Streets of New York, Solidarity Reigns," *New York Daily News*, May 2, 2006; R. Morris, "Immigrants Go Back to Work in South Florida After One-Day Walkouts," *Sun-Sentinel*, May 3, 2006.

60. "Local Workers Protest for Rights, *Ledger* (Lakeland, FL), April 11, 2006.

61. Chris Kutalik, "As Immigrants Strike, Truckers Shut Down Nation's Largest Port," *Labor Notes* (June 2006); Dan La Botz, "Millions March for Immigrant Rights; Virtual Strike in Some Cities," *Labor Notes* (May 2006); "We Say We Don't Want Illegals Here," *Palm Beach Post*, April 30, 2006.

62. On the importance of workers' centers in this organizing, see Ruth Milkman, "Critical Mass: Latino Labor and Politics in California," *NACLA Report on the Americas* 40, no. 3 (May–June 2007): 30–38; Miriam Ching Yoon Louie, *Sweatshop Warriors: Immigrant Women Workers Take On the Global Factory* (Cambridge, MA: South End Press, 2001); Janice Fine, "Worker Centers: Organizing Communities at the Edge of the Dream," EPI Briefing Paper 159 (Washington, DC: Economic Policy Institute, December 14, 2005).

63. Milkman, "Critical Mass."

64. María Elena Durazo, *Living Wage for All: A Plan for a New Living Wage Movement* (Los Angeles: Center for the Working Poor, May 12, 2006) http://www.centerfortheworkingpoor.org/living-wages/living-wage-for-all-a-plan-for-a-new-living-wage-movement (accessed May 11, 2017).

65. Ibid.

66. Robin Abcarian, "Obama Gets Major Labor Endorsement," *Los Angeles Times*, January 16, 2008, http://www.latimes.com/nation/la-na-labor 16jan16-story.html; Randy Shaw, "Cesar Chavez and the Roots of Obama's Field Campaign," *In These Times*, November 6, 2008, http://www.inthese times.com/article/4024/cesar_chavez_and_the_roots_of_obamas_field_cam paign.

67. Joel Gehrke, "Obama Took 'Yes, We Can' from Dolores Huerta," *Washington Examiner*, May 29, 2012.

68. Danae Tapia, "My Experience," August 10, 2010, unpublished essay (in author's collection). See also S.I.N. Collective, "Students Informing Now (S.I.N.) Challenge the Racial State in California without Shame . . . Sin Vergüenza!," *Educational Foundations* (Winter–Spring 2007): 71–90.

69. Ibid.

70. "Regional Leadership Development Conferences," Labor Council for Latin American Advancement, January 29, 2009, http://www.lclaa.org/65 -calendar/calendar.

71. William Johnson, "Smithfield Meatpackers Stay Off Work to Demand Martin Luther King Holiday," *Labor Notes* (January 26, 2007).

72. David Bacon, "Unions Come to Smithfield," *American Prospect*, December 17, 2008, http://prospect.org/article/unions-come-smithfield.

73. "Hispanic Women Energize Unions," *Baltimore Sun*, June 23, 2002; John Trumpbour and Elaine Bernard, "Unions and Latinos: Mutual Transformation," in Suárez-Orozco and Mariela Páez, *Latinos: Remaking America*, 126–45.

74. UC Berkeley Labor Center, "Data Brief: Blacks in Unions: 2012," April 8, 2013, 2–3.

75. Jerry Mead-Lucero, "Chicago Sitdown Strike Produces Wins for Workers, Not Banks," *Labor Notes* (December 22, 2008), http://labornotes .org/2008/12/chicago-sitdown-strike-produces-win-workers-not-banks.

76. The workers subsequently "decided to buy the factory for ourselves and fire the boss." See "Our Story: New Era Windows Cooperative," http://newera windows.com/about-us/our-story (accessed January 4, 2017); Kari Lydersen, "Chicago Window Workers Who Occupied Their Factory in 2008 Win New Bankruptcy Payout," *In These Times*, January 25, 2016, http://inthesetimes .com/working/entry/18802/republic-windows-doors-factory-occupation-bank rupcty-ue-union.

77. CNNPolitics.com, Election Center 2008, "CNN Electoral Map Calculator: You Call the Race," exit polling data, http://www.cnn.com/ELECTION /2008/calculator (accessed, May 11, 2017).

78. David Moberg, "Obama and the Union Vote," *In These Times*, November 10, 2008, http://www.inthesetimes.com/article/4035/obama_and_the _union_vote/.

79. Mark Hugo Lopez, *The Hispanic Vote in the 2008 Election* (Washington, DC: Pew Research Center, November 5, 2008), http://www.pewhis panic.org/2008/11/05/the-hispanic-vote-in-the-2008-election/; Casey Woods, "Obama Wins Florida's Hispanic Vote," Hispanic Business.com, November 5, 2008.

80. Paul Ortiz, "On the Shoulders of Giants," *Truthout*, November 25, 2008, http://www.truth-out.org/archive/item/81229:on-the-shoulders-of -giants.

81. Dara Kam, "Early Voting Limits Motivated Democrats, Minorities to Turn Out," *Palm Beach Post*, December 1, 2012.

82. Bureau of Labor Statistics, *Bureau of Labor Statistics*, "Union Members—2012," https://www.bls.gov/news.release/archives/union2_01232013 .pdf (accessed June 15, 2017).

83. "Buoyed by the Election Results, Unions Take Stand," *Gainesville Sun*, November 23, 2012.

84. "Early Voting Limits Motivated Democrats, Minorities to Turn Out."

85. Benjy Sarlin, "Poll: Latino Vote Devastated GOP Even Worse Than

Exits Showed," *Talking Points Memo* (blog), November 7, 2012, http://talking
pointsmemo.com/election2012/poll-latino-vote-devastated-gop-even-worse
-than-exits-showed; Mark Hugo Lopez and Paul Taylor, *Latino Voters in the
2012 Election* (Washington, DC: Pew Research Center, November 7, 2012),
www.pewhispanic.org/2012/11/07/latino-voters-in-the-2012-election.

86. Manu Raju et al., "Immigration Reform Returns to Fore," *Politico*,
November 8, 2012, http://www.politico.com/story/2012/11/2012-election
-puts-spotlight-on-immigration-reform-083552.

87. "Immigration Raid Breaks Up Organizing Drive at Iowa Meatpacking
Plant," *Labor Notes*, August 26, 2008.

88. David Bacon, "Mass Firings, the New Face of Immigration Raids," *Progressive*, December 2009–January 2010.

89. David Bacon, "Feds Crack Down on Immigrant Labor Organizers,"
American Prospect (May 9, 2007).

90. "Abuses Against Workers Taint U.S. Meat and Poultry," news
release, Human Rights Watch, January 24, 2005, https://www.hrw.org/news
/2005/01/24/abuses-against-workers-taint-us-meat-and-poultry.

91. J. Morgan Kouser, *Colorblind Injustice: Minority Voting Rights and the
Undoing of the Second Reconstruction* (Chapel Hill: University of North Carolina Press, 1999), 58–68; "Voting Rights Act of 1965," *Harvard Law Review*
122, no. 1 (November 2008): 495–96.

92. "Voting Laws Roundup 2013," Brennan Center for Justice, New York
University School of Law, August 6, 2013, http://www.brennancenter.org/analy
sis/election-2013-voting-laws-roundup.

93. "Illegal Voters: The Winning Edge," *Washington Times*, editorial, June
4, 2012, http://www.washingtontimes.com/news/2012/jun/4/illegal-voters-the
-winning-edge.

94. Luis Carlos Lopez, "Latinos Upset About Supreme Court's Voting
Rights Decision," *Huffington Post*, June 26, 2013, http://www.huffingtonpost
.com/2013/06/26/latinos-voting-rights-act_n_3502303.html.

95. Jim Rutenberg, "A Dream Undone: Disenfranchised," *New York Times
Magazine*, July 29, 2015.

96. "Voter Protection Efforts," Mexican American Legal Defense Fund,
http://maldef.org/voting_rights/public_policy/voter_protection/ (accessed
August 4, 2015).

97. Joseph Shapiro, "Jail Time for Unpaid Court Fines and Fees Can Create Cycle of Poverty," *Code Switch*, National Public Radio, February 9, 2015,
http://www.npr.org/sections/codeswitch/2015/02/09/384968360/jail-time-for
-unpaid-court-fines-and-fees-can-create-cycle-of-poverty; Joseph Shapiro, "In
Ferguson, Court Fines and Fees Fuel Anger," *All Things Considered*, National
Public Radio, August 25, 2014, http://www.npr.org/2014/08/25/343143937
/in-ferguson-court-fines-and-fees-fuel-anger; Mark Jay, "Policing the Poor in
Detroit," *Monthly Review* 68, no. 8 (January 2017): 21–35.

98. For a critique of the broken-windows theory, see Robert J. Sampson and
Stephen Raudenbush, "Systematic Social Observation of Public Spaces: A New
Look at Disorder in Urban Neighborhoods," *American Journal of Sociology*
105, no. 3 (1999): 603–51; Eric Boehm, "Nanny State of the Week: City Fines

Residents for Chipped Paint, Mismatched Curtains," Missouri Watchdog.org, December 21, 2015, http://watchdog.org/252413/nanny-state-pagedale-mis souri-fines.

99. Laura Sullivan, "Prison Economics Help Drive Ariz. Immigration Law," *Morning Edition*, National Public Radio, October 28, 2010, http://www.npr .org/2010/10/28/130833741/prison-economics-help-drive-ariz-immigration -law.

100. NAACP, *Born Suspect: Stop-and-Frisk Abuses & the Continued Fight to End Racial Profiling in America* (Washington, DC: NAACP, September 2014), 1.

101. Bryan Stevenson, "We Need to Talk About an Injustice," *TED: Ideas Worth Spreading*, March 2012, https://www.ted.com/talks/bryan_stevenson _we_need_to_talk_about_an_injustice/transcript?language=en (accessed June 11, 2016).

102. Charlie Spiering, "Obama Lectures Hollywood for Perpetuating Muslim Stereotypes," *Breitbart*, February 3, 2016, http://www.breitbart.com /big-government/2016/02/03/obama-lectures-hollywood-for-perpetuating -muslim-stereotypes.

103. "Al Sharpton Wears 'Los Suns' Jersey During March to Arizona Capi- tol Protesting SB 1070," *Phoenix New Times Blogs*, May 6, 2010 http://blogs .phoenixnewtimes.com/bastard/2010/05/al_sharpton_wears_los_suns_jer .php.

104. "Chuck D Calls Jan Brewer a Hitler," *Resistance to SB 1070: No Borders, No State, No Papers* (blog), June 21, 2010, http://sb1070resistance .blogspot.com/2010/06/chuck-d-calls-jan-brewer-hitler.html.

105. "Immigration Advocates Rally for Change," *New York Times*, May 1, 2010.

106. "Dems: Ariz. Law Like Jim Crow, apartheid," *Politico*, April 28, 2010, http://www.politico.com/news/stories/0410/36503.html.

107. "Rewriting History? Texas Tackles Textbook Debate," *CBS News*, Sep- tember 16, 2014, http://www.cbsnews.com/news/rewriting-history-texas-tack- les-textbook-debate/; Ellen Bresler Rockmore, "How Texas Teaches History," *New York Times*, October 21, 2015; "Arizona Gov. Signs Bill Targeting Ethnic Studies," *Yahoo News*, May 12, 2010, http://news.yahoo.com/s/ap/20100512 /ap_on_re_us/us_arizona_ethnic_studies (accessed, May 20, 2010).

108. For the success of ethnic studies in improving student learning and suc- cess, see A. F. Romero, "Towards a Critically Compassionate Intellectualism Model of Transformative Education: Love, Hope, Identity, and Organic Intel- lectualism," PhD diss., University of Arizona, 2008; Conrado Gómez and Mar- garita Jiménez-Silva, "Mexican American Studies: The Historical Legitimacy of an Educational Program," *Association of Mexican-American Educators Journal* 6, no. 1 (2012): 15–23.

109. Stephen Ceasar, "L.A. Unified to Require Ethnic Studies for High School Graduation," *Los Angeles Times*, September 4, 2016.

110. Susan Chandler and Jill B. Jones, *Casino Women: Courage in Un- expected Places* (Ithaca, NY: Cornell University Press, 2011); Paul Ortiz, "Charging Through the Archway of History: Immigrants and African Ameri-

cans United to Transform the Face of Labor and the Power of Community," *Truthout*, February 16, 2013, http://www.truth-out.org/opinion/item/14540 -charging-through-the-archway-of-history-immigrants-and-african-americans -unite-to-transform-the-face-of-labor-and-the-power-of-community.

111. Steven Greenhouse, "Obama Receives Union Endorsements," *New York Times*, January 9, 2008; "Obama Gains Key Labor Backing in Nevada," *NBC News*, January 9, 2008, http://www.nbcnews.com/id/22575934/ns/poli tics-decision_08/t/obama-gains-key-labor-backing-nevada.

112. "Obama Statement on the Culinary Workers Union Local 226 Strike Authorization Vote," September 12, 2007, online at *American Presidency Project*, http://www.presidency.ucsb.edu/ws/?pid=90992 (accessed September 5, 2016); "Obama Statement on the Culinary Workers Union Local 226 and their Negotiations with the Grand Sierra Resort," August 20, 2007, online at *American Presidency Project*, http://www.presidency.ucsb.edu/ws/?pid=90989 (accessed September 5, 2016).

113. Chandler and Jones, *Casino Women*, 55–56.

114. "Nation's Longest Strike Comes to an End," *Las Vegas Sun*, September 5, 2016.

115. "Student Activism Leads to Undocumented Scholarship," *Oberlin Review*, February 23, 2017, https://oberlinreview.org/8844/opinions/student -activism-leads-to-undocumented-scholarship.

116. "Newswatch," *Labor Notes* 450 (September 2016): 5.

117. Jana Kasperkevic, "Workers Rally Around Wages, Race and Plans to Protest Presidential Debates," *Guardian*, August 14, 2016.

118. Dream Defenders, "About," http://www.dreamdefenders.org/about (accessed October 12, 2015); Keeanga-Yamahtta Taylor, *From #BlackLives- Matter to Black Liberation* (Chicago: Haymarket Books, 2016); Wesley Lowery, *"They Can't Kill Us All": Ferguson, Baltimore, and a New Era in America's Racial Justice Movement* (Boston: Little, Brown, 2016).

119. Movement for Black Lives, "Invest-Divest," https://policy.m4bl.org /invest-divest/ (accessed September 4, 2016).

120. Vijay Prashad, "Powder Keg: the Rage in Urban America," *Counter- punch*, September 2, 2016, http://www.counterpunch.org/2016/09/02/powder -keg-the-rage-in-urban-america/.

121. James Brown and Vanessa Brown, interviewed by Paul Ortiz, December 10, 2016, SPOHP.

EPILOGUE: A NEW ORIGIN NARRATIVE OF AMERICAN HISTORY

1. Carlos Fuentes, "Land of Jekyll and Hyde," *Nation*, March 22, 1986, 337.

2. King, "Beyond Vietnam."

3. "Discurso de Evo Morales al asumir la presidencia de Bolivia," January 22, 2006, http://www.democraciasur.com/documentos/BoliviaEvo MoralesAsuncionPres.htm (accessed August 22, 2015).

4. For a discussion of the Black Workers for Justice and Farm Labor Organizing Committee's "Juneteenth" commemoration, see chapter 8.

5. William Darity Jr., "Forty Acres and a Mule in the 21st Century," *Social Science Quarterly* 89, no. 3 (September 2008): 656–64; William Darity Jr. and Dania Frank, "The Economics of Reparations," *American Economic Review* 93, no. 2 (May 2003): 326–29; William Darity Jr. and Samuel L. Myers Jr., *Persistent Disparity: Race and Economic Inequality in the United States Since 1945* (Cheltenham, UK: Edward Elgar, 1998).

6. Darrick Hamilton and William Darity Jr., "Can 'Baby Bonds' Eliminate the Racial Wealth Gap in Putative Post-Racial America?," *Review of Black Political Economy* 37 (2010): 215.

7. Lake Research Partners, *Hunger in America's Classrooms: Share Our Strength's Teachers Report* (Washington, DC: Share Our Strength, 2013), 3; Yang Jiang, Maribel R. Granja, and Heather Koball, *Basic Facts About Low-Income Children: Children Under 3 Years, 2015* (New York: National Center for Children in Poverty, Columbia University School of Public Health, 2017), 1.

8. Martinez, *De Colores Means All of Us*, 48.

INDEX

Act of Chapultepec. *See* Chapultepec
 Conference
Acuña, Rodolfo, 141
Adams, Charles Francis, Jr., 92
Adams, John, 30
Adams, John Quincy, 36–38, 43–44
Adams-Onis Treaty, 39
African Americans: activist traditions,
 13–14, 36–38, 43, 81–82, 106–7,
 114–15, 244n31; discrimination against/suppression of, 18,
 54, 58–59, 84, 128–29; 215n3;
 and the election of Obama, 177;
 financial racism/poverty, 56, 123,
 125–26, 130–31, 151, 169; and
 Latinx heritage, 161; leadership
 role of women, 221n29; and
 Mexican independence, 45, 97;
 post–Civil War gains, 89–90;
 "quasi-free Blacks," 205n72; role
 in Northern success during Civil
 War, 66–67, 69–70, 186; terms
 used to refer to, 9–10; understandings of emancipatory internation-
 alism/racial capitalism, 40, 63,
 72–73, 80, 87–88, 103–6, 113–14,
 200n12, 206–7n87, 228n27. *See
 also* antislavery activism and resistance; civil rights movement; Jim
 Crow/Juan Crow segregation;
 Ku Klux Klan; labor organizing/

unions; mass incarceration;
 slavery/enslaved people
African Communities League. *See*
 Universal Negro Improvement
 Association and African Communi-
 ties League
African Methodist Episcopal Church.
 See *Christian Recorder*
"The African Roots of War" (Du Bois),
 103
African Slavery in America (Paine), 15
Afro-American (Baltimore): demands
 for public relief during the Great
 Depression, 133; on Hoover's
 imperialist policies, 115–16; on size
 of urban slums, 126–27; tribute to
 Máximo Gómez, 30; on US investments in the Global South, 111
Afro-Mexicans, 10
agribusiness: and the Associated Farmers of California, 133; and the
 Bracero Program, 141; and farm
 consolidation, 235n19; "guest
 worker" programs, 151–52; and
 theft of African American–owned
 farmland, 236n36
agricultural workers: disenfranchisement and impoverishment of, 57;
 exclusion from New Deal protections, 141–42; exploitation and
 terrorizing of, 5, 120–22, 131–32,